FAMILY PLANNING IN CANADA

BENJAMIN SCHLESINGER

Family Planning in Canada

A SOURCE BOOK

University of Toronto Press

© University of Toronto Press 1974
Toronto and Buffalo
Printed in Canada
Reprinted in 2018
ISBN 0-8020-2160-3 (cloth)
ISBN 978-0-8020-7708-0 (paper)

Preface

I am grateful to the Department of National Health and Welfare, Family Planning Division, for their Family Planning Grant #4490-5-4, which enabled me to produce this book.

Special thanks go to Dr R.W. Tooley, the Director, Mr C.N. Knight, the Grants Officer, and Cenovia Addy, Social Work Consultant, of the Family Planning Division, for their encouragement of this project and valuable suggestions.

I had the help of Sadie Gerridzen and Diana Swift as editors, and R.I.K. Davidson of the University of Toronto Press as general editor, in polishing the content and style of presentation. The typing at various stages of preparation was done by Muriel Allan and Dorothy Jenkins. The final copy was prepared by Helen Romanick. I am also grateful to the authors, and publishers, for allowing me to reproduce their material in this volume.

Last but not least, I am indebted to Dean Albert Rose of the Faculty of Social Work for his continued support and encouragement in allowing me to work on this endeavour.

B.S.
Toronto, March 1974

This book is dedicated to the following
Canadian Pioneers in Family Planning

Dr Elizabeth C. Bagshaw
George C. Cadbury
Barbara Cadbury
Dr Lise Fortier
A.R. Kaufman

We are grateful for their untiring efforts
on behalf of our Canadian families.

Contents

x

Introduction

The importance of family planning has become increasingly evident to more Canadians during the past few years. To the individual family it can mean greater health and happiness and the ability to bring up children with love, dignity, and the capability of reaching their full potential. To a nation it may mean a stabilized and optimistic society. To the world it may mean survival. Today, many couples, for social, economic, or medical reasons, feel a need to limit the number of children they will have. If couples are to be able to plan their ideal families, they must have access to information and counselling. Because people have different needs, there must be a choice, not only of methods but also of advisers.

The federal government defines family planning as the knowledge and practices that enable couples to attain the following:

to avoid unwanted pregnancies

to bring about wanted births

to regulate the interval between pregnancies

to control the time at which births occur in relation to the ages of the parents

to decide the number of children they wish to have.

The federal government is now financing the dissemination of information, training of personnel, and research in this area: provincial and municipal levels are slowly following the federal lead.

The First National Conference on Family Planning was held in Ottawa from February 28 to March 2, 1972. Among the recommendations made at that conference was that we should provide curriculum, materials, and courses in family planning and family life education, in education, social work, health, and other university faculties and departments.

The editor of this volume of Canadian readings hopes that this book is one response to that request. This volume contains 33 selections. The authors include doctors, psychiatrists, nurses, psychologists, sociologists, and social workers. The articles have been selected from governmental and non-governmental sources. Thirteen of the contributions have been previously published in Canadian journals (one in an Australian journal), three are from published governmental reports, and 17 selections were unpublished and appear for the first time in this book. The book is divided into six parts and an appendix.

PART ONE: AN OVERVIEW, primarily examines the whole area of family planning as seen by medical, sociological, religious, and women's rights viewpoints.

PART TWO: PROFESSIONALS AND VOLUNTEERS, looks at the roles of medical personnel, social workers, and volunteers in family planning.

PART THREE: GOVERNMENT REPORTS, highlights family planning content from the Royal Commission on the Status of Women, the Senate Committee on Poverty, and the recommendations of the First National Conference on Family Planning.

PART FOUR: CONTRACEPTION, surveys the various available methods of contraception and services and reports on a few selected studies in this area.

PART FIVE: ADOLESCENTS AND YOUNG ADULTS, reports on the problem of pregnancies and contraceptive services for teenagers and single university students.

PART SIX: ABORTION, presents the views and attitudes of various Canadian groups towards abortion. An analysis of abortion as a public health problem is also included.

The Resources section was developed to serve as a guide to the topic of family planning in Canada. It includes a glossary of terms, addresses of Canadian and American journals containing family planning content, addresses of major Canadian agencies dealing with family planning, films, and teaching materials. For further study we also included a 67-item annotated bibliography of Canadian articles, and a basic paperbound library of 75 books related to the topic of family planning.

We foresee that this resource book will be of use in community colleges, universities, in-service training courses, and professional seminars. This book is the first Canadian effort of its kind in the area of family planning and it is hoped that it will be of help in counselling, research, teaching, and training at all professional and inter-professional levels in the Canadian context.

PART ONE

AN OVERVIEW

COPE W. SCHWENGER

The need for family planning

and population control in Canada

Because of continually decreasing birth and fertility rates[1] there is a danger of overlooking the persistent and still urgent reasons for offering more adequate Canadian family planning services. Some of these reasons are:

a There is still a definite relationship between the too frequent and ill-timed arrival of unplanned children and physical, mental, and social ill health in the mother, father, children, family, and indeed in the whole community affected [2]. Although the relationship between maternal mortality and family planning has been obvious to almost everyone, it is only relatively recently that the close connection between the prevention of unplanned pregnancies and the reduction of infant mortality has been and fully recognized emphasized by community health authorities [3]. Canada still has a long way to go in lowering its excessively high infant mortality rate.[2]

b Unplanned pregnancies may lead to some of the following socio-medical problems: 'shotgun marriages'; illegitimacy and marital disharmony (including divorce, separation and conflict within marriage); abortion; infanticide and battered children (physically or emotionally). Concern has been expressed for the high rate in Canada of illegitimacy[3] and abortions,[4] both of which are (theoretically at any rate) completely preventable by family planning. There is a distinct possibility that unless more acceptable and effective family planning services are rapidly made much more available, then abortion on request ('demand') may become established as a leading and accepted primary method of birth control as has been the case in Eastern Europe and Japan.

c Parents have been too prone to say that children are no doubt the same as their parents and grandparents were, with exactly the same basic urges needing satisfaction. This may be good for our own tottering egos, but unfortunately it is not true. Our children are actually different from us and from our ancestors in one important respect – the average age of development of puberty appears to be dropping slightly decade by decade in boys and girls as a result, for one thing, of better nutrition. There is a distinct difference between the situation faced by one's Victorian ancestors who were functionally ready to produce children at perhaps 17 or 18 years of age and today's young women who are beginning their menstrual periods at an average age of 12 to 13 but are not married until about 23. Here is a ten-year period in which, physiologically, getting pregnant would be the most natural thing in the world. Adolescents therefore need more help than formerly if this eventuality is to be prevented.

d Many have referred to our society as sex-obsessed. The socio-cultural pressures in the mass media and elsewhere on young people to 'go ahead' are considerable and much greater than previously. At the same time as an increase in sexual candour, there has been an additional rejection of adult values, at least in some subcultures, and the generation gap appears to be widening. Along with this go the use of drugs, including alcohol, much more money and leisure, increasing accessibility of automobiles and motels, and much more readily available contraceptives and access to abortion. It would indeed be surprising if the rate of premarital intercourse had *not* increased.

e There appears to have been a relatively recent acceleration in the change of sexual mores in North America. Up until the past few years there was said to have been a lot more talk than action on the part of university students. However, since 1965, studies in the United States and Canada have shown a rise in rates of premarital intercourse. One Canadian sociologist has shown an increase from 1965 to 1969 on one Canadian campus of from 22 to 37 per cent of female students admitting to premarital intercourse [6]. Studies in the United States show the same upward trend [7].

f Much more reliable indicators of unplanned pregnancy have been obtained from the United States National Fertility Study. At least 27 per cent of all first-born white births from 1964 to 1966 in the United States were unplanned as evidenced by the fact that 2/3 (18 per cent) of these conceptions resulted in a 'shotgun marriage' (i.e., births occurred less than 8 months after marriage) and 1/3 (9 per cent) in illegitimacy [8]. Canadian rates are very likely much the same. One must keep in mind that these enforced marriages are fraught with potential breakdown and that the children in either case are much more prone to develop problems than are planned children. Pregnant married females were asked whether their pregnancy was planned or not. The rate for white couples from 1964 to 1968 rose from an average of 6 per cent unplanned for the second child to 38 per cent for the fourth and 50 per cent for the sixth (or more) child [9]. What about the availability of adequate contraceptive advice to these married females, many of whom were bearing children at an advanced and hazardous age?

g Although our birth and fertility rates have fallen to much lower levels than during the depths of the Depression (and may fall even lower), this decrease has not been shared equally by all segments of society. Statistics still indicate an inverse relationship between income and family size in Canada as a whole, between different provinces, within individual provinces and in certain municipalities [10]. Discrepancies, although they are less than formerly, are still present. Family planning services are definitely not yet geographically and economically available to all Canadians. A significant number of Canadian men and women (particularly in the lower socio-economic groups) still do not have the advantage of readily available information on family planning and have more children than they desire or can look after properly. It is most important that a real opportunity be given for everyone to get equal access to services. Research shows that the poor in North America will make use of such information if it is properly presented and will not necessarily be pressured into having fewer children [11].

h Of course along with this emphasis on the quantity of births we must surely at the same time improve the quality of life both for the parents and children who are brought into this world – otherwise the whole exercise of family planning is not only immoral but completely futile. Family planning has been referred to as cheaper than welfare handouts. Be that as it may, the important thing is to give the impoverished mother something enriching as an alternative to her creative maternal instinct. As for the children, there is no real advantage unless increased opportunities are indeed available to these fewer, better-spaced and well planned children to realize their full potential, physically, mentally, and socially.

The message of individual family planning appears to be getting through to more and more Canadians. The necessity for international population control is also evident to most. When it comes, however, to the need for a Canadian population policy, there is still a lot of opposition both active and passive. 'Canada is certainly one country which doesn't have to worry about population control' is a typical response; 'Look at all those wide open spaces.' Fear is expressed about continuously decreasing birth and fertility rates, varying from 'We're going to become a nation of old crocks or under-breed ourselves out of existence' to 'Our standard of living is going to drop – the economy needs more and more consumers.'

First of all about those famous wide open spaces – the great majority of this space is either inhospitable for settlement (Pre-Cambrian shield, tundra) or if desirable could be developed only at great ecological cost. There is already evidence of overuse and abuse of our existing natural resources – air, water, land, forest, and animals – leading to shortages on the one hand and pollution on the other. There are in Canada problems of inadequate housing, hospitals, schools, jobs, transportation, and recreation, in addition to a reduction of personal freedom, loss of dignity, and identity. All of these are certainly in part due to too many people in addition to their maldistribution, to general technological development, and to excessive individual consumption.

From the international point of view, the term 'global spaceship' has become familiar, signifying the interdependence of the world's population and finite resources. Other countries already depend on Canada's surplus food, water, forests, and air. The ecological damage inflicted on this planet by filling up Canada with more and more people might in the long run prove disastrous. Also there is little possibility of persuading other countries to limit their population unless we have an aggressive, serious population policy of our own; otherwise we could quite rightly be accused of pursuing a policy of international genocide. Should we not develop a reasonable population policy that can be an example to the whole world including the United States, which at this point, although possessing some 6 per cent of the world's population (a proportion that is continually decreasing), is consuming well over 40 per cent of the world's resources (a proportion that is continually increasing)? In addition to developing an appropriate population policy, an earnest attempt must be made to curtail our own excessive individual consumption and general technological development.

As for becoming 'a nation of old crocks' this is certainly very unlikely. The 1971 Census revealed that in Canada a mere 8.1 per cent of the population was 65 years of age and over [1]. This figure is only 0.3 per cent more than it was in 1951, is less than the US figure, and is far less than many countries in Western Europe. For example, Sweden is reported to have had 15.8 per cent of its population 65 years of age and over in 1970 [12]. This is almost twice the proportion of older people in Canada.

As for the argument that we are going to 'breed ourselves out of existence' this also appears to be a myth. It has been correctly pointed out that Canada has recently reached the 'replacement level' with an average total number of 2.1 births per woman. It will however take at least 40 to 50 years at the present rate of child-bearing before this will lead to what is called zero natural increase. This means that Canada's population will still reach at least 29 million by the turn of the century *if* we maintain our present rate of child-bearing and *if* we sustain a policy of zero net migration [13].

The most difficult argument perhaps to counteract is economic: 'The economy needs more and more consumers.' Canadians are said to be too materialistic to accept a drop or even a levelling off of their present high standard of living. Increasingly, however, we are hearing criticism of our dependence on technology and economic expansion. The feasibility of zero economic growth has been discussed by economists more recently. Politicians are critically examining certain cherished capitalist and other political dogmas. The Judaeo-Christian ethic of a man-dominated (and exploited) environment has been condemned. It may be somewhat reassuring to note that Sweden, which has a higher standard of living than Canada, is much closer than we to Zero Population Growth.[5]

Canada must establish a population policy as soon as possible. What, for example, is an optimum population for Canada? Have we already reached or passed this optimum? Now that we have reached (temporarily at any rate) the birth replacement level, there will be much greater pressure for increased immigration to Canada (depending on the current rate of unemployment). How much assistance can Canada be reasonably expected to give in solving the world's annual natural increase of over 70 million people per year [14] ? When immigrants move from a developing country (particularly if it is from a rural area) to Canada, there is a very significant rise in their per capita consumption and a much greater drain on world resources. If children for adoption are scarce in Canada it would be ecologically far more acceptable, and indeed more unselfish in the long run, to 'adopt' children actually within developing countries and leave them there, rather than to bring them to Canada (through, e.g., Canadian Save the Children Fund, Foster Children Plan).

Zero Population Growth (ZPG) is an organization which believes that in Canada the natural population increase (births minus deaths) plus the net population migration (immigration minus emigration) must tend toward zero and that Canada must establish a population policy as soon as possible [15]. Included in its aims are the following: *a* universal access to voluntary family planning, including contraception, sterilization, and abortion; *b* social acceptance and encouragement of no-child, one-child, and two-child families ('stop at two'); *c* concern for net migration and internal migration (urbanization); *d* a Canada based on a stable population and ecologically sound practices with less emphasis on economic and material growth; *e* the achievement of population stabilization in all 'developed' as well as developing countries.

NOTES

1 In 1961 there were 475,700 births in Canada giving a birth rate of 26.1/1000 population and a fertility rate of 111.5/1000 women 15–44 years. In 1971 there were 362,187 births giving a birth rate of 16.8 and a fertility rate of 67.7 [1]. Numbers in square brackets refer to References which are given below.
2 In 1969 the Canadian infant mortality rate was 19.3/1000 live births; 10 countries had lower rates (including Sweden in first place with 13.0) [4].

3 In 1970 there were 35,588 illegitimate births in Canada, accounting for 9.6 per cent of total live births [1].
4 From January to June 1972 there were 18,801 therapeutic abortions performed in Canada, equivalent to 10.1 per cent of total live births [5].
5 1971 Sweden: crude birth rate 14.1/1000 population (Canada 16.8); 1970 Sweden: fertility rate 52.3/1000 women 15–49 years (Canada 70.5) [13].

REFERENCES

1 Vital Statistics, *Preliminary Annual Report 1971*. Statistics Canada, Cat. no. 84-201, March 1973.
2 Schwenger, C.W., 'Population and Family Planning in Public Health,' editorial, *Canadian Journal of Public Health,* July 1968.
3 Wallace, H.M., E.M. Gold, and S. Dooley, 'Relationship between Family Planning and Maternal and Child Health,' *American Journal of Public Health,* 59, no. 8 (August 1969).
4 Summary of Vital Statistics. Reprinted from *Canada Year Book 1972.*
5 'Therapeutic Abortions in Canada, January–June 1972,' Statistics Canada, December 11, 1972.
6 Mann, W.E., 'Sex and York University,' in his *The Underside of Toronto* (Toronto, 1970).
7 Bell, R.R., and J.B. Chaskes, 'Premarital Sex Experience among Coeds 1958 and 1968,' *Journal of Marriage and the Family,* February 1970.
8 Kovar, G.K., 'U.S. National Fertility Survey 1964-1966,' *Monthly Vital Statistics Report* 18, no. 12, Supplement 1970.
9 Bumpass, L., and C.F. Westoff, 'The Perfect Contraceptive Population,' *Science* 169, September 1970.
10 Schwenger, C.W., 'Social and Demographic Trends in Canada.' Paper presented at the 14th Annual Refresher Course, School of Hygiene, University of Toronto, February 1971 (mimeographed copy on request).
11 Jaffe, F.S., and S. Polgar, 'Family Planning and Public Policy: Is the "Culture of Poverty" the New Cop Out?' *Journal of Marriage and the Family* 30 (May 1968).
12 Svala, G., *Sweden* (Country Profile), The Population Council, New York, July 1972.
13 Romaniuc, A., 'Potentials for Population Growth in Canada: A Long Term Projection,' Statistics Canada. Unpublished paper presented at Population Seminar, Toronto, 1972.
14 *Demographic Yearbook 1971,* United Nations, New York, 1972.
15 Taylor, C., *Zero Population Growth*. Department of Zoology, University of Toronto (information available on request).

CONSTANCE SWINTON

Population and family planning: an overview

Uncontrolled population growth has been said to be the greatest threat to man's survival in the world today. Over-population, environmental pollution, and the depletion of the world's natural resources are three major factors in this struggle for survival. How do Canadians react to these population issues? Many people feel that Canada is a very large country with a relatively small population, that we have room to grow, and that our economy needs more people to ensure continued economic growth and prosperity. It is difficult for some people to accept the concept of population control on a rational basis, and with an understanding that today's decisions on population will have effects for generations ahead.

Over 200 years ago, Malthus stated that a population when unchecked increases by exponential growth rather than by linear growth. Linear growth is characterized by an increase of a constant amount in a constant period of time. For example, a miser hides $10.00 each year in an old sock. This money increases in a linear way by $10.00 per year so that in five years he will accumulate a total of $50.00. But a quantity exhibits exponential growth when it increases by a constant percentage of the whole in a constant time period. If the miser took his $50.00 and invested it at 7 per cent interest per annum, in ten years his $50.00 capital would have doubled to $100.00 without any further investment on his part. There is a simple mathematical relationship between rate of growth, in this case 7 per cent per year, and the time it will take a quantity to double in size. Doubling time is approximately equal to 70 divided by the growth rate. In terms of exponential growth, the world's population will double by the year 2000 to seven billion people. It has taken the world 18 centuries to increase its population to one billion persons and it is growing at a rate 30 times as high as the average rate of growth between the first century AD and 1650. It has been estimated that the population doubling time for the United States, Japan, and the Soviet Union is approximately 69 years, Canada 46 years, Africa 28 years, and South America 17 years.

The time required to double a population depends on two variables: the birth rate as it relates to the death rate and the age structure of the population. The birth rate is the number of births per 1000 people per year in the population. The death rate is the number of deaths per 1000 people per year. Subtracting the death rate from the birth rate (ignoring migration) gives the rate of natural population increase. If the birth rate is 30 per 1000 per year, and the death rate is 10 per 1000 per year, then the rate of natural increase is 20 per 1000 per year. Expressed in percentage or rate per 100 people per year the rate is 2 per cent with a doubling time of 35 years. If the same number are born each year as die, a condition of zero population growth is said to exist.

The age structure of a population is an important factor in population growth. In the developed countries, there are fewer people in the under-15 age groups than in the underdeveloped countries. This means that in countries such as India, Africa, or South America, there will be a surge of population as these people reach their reproductive years.

The spectacular growth of world population since the Second World War is due chiefly to the sudden decline in death rates without a corresponding decline in birth rates. In the industrialized nations with higher standards of living, reduced infant mortality rates have been accompanied by decreasing birth rates. However, in the underdeveloped countries the decline in infant mortality has occurred independent of any real improvement in social or economic conditions or changes in fertility levels. This situation has resulted in unprecedented population growth, with the age structure of the population showing a substantial increase in the number of young people.

In Canada many demographic factors are now being recognized as having a direct bearing on social problems such as illegitimacy, infant and maternal mortality, abused or neglected children, and juvenile delinquency. A 1971 report gave Canada's population as 21,568,310. The birth rate declined from 26.8 per 1000 population in 1960 to 16.8 per 1000 population in 1971. The death rate for the same period dropped from 19.0 per 1000 population in 1960 to 9.5 per 1000 population. General fertility rates, which is the rate of birth per 1000 women between the ages of 15 and 49, also declined from 114 in 1960 to 68 in 1971. The significance of these figures is the contrast between the national rates and corresponding figures in various parts of the country. In 1971 the natural increase in the Northwest Territories was 30.4 compared to the national increase of 9.5 for the same year. The national infant mortality rate in 1971 of 17.5 is still high in comparison with other countries of the world with similar standards of living. England and the Scandinavian countries have lower infant mortality rates. In Canada in 1971, Ontario had the lowest infant mortality rate, 15.3, while in the Northwest Territories the rate was 49.0, more than triple the Ontario figure. Maternal mortality has decreased from 4.5 per 10,000 live births in 1960 to 1.8 per 10,000 live births in 1971. In 1960 the illegitimate birth rate was 4.3 per cent of the total live births and in 1971 9 per cent.

These demographic data are important for our understanding of the need to control fertility in order to cope with the social and economic consequences of excessive human growth. Throughout most countries of the world, the development of fertility planning services has received the widest acclaim and support in the search for effective control measures.

FAMILY PLANNING SERVICES

Family planning has been defined in a number of ways. The universal theme in these definitions is that the decision to limit fertility and the method selected should be a voluntary one. Related to this concept of family planning is the use of contraception to prevent unwanted births, to control the spacing of children, and to limit family size. Some organizations have defined long-range objectives as they relate to family planning in terms of maintaining the quality of family life, protecting the human rights of women and children, benefiting society by improving maternal and child health, reducing poverty, and promoting the welfare of the public. Less well defined in these definitions is the place of abortion and sterilization, infertility, treatment, and genetic counselling.

Family planning is not a new concept. From earliest times, man has been trying to find ways to control fertility. Some of the very earliest attempts at fertility control were based on superstition and ignorance. Around 1100 BC, a popular belief in Egypt and parts of Europe was that a woman was rendered sterile for one year by swallowing a castor bean. An interesting variation of today's rhythm method was practised by the East African Masai tribe who believed a woman's fertile period coincided with the blooming of a certain tree.

Other less fanciful methods of contraception were tried by ancient peoples, some of which formed the basis for the development of modern contraceptive techniques. Mechanical barriers and spermicides of various kinds have been used for thousands of years and a device similar to the modern intrauterine device (IUD) was described by Hippocrates over 2000 years ago.

A growing understanding of reproductive physiology and the development of simple and effective contraceptive methods such as the diaphragm, the intrauterine device, and the 'pill,' have made family planning theoretically possible for every couple today. The challenge remaining, however, is to ensure that modern birth control methods are made known and available to everyone who could profit from them.

FAMILY PLANNING IN CANADA BEFORE 1969

The dissemination of birth control information and the sale of contraceptives was a criminal offence in Canada until 1969 under a section of the Criminal Code. The law, however, was largely ignored during the late 1950s; contraceptives were available in drugstores, and oral contraceptives, IUDs, and diaphragms prescribed freely by doctors. In effect, what happened was that the state of affairs under the law favoured the highly motivated and more informed members of society. Family planning was available to upper and middle class couples who could afford the services of a private physician, but to the couples least able to support large families, birth control information and means were not usually accessible.

The law was tested in 1936 in Ontario and the defendant acquitted. The case in point involved Miss Dorothea Palmer, a nursing fieldworker in Eastview, Ontario, whose job was to visit the homes of poor families and offer needy mothers contraceptive information and supplies. Miss Palmer was an employee of A.R. Kaufman, a manufacturer in Kitchener, whose interest in family planning began during the depression. During this period Mr. Kaufman was forced to lay off large numbers of employees, many of whom had large families and were desperately in need of assistance. Concluding that the most constructive help he could give was assistance in family planning, he established the Parents' Information Bureau to distribute birth control information and supplies. This Bureau provided contraceptives service and is in operation at the present time.

VOLUNTARY ACTIVITIES

The first organized activities in the field of family planning were under the auspices of voluntary agencies. Hamilton, Ontario, claims the honour of operating the oldest continuous birth control clinic in Canada. Its Planned Parenthood Society has been active since 1932 and preceded even the Parents' Information Bureau of Kitchener. The Family Planning Association of Winnipeg was established in 1934. This group did not conduct a clinic but established a home visiting service staffed entirely by volunteers who provided assistance for approximately 150 new patients each year.

In 1955, Gilles and Rita Breault from Lachine, Quebec, undertook the establishment of a family planning movement whose dual objectives were to inform married couples of a birth control method which would be in accordance with their religious principles and to provide counselling in all aspects of married life. The new movement was given the name Serena, an abbreviation of Service de Regulation des Naissances. The aim of the Serena movement was to train couples in the use of the sympto-thermal method of birth control which is based on the slight drop in temperature in the female during ovulation. These couples would, in turn, form teams of volunteers to provide information on this method to interested families in their own areas. Between 1964 and 1965 more than 40 such teams were formed.

The Planned Parenthood Association of Toronto was organized in 1961 and the following year submitted a brief to the Royal Commission on Health Services. Its brief recommended that the Commission consider contraceptive services among the other personal health needs of the Canadian people; that consideration be given to the need for dissemination of contraceptive information in hospitals and clinics and through public health units and departments; and that Section 150 of the Criminal Code be amended and any references to contraception eliminated.

In 1963 a provincial charter was granted to the Society for Population Planning, now the Family Planning Association of British Columbia. It was the first family planning association to achieve this mark of respectability. Other local associations were formed in Edmonton, Calgary, Ottawa, and Montreal. In the same year the Family Planning Federation of Canada was organized under the name of 'The Canadian Federation of Societies for Population Planning.' The Federation is credited with stimulating public awareness and organizing voluntary activities in the family planning field in Canada. Since 1969 new voluntary organizations such as Zero Population Growth have been formed.

PROVINCIAL ACTIVITIES

The Quebec provincial government was among the first in Canada to enter the field of family planning when its Minister of Family and Social Welfare made funds available for the founding of Le Centre de Planification Familiale in May 1967. In April 1967 the Ontario Minister of Health announced legislation to encourage Ontario's 43 local health boards to open family planning clinics and to provide municipal health units with money to do this. The governments of British Columbia and Alberta gave considerable encouragement to family planning activities in those provinces. In the Atlantic provinces, Saskatchewan, the Yukon, and the Northwest Territories virtually no activity in the field of family planning existed during this pre-1969 period.

MUNICIPAL ACTIVITIES

Municipal governments in Scarborough and East York (boroughs of Metropolitan Toronto), Montreal, Vancouver, and Winnipeg, took the first steps towards establishing family planning facilities in the few years preceding 1969. Scarborough established a program that included monthly clinics at 15 child health centres in different areas of the township. In Vancouver, the Family Planning Association gave aid to patients in two Vancouver public health units. The Winnipeg City Council authorized its Departments of Welfare and Public Health to set up a family planning clinic. The City of Montreal had as many as nine clinics open at one time in 1967.

COMMERCIAL AGENCY ACTIVITIES

During the 1960s, there was an upsurge of published material on family planning from commercial sources. Canadian drug companies made several brochures available for the general public explaining family planning and describing the various methods of birth control. They also produced literature, films, slides, and other audiovisual aids for physicians, nurses, and social workers. At least two companies sponsored workshops and seminars for professionals involved in family planning.

PROFESSIONAL TRAINING IN FAMILY PLANNING

In 1966, Dr Robert Kinch, then Professor of Obstetrics and Gynaecology at the University of Western Ontario, conducted a poll of the chiefs of Obstetrics and Gynaecology in all 12 medical schools in Canada. Of the 12, all but one were offering instruction in premarital and marital counselling in family planning.

The main criticism levelled against medical schools at this time was that direct clinical instruction in birth control methodology was lacking. Although all but one reported some effort to teach the various aspects of family planning, the lack of curriculum integration of the disciplines bearing on family planning was evident. It was pointed out that the matrix for teaching a broad understanding of family planning has long existed in medical schools, and that professors needed to help students see the relationship existing between disciplines and to underlie opportunities for promoting family planning.

It is doubtful if family planning was taught in Canadian schools of nursing prior to 1969. Nursing teachers were not prepared to teach it nor were they encouraged to do so. The only other resource for professional training in family planning was provided by commercial companies. Scholarships were made available for public health nurses to attend training courses in family planning at clinics in the United States. Several seminars, symposia, and training workshops were also sponsored by the companies.

In almost all areas, family planning services and activities were minimal before 1969. Voluntary agencies suffered from lack of funds and from lack of governmental and public support. Many family planning associations could not realistically operate clinics, but acted only as referral centres on family planning.

Government activity, as we have seen, was almost negligible. Indeed, the federal government could not participate in or initiate a family planning program until the Criminal Code had been changed. On September 18, 1970, the Minister of National Health and Welfare announced the initiation of a government-sponsored family planning program of public information, training, and research. This substantial program launched by the federal government through the Family Planning Division of the Department of National Health and Welfare has had considerable impact on the development of new services, training of personnel, and research across Canada.

Underlying these objectives is the government's growing concern with Canada's high rate of infant mortality and the allegedly high incidence of unwanted children. The program stresses child-spacing and limitation of family size in an effort to reduce these rates. The emphasis of the government's program is on making family planning information and services available to all citizens, with no suggestion of coercion. Family planning in Canada remains strictly a matter of choice for every individual and every family.

VIEWPOINTS

Is family planning in rural areas adequate?*

C.J.G. MACKENZIE, MD, Associate Professor and Chairman, Department of Health Care and Epidemiology, Faculty of Medicine, University of British Columbia, Vancouver, BC:
When educational factors, age, socio-economic factors etc., are matched, rural populations tend to have more children than urban populations. This fact is demonstrable. Less clear cut is why this should be the case.

One obvious explanation is that rural people want more children than city people. Children in an agrarian setting can still be of some economic assistance before they reach maturity. Out-of-pocket expenses for child rearing may be less in a rural setting. Older traditions may still survive in a rural region after they die in an urban setting. Methods and advice for family limitation may be harder to obtain in rural regions. While these social reasons for the number of children in a family may be nebulous and hard to assess, the lack of medical or family planning services should be easier to study.

Do adequate family planning services exist in rural areas of Canada?

The most usual source of family planning services in Canada is the private medical practitioner. Other sources of such services are public health nurses, pharmacists, public family planning clinics, hospital outpatient departments, public and private welfare agencies, and members of the clergy, etc. Many of these services exist in rural areas but where they do exist there may be some special rural problems in their use.

*Reprinted from *Medical Aspects of Human Sexuality* 2 (March 1972).

In an urban setting the individual has access to a large number of physicians. In the rural setting, even in an area as fortunate in its number and distribution of physicians as British Columbia, the individual's choice of physician may be limited to one or perhaps a small group. Even this physician or group may be some distance from the individual seeking assistance. This situation can present a number of potential problems which would not arise or could be easily overcome in an urban setting:

1 The physician may have some limitation on the circumstances under which he will prescribe birth control methods. This can range from a complete disapproval of any methods for anyone (now fortunately rare) to limitations on parity, marital status or age. Lacking the urban alternative of easy access to another physician, limitations of this type may deny information or prescription to an individual.

2 The individual may not wish to raise the very personal matter of birth control with a physician who knows the family intimately. This lack of anonymity, so easily overcome in an urban setting, may be a severe block to service for young and unmarried rural people.

3 The rural physician, caught in a heavy and busy practice, may not have had the time and opportunity to keep abreast of modern methods of birth control.

Similar problems can intervene in rural areas when other services are considered. The fact that mail order houses will send nonprescription birth control methods is not well known. These items are usually 'hidden' in the catalogues among many products for 'feminine hygiene.' It would take a sophisticated individual to separate one from the other and a brave person to commit himself to the rural mails.

In metropolitan areas such as Vancouver or Victoria, public birth control clinics are well patronized. But there are difficulties in adapting them to rural areas. One suggested solution is the mobile clinic.

The usual mobile clinic is a tractor-trailer-truck similar in outward form to a mobile tuberculosis detection unit. Such a unit would be well equipped and expensive. It would also be obvious. So obvious that only the most brave and brazen woman would enter it in her own region. Even if the sides of the unit were unmarked, everyone in a rural area would know what it was.

To provide good 'public' services for birth control in rural areas some degree of anonymity must be provided. At the least, some ambiguity and an opportunity for rationalization or plausible lying must be provided. A travelling 'well woman' and gynecological consultant service setting up shop in a local health unit building or hospital might be acceptable and useful. Such facilities do not now exist to any extent in Canada.

The rural population of Canada is of two main types – rural farm and rural non-farm. In areas such as British Columbia, rural non-farm is the prevalent classification. These are people living in a rural or village setting but occupied in rather urbanized pursuits of forest product industries, mining, transportation, etc. These people are easier to reach than the true farm population. There has been some limited success with birth control clinics centred in the principle trading towns.

Ultimately, we may be able to offer our rural populations travelling consultant clinics, fixed clinics in local health units or hospitals in the principle towns, printed material available through government sources, mail order pharmaceuticals, person to person teaching as practiced by SERENA and similar services.

Given adequate services and information, it may turn out that rural people are having more children, legitimate and illegitimate, than they actually want.

BRUNO RIVARD, MD, Family Physician, Drummondville, Quebec:
It is my opinion that family planning in rural areas, and also urban areas, except for large cities, is inadequate. Most rural communities do not provide any service at all. Where family planning is available, we can reach only a minority of the population.

In my area, an urban community of 50,000 people, we have organized a family planning service. People from the town and also from rural communities visit us. After eight months of operation, we can draw the following conclusions:
1 Many people do not see that there are problems in providing adequate service.
2 The population is badly informed regarding family planning.
3 Many people consider sexuality and family planning 'taboo.'
4 The people we see are not always the ones who really need our help.

IAN SMITH, MD, Edam, Saskatchewan:
No! It is only as adequate as the local doctors can make it. I discuss family planning with young people who come for premarital examinations, and also with couples after each pregnancy.

I feel there should be more education especially in schools. In this 'permissive society,' the moral and social problems which arise with unwanted pregnancies are becoming more complex. Should the pill be given to young teenagers who request it? Should abortion be given on demand? These questions pose quite a dilemma for many physicians. The answers may go against their beliefs and what they have been taught regarding the preservation of life.

In urban areas it is much easier to operate family planning clinics. In rural areas, especially with a scattered population such as there is in Saskatchewan, it is not feasible. A community has therefore to rely on the attitude of the local doctor and his rapport with his patients.

J.M. SOOD, MD, Family Physician, Weyburn, Saskatchewan:
The answer to the question is far from it, although the importance of family planning has been recognized for a long time. It is one of the ways we can avoid population explosion in general and raise the social standard of some families in particular.

People are aware of family planning and most of them are eager to make use of it, but find it difficult to do so. In rural areas, for instance, family planning is carried out by family physicians who are already busy treating acutely ill patients. Therefore, there is little time to help the couples in need of family planning.

In my view, family planning should be carried out in family planning clinics with staffs adequately trained to educate the public, do proper check-ups on people using family planning methods and keep precise records. I am sure this sort of system would prove a better set-up – and be worth the dollars we put into it.

D. MURRAY, MD, Medical Clinic, Hinto, Alberta:
I practise in a group medical clinic of five doctors in an industrial town of 5,000, situated in west central Alberta, about 200 miles west of Edmonton. Four members of the group graduated from Aberdeen, Scotland. We were all influenced by the teaching of Sir Dugald Baird. Consequently we all have liberal views on male and female sterilization.

I feel that family planning, in this area, is as adequate as anywhere in Canada – but, that also means it is very inadequate. The areas needing our greatest attention are: the legal difficulties that may be encountered in prescribing contraceptives to minors without their parents' consent, the failure of public health authorities to get involved in family planning and the total lack of sex education in the schools.

C.H. OPIE, MD, Pinawa, Manitoba:
Probably yes, in the majority of communities. However, there is variation influenced by the adequacy of the local medical services and the personality of the local doctor, in a one-doctor community.

In an area serviced by one doctor, even if he is able to provide adequate advice, there will always be a proportion of the local people who will either not like him or will find him difficult to talk to.

R.M. COLLINS, MD, Family Physician, Pincher Creek, Alberta:
Is family planning in rural areas adequate? Apparently not, for we are seeing unplanned, unwanted pregnancies, mostly in unmarried girls. Our doctors are quite willing to discuss contraception with the young people, but we are told by them

that they are afraid the word will get back to their parents. Some are embarrassed to ask for fear of being lectured.

A street clinic concept has been discussed by the local family life centre, but has not been followed through, due partly to the extra work load it would impose on the medical profession.

There is also a great need for more education regarding venereal disease - which is on the increase here.

WILLIAM D. FLATT, MD, CRCS (C), Stanton Yellowknife Hospital, Member of the Board of Directors of the Yellowknife Family Planning Clinic, Yellowknife, NWT: Family planning is no longer a phantasmagoric dream. Its success is our only hope of survival. It is the sacred responsibility of the medical profession to help control the current population explosion with its accompanying pollution and starvation.

Family planning centres are totally inadequate and unauthoritative in urban centres and totally ineffectual in rural areas. All married or unmarried people today should either voluntarily prevent or plan conception and should introduce their own regulations for quantitative reproduction, with the guidance and assistance of a family planning clinic.

As the population increases, personal freedom decreases. Therefore, governments of the future will be forced to take complete control of reproduction, not only in the cities, but throughout every urban area of our vast country.

Family planning centres of the future will possibly be called Donor Fertilization, Abortion, and Conception Permission Centres, and will have the power and jurisdiction to regulate the number of children born to each family or to any individual, to sterilize and abort any citizen, and more important, to sterilize and abort those who have chromatin anomalies, mental deficiency, and those who are incorrigible. Desirable females will be required to be fertilized by highly selected spermatozoa, and possibly the authorities might then give equal status to the vast and sadly neglected rural areas.

W.R. ABELL, MD, and M.E. ABELL, MD, Wawanesa, Manitoba:
In our practice we find that family planning is adequately provided for married adults. Pregnancies that are not planned are due to the failure of the contraceptive method.

However, young people and unmarried adults are not adequately served. We feel there is a need for an impersonal service, as this group does not want to approach the local doctor with contraceptive problems - even if the doctor is sympathetic to their needs. (As we are.)

W.A. NORMAN, MD, Provost Medical Centre, Provost, Alberta:
The answer to this question is 'no,' but unwanted pregnancies are occurring in both city and rural areas – because family planning in general is inadequate. There may be many reasons for the inadequacy: religious background may influence a doctor's views; a physician may be known to be unwilling to give contraceptive advice to a minor, with or without parental consent. The time factor is important. Counselling unmarried people may take up more time than office hours permit.

I believe the answer lies in better education of the public and involvement of doctors in sex education/family life education programs in the schools.

J.R. HESELTINE, MD, Watrous, Saskatchewan:
In effect this question asks if I think my work is adequate! The answer in our area is certainly, yes. We provide service to an area bounding on a district serviced by three other physicians, two of whom are Catholic. One of the doctors gives contraceptive advice, the other does not.

In our clinic we prescribe all the various methods of contraception. I personally prescribe contraceptive pills for any female over 16 years of age who comes to me for that purpose.

P.A.R. SUKHIBIR, MD, Morris, Manitoba:
For the average family, counselling appears to be adequate. However, the poorer classes and the Indians are not provided with an adequate service.

I recommend the following: improved education for social workers which would motivate them to give better counselling; removal of restrictions on sterilization operations to allow physicians to assist people unable to use contraceptive methods successfully. This inability to use contraceptives may be due to ignorance, poverty, lack of transportation to acquire information and service, or people's inability to communicate their needs.

N. JACKSON, MD, Milden, Saskatchewan:
Family planning is adequate and really quite well organized among educated and high income groups in Canada. Nevertheless there is great need to supply counselling for the chronic unemployed, delinquent alcoholics and other underprivileged people who seem unreasonably anxious to share their misfortunes with numerous offspring.

Sexuality and the role of intercourse in the life pattern of the individual is rarely understood and virtually never discussed. In many rural areas the clergy are equally ignorant and in their narrowness denounce sexual aspects of social life as a vice.

MICHAEL J. BALL

Obstacles to progress in family planning*

The words 'prevention of conception' were removed from the Canadian Criminal Code in 1969, and legalization of therapeutic abortion occurred in the same year. Many prefer to consider contraception and abortion as entirely separate issues, but in practice they are so closely interrelated that the terms 'birth control' and 'planned parenthood' are now widely taken to include both contraception and abortion. Thus the rising demand for abortion may be interpreted either as failure of a family planning program, or as a growing tendency for the public to choose a method of birth control that is less desirable than alternative methods.

If the public is to have ready access to family planning, this being stated federal government policy,[1] then one must consider whether such an objective appears attainable in the light of the situation in Canada at the present time and in the foreseeable future. Some of the factors likely to impede progress in family planning in Canada are here considered.

CLINICAL RESOURCES

The Criminal Code section that prohibited birth control has been blamed for the delayed growth of family planning in Canada, but even 30 to 40 years ago a few voluntary agencies, municipalities and individuals were showing that they could operate family planning clinics without fear of prosecution. In other agencies, public health nurses might advise patients or refer them to sympathetic physi-

*Reprinted from *CMA Journal* 106 (February 5, 1972), 227ff.

cians in defiance of the instructions of their employers, but this was the exception rather than the rule. Medical education also suffered from strict interpretation of the law, so that interested physicians even today tend to be largely self-taught.

Most Canadian physicians now appreciate the need for family planning, but this acceptance may be qualified. Some maintain that universal health insurance already gives every woman unrestricted access to family planning through the general practitioner or gynecologist of her choice. Others insist that the gynecologist is the only person qualified to provide family planning services. Many health-unit medical officers do not see the need for family planning clinics in spite of arrangements whereby certain provincial governments will provide 75 per cent to 80 per cent of the cost. Others would open clinics, but are fearful of competing with local physicians. In the voluntary field, the organization now known as the Family Planning Federation of Canada was formed less than 10 years ago when local and provincial associations joined forces with some of the churches. Member family planning associations now number over 20 and are increasing steadily, aided by a federal grant. Their role is primarily provision of information and referral, although a few provide clinic services. No great increase in voluntary association clinics seems likely on a national scale, but provincial associations that have proved successful may attract further support.

The Royal Commission on the Status of Women in Canada reported that only 23 of over 900 general hospitals in Canada operate family planning clinics.[2] The Family Planning Federation of Canada, in a recent survey, confirmed this and identified a total of some 66 clinics across the country divided approximately equally between hospitals, health departments and private organizations, including local family planning associations[3] (see Table below). (This figure does not include clinics teaching the rhythm method only.)

What would represent a desirable number of birth control clinics is difficult to determine. A ratio of one clinic to 55,000 population has been found to be quite inadequate in Britain, and special legislation was passed to encourage hospitals and health departments to open more clinics. Three-fourths of Canada's population were urban dwellers in 1966, and this proportion is rising steadily.

If one clinic to 30,000 population is made the objective for Canada - including mobile clinics or teams for more remote areas - then some 700 clinics would be required for the country as a whole. This figure would be attainable without much capital expenditure if general hospitals and health units were to open clinics in existing premises. The cost-benefit in Aberdeen, Scotland, has been calculated as a tenfold saving in health and welfare costs over the combined expenditure on contraceptive services and health education over a five-year period.[4]

FAMILY PLANNING CLINICS IN CANADA

	Nfld.	PEI	NS	NB	Que.	Ont.	Man.	Sask.	Alta.	BC	Yukon and NWT	Canada
Family planning clinics*	1		2	1	13	17	6		2	13	1	66
Population (thousands) per clinic	500		380	620	450	400	160		730	140	43	320
Required number of clinics** for 1 per 30,000 population	16	4	25	21	193	232	32	32	49	62	2 plus	700 (668)

*Including mobile clinics and teams. (See text.)
**Excludes 'rhythm method only' clinics.
SOURCE: Family Planning Federation of Canada survey, 1971.

TEACHING FACILITIES

Very few facilities exist in Canada for training of health professionals and social workers in family planning, and only in the province of Quebec is there an organization set up expressly for education and research, Le Centre de Planning Familial du Québec Inc. This centre was started with government funds even before the law was changed.

There is as yet no such centre for English-speaking Canadians, who can only compete for a limited number of places at centres in the United States. The need for training facilities is such that every family planning clinic in Canada should be equipped for teaching. It is worth noting the amount of training carried out by the British voluntary Family Planning Association. In one year (1969), 600 doctors and 800 nurses completed certificate courses in contraceptive technology in 182 teaching clinics. Twenty-four hundred lay workers were also trained that year, as well as 190 lay speakers. Over the past 13 years, some 4500 doctors and 5500 nurses received family planning training.[5] Even so, there is much concern in Britain over the inability of family planning services to meet the needs of the public.

Teaching facilities can serve another purpose, the training of overseas personnel as a form of foreign aid. But it should not be overlooked that certain 'underdeveloped' countries are now more knowledgeable in birth control than many wealthier nations.

TECHNOLOGICAL DEFICIENCIES

Some contraceptive methods have failure rates that are unacceptably high, yet they are regularly prescribed for, or chosen by, women who can least afford to become pregnant. Family planning literature tends to understate the negative aspects, though many parents can, on enquiry, list the birth control methods used at the conception of each of their children.

The undesirable and hazardous side effects of oral contraceptives have been so publicized that large numbers of women have unwanted pregnancies and subsequent abortions before they see the evidence in perspective.

Oral contraceptives and many intra-uterine devices have the advantage of very large, long-term effectiveness studies. Effectiveness rates for other contraceptive methods tend to be determined from selected or unrepresentative populations, but once having appeared in print are quoted and accepted. Failure rates of 15 per 100 women-years of exposure for condoms and diaphragms, and 25 per cent for spermicides, calendar rhythm and coitus interruptus, given by Potts and Swyer,[6] are probably much more realistic.

If pregnancy were recognized as a serious adverse side effect of a contraceptive, it would follow that a warning of the percentage risk of pregnancy should be prominently displayed on the package, using Food and Drug Directorate figures rather than manufacturers' claims. If manufacturing standards for condoms and diaphragms[7] and expiry dates were mandatory, and sale of substandard imports prohibited, many unplanned pregnancies could be prevented.

The ideal contraceptive has not yet been developed, for it must be safe, effective, free from side effects, aesthetic and render the subject completely infertile until deliberate measures are taken to restore fertility.

MOTIVATION

The success of family planning programs appears to be limited by motivational factors affecting both the patient and the health professional.

The Chicago sociologist Bogue describes five steps to the successful practice of family planning: information, acceptance, consultation, initiation and habituation. An illustration of the distance separating the first three steps is provided by young women attending universities and colleges. They are now subjected to an abundance of accurate and detailed birth control information distributed by their peers with evangelical zeal, and they have ready access to physicians and gynecologists, yet the frequency of sexual intercourse without contraception shows no signs of diminishing.

Neither the traditional philosophies of family planning nor the technology of contraception pay sufficient attention to the realities of human psychology. Planning is the antithesis of spontaneity, yet spontaneity in sexual matters is in general thought to be desirable, and is often unavoidable. Family planning requires foresight, but few young women would consider a birth control method, and few physicians would prescribe one, if there were only a possibility of sexual activity. Even when this possibility is a statistical probability much greater than 5 per cent, patient and doctor usually wait for at least one mistake before deciding on contraception.

Too few obstetrical units view family planning as an essential part of pre- and post-natal care that should be offered to every woman.

The amount of forethought required for most methods of contraception makes preliminary reports on the prostaglandins particularly interesting. If confirmed, then their administration immediately after a missed menstrual period will require their acceptance by the woman, the physician and the legislature, as a form of abortion. The question of self-administration may also arise. If given as a 'morning after pill' prior to implantation, then menstrual cycles could be put out of phase, but since patient- and method-failure in contraception are so common, any alternative to therapeutic abortion is welcome.

Post-coital estrogens in high dosage are very effective as a secondary birth control measure if administered within 72 hours of exposure. Failure rates of only one or two per 1000 cases have been reported in studies involving many thousands of women. However, access to a physician familiar with the technique is necessary within the time limit.

Abortion is believed to be the commonest form of birth control in current use throughout the world, and women are increasingly ready to choose therapeutic abortion as an alternative to illegal abortion or an unwanted child. Therapeutic abortion as a form of tertiary birth control is gaining gradual acceptance amongst patients and physicians.

Such observable factors as lengthening gynecological waiting lists seem to provoke more concern amongst physicians than religious or aesthetic considerations. Motivation of those responsible for health services planning will be necessary to ensure that other gynecological patients do not suffer from inappropriate use of general hospitals for pregnancy terminations where alternative facilities would suffice.

DISCUSSION

A high priority is now accorded to family planning at the federal level and in most provinces, but a close look at resources and funds suggests that it will be many years before contraception will become readily available to all in this country.

As women become less willing to accept unplanned pregnancies, the shortage of family planning services will inevitably be reflected in a rapidly rising demand for abortion, which will only diminish when these services are adequate.

The unwanted pregnancy results from failure to practise contraception or failure of a method of contraception. The argument that a woman will deliberately choose a therapeutic abortion as an alternative to contraception is difficult to accept, other than as an indictment of the amount, accessibility and quality of the family planning services that are offered.

In Japan, high abortion rates are associated with prohibition of the sale of oral contraceptives and intra-uterine devices, and the limitation of their use to clinical trials.[8] Nevertheless ready availability of abortion has resulted in birth rates, perinatal and infant mortality rates and illegitimacy rates that now rank amongst the lowest in the world. Abortion rates peaked in 1955 but have been falling steadily as contraception becomes more available.

In Britain, family planning clinics are proportionately six times more numerous than in Canada, with training facilities and skilled personnel even more abundant, yet abortion rates are still rising, though not as steeply as in Canada. In 1971, for the first time, illegitimacy rates showed a fall.

Abortion rates may be expressed per 1000 population, per 100 live births, per 1000 women aged 15 to 49 or otherwise, making international comparisons difficult;[9] but with the post-war bulge in the population expansion now entering the reproductive age, Canadian abortion numbers can be expected to rise rapidly to at least 10 times the 1970 figure, and it would be inappropriate to evade the problem by leaving it to individual Canadians and provincial health insurance schemes to pay United States physicians and clinics for providing the services.

Family planning programs directed mainly towards information cannot be expected to solve the problem of shortage of services, and it will soon become necessary to re-organize Canadian abortion procedures and facilities, not on the British pattern, but on out-patient lines already commonplace in eastern Europe, Japan and, more recently, in New York and California. Such centres should incorporate comprehensive family planning services, including vasectomies and tubal ligations, since every abortion represents a failure to prevent conception. Unfortunately, under the law as it now stands, provincial ministers of health may arbitrarily decide not to approve any place for abortions, other than accredited hospitals, however high the standards of the proposed facilities and staff.

It would appear to be time to take a fresh look at the situation from a logistic standpoint.

NOTES

1 Government of Canada, Document on Family Planning (news release), Ottawa Department of National Health and Welfare, May 6, 1971.
2 Royal Commission on the Status of Women in Canada, *Report* (Ottawa, 1970).
3 Family Planning Federation of Canada: Family Planning Clinics – preliminary list (Toronto, 1971).
4 Editorial: 'How to Forward Family Planning,' *Medical Officer* 125, no. 18 (1971), 225.
5 Family Planning Association, 38th Report and Accounts 1969-70 (London, 1970).
6 Potts, D.M., and G.I.M. Swyer, 'Effectiveness and Risks of Birth Control Methods,' *Br. Med. Bull.* 26, no. 1 (1970), 26-32.
7 Review: 'Which?' Contraceptive Supplement, *International Planned Parenthood News* (1970), 123.
8 Matsumoto, S., 'Contraception in Japan,' *I.P.P.F. Medical Bulletin* 3, no. 4 (1969).
9 Dominion Bureau of Statistics, 'Therapeutic Abortions in Canada 1970,' *D.B.S. News* (Ottawa, 1971).

C.J.G. MACKENZIE

Some mythology of birth control

There is a sudden and massive official interest in family planning in Canada. This interest is manifest in a series of governmental conferences, courses and programs which have come into existence since November 1969. That month was the magic one in which a number of long overdue amendments were made to the Criminal Code. Among these changes was the so-called legalization of birth control and an easing of the iron-clad illegality of abortion as a medical procedure. In point of fact, birth control was not illegal in Canada prior to November 1969 if it was in the 'public good.' No convictions had been made under the law and birth control information and material were widely available to the people.

Today, in this period of renaissance in Canadian family planning, a number of myths have sprung up full-blown. These myths are not really believed by those who mouth them but they are put forward at policy-making conferences as though they were facts.

Myth 1. No birth control or family planning existed in Canada before November 1969 because it was illegal. The corollary of this myth is more specific.

Myth 1α. No official agency engaged in the dissemination of birth control information prior to November 1969 because it was illegal.

Myth 1 is of course untrue and absurd. Canada's birth rate fell steadily from the beginning of this century to 1932 when an all-time low was reached. It then rose steadily (with a few peaks and valleys during the war) until 1958 when it again turned down and fell steadily to its present level, which is close to the 1932 level. The reasons for the trends are no doubt complex but the means of their accomplishment must in part have been by birth control, both conception control and abortion. Since the rate fell, rose and fell again, the means must be in the hands of the people and subject to their control.

Myth ɪα seems closer to the truth. All too few official agencies or private societies interested in health had programs prior to November 1969. There were some, however. All the law did was keep reports of these activities out of official documents but not out of the scientific literature.

Myth ɪɪ. Family planning is acceptable to governments because it is what the people want. Birth control is not acceptable to governments because the people see that it implies provision of services to unmarried persons, or worse to minor unmarried persons, and worst of all, could imply the use of abortion and sterilization.

This myth is accurate in that it points to the misconceptions of government. The people, however, do not seem to be so squeamish. They seem to want birth control for themselves and their daughters. They would prefer that their daughters remain chaste before marriage but are realistic enough to see that if this is not the case, discreet conception control or even abortion is better than a bastard in the family. For themselves they prefer conception control to abortion just as they prefer medical to surgical treatment. If the less uncomfortable solution fails, for whatever reason, they will undergo surgery rather than produce a grossly unwanted baby.

There are those who point with great alarm at the growing number of abortions being recorded in Canada. There seems to be some evidence that where abortions are freely available in Canada, younger women than formerly are having them. This is reflected in an obvious decline of illegitimate births in these regions. There is no way of telling whether the overall number of abortions in Canada is increasing. The operation was obviously a prevalent one in the land prior to November 1969. The number of deaths, near deaths, and hospital admissions for complications was the only true measure of what was probably going on. Making abortion a nearly legal procedure has reduced these complications but it may not have increased the abortion rate. In any event, the people do not seem to hold the same view about abortion as their government. They just go on quietly doing what they do.

Myth ɪɪɪ. The family planning problem can be solved by establishing numerous public clinics. This will allow the poor to avail themselves of the advantages of family planning.

Corollary Myth ɪɪɪα. The poverty problem will be solved or greatly lessened if the poor have family planning services available to them.

Family planning is not too much of a problem for a large number of Canadians. They have solved it for themselves. A few of 'the poor' have come to public clinics but they seem to make up a relatively small part of the overall clientele. Whenever clinics are set up they are usually patronized.

The biggest function of public birth control clinics in Canada is to provide services to young, nulliparous, single women. These women frequently do not have a private physician. They have left their parents' home where the family physician used to care for them. Even if they have not left the parental home physically, the fact that they have become sexually active and seek birth control services constitutes a psychological marriage. Their new status is almost always clandestine – at least with respect to the parents. The young woman does not want a charge put through on her father's medical insurance. She does not want to attend her mother's physician for the help she needs.

Conversely, the ill-defined poor do, usually, have a physician. Even before the advent of general medicare in Canada, this group often had medical and drug cost coverage. Such birth control information as they request, they get through their private physician. The establishment of public clinics geographically near to them does not markedly improve their performance. This group is hard to reach. Members of it are married either according to law and custom or by common law. They are housebound in the urban society, chained to their dwellings by children, a lack of resources, few or no friends capable of helping; an attitude of quiet hopelessness is the result. The best hope for these people in meeting their health and welfare needs, including birth control, seems, at the moment, to be an outreach program. This can be some new and innovative type, or a use of existing public health and welfare resources.

Even if this low-income group is reached effectively with good family planning services it may not greatly help them. It may not even have a visible effect on the number of pregnancies they experience. These people must first be reached. When this is accomplished they must be supported. Planning of any sort has long ceased to be an option open to them. Planning requires some degree of reserve resources or some prospect of a stable situation in which to work. These people have often passed beyond this possibility into a situation of living from crisis to crisis. Pregnancy is one such crisis. When it occurs they need a 'cure,' either in the form of abortion, or increased resources for the gestational period and the resulting infant.

In this group of house-bound, impoverished, demoralized persons, family planning has already passed them by. They have families. These families were rarely planned but represent the results of earlier crises. What they now seek is family limitation or termination. The solution lies in sterilization and many would welcome this. In this group, female sterilization is the best solution since there tends to be a certain lability of male partners. This lability is not the promiscuity so often deplored and practised by the middle class. It is instead a relatively slow process of desertion or death followed by subsequent semi-permanent liaisons which terminate in desertion or death. This group wants and needs help but this help must be on their terms. Public birth control clinics do not meet these terms to any great extent. Outreach contacts are better, but without a follow-up friendship they only succeed in postponing the next crisis by a few weeks or months.

Myth IV. Mobile birth control clinics will do much to solve the rural family planning problems.

The form and nature of mobile clinics usually postulated is a large tractor trailer truck much like a mobile x-ray unit for tuberculosis. The question is, what will be painted on the side of these vans? Even if their planks are blank they will be identified as birth control units. In a village or rural area it will be a brave or brazen young woman who will step into one in her own community. For a rural young man, married or single, the trauma of entry would be intolerable.

This myth could be brought closer to a reality if the van concept is abandoned. If the clinic becomes a 'floating' general clinic or a visiting consultative service, if it travels in an unobtrusive station wagon or by public transport, it could be very useful. People entering a rural health unit or hospital have a degree of anonymity or at least ambiguity surrounding their actions. These units give a number of socially acceptable and not very private services such as weighing babies, taking x-rays, or giving vaccinations. The visitor can have an excuse for going and a plausible lie to explain his actions later.

Myth V. Once an individual gets to a physician or nurse the service chain is complete and the problem is solved.

This myth should be fact and in some cases is fact. There are, however, some problems at the present time that still keep this statement in the realm of myth. These are:

1 For some individuals knowledge and prescription, no matter how effective and skilfully imparted, are of little use if follow-up services are not available.

2 The individual may be too shy, overwhelmed, or incapable of finding words to express his or her problem to the professional. Coupled with this is the feeling by some health (and welfare) professionals that they should not raise the question with people but should respond only if they are asked. The impasse develops. The patient feels that the professional would raise the subject if it were good for him. The professional feels that he should not discuss the subject unless the patient raises it. In the resulting silence, the opportunity is lost.

3 A number of physicians and nurses place limitations on the type of patient to whom they will give advice and prescriptions. Service may be given only to married people, to people over a certain age or parity, etc. There may be legal barriers (real or imagined) that the professional feels forbid the dissemination of

information or material. These barriers seem particularly prevalent in the case of minors or in the matter of sterilization of both males and females.

4 Many professionals, particularly in the older age groups, have not been trained in birth control methodology and have not had the opportunity to make good their lack.

Myth v can and should be converted to fact as soon as possible. Training courses at both the undergraduate and continuing education level should be frequent, specific, and readily available. Financial barriers to such courses should be kept to a minimum.

To sum up, Myth I, which is a misinterpretation of history, is now relatively harmless. It may even have several beneficial side effects in that it may impart a certain urgency to the interest of government at all levels in the socio-medical problem of birth control. It is hopefully a harmless little myth and could have a happy fairy-tale ending. Myth II may have to remain in the realm of the metaphysical. It perhaps should be accepted as a polite and simple way of allowing government and citizens alike to protect their psyches with a little harmless hypocrisy. Myth III should be brought to reality and more family planning clinics should be established to fill a gap in the services for the group they now serve. Vigorous face-to-face programs should be implemented to fill other gaps. Myths IV and v should be converted to reality with good rural consultative services available in all areas and a well trained professional group to give birth control service to the nation.

Sex has always been surrounded by myths and myths make culture. Perhaps we can use our new myths to produce a good culture.

VIRGINIA THOMPSON

Some religious views on family planning*

INTRODUCTION

Anything as fundamental as the birth of new life is inescapably related to man's
religious instinct. At the core of mankind's survival, and intimately connected to
the dynamic and the creative in the universe, procreation is a point of intersec-
tion of such powerful forces as sex and state, religion and science, individual and
society.

Examination of religious views and doctrines regarding procreation and contraception reflects the importance of various systems of ideas as grounds for debate. While directly affecting many, and as such viewed as broad social forces,
religious doctrines can also be seen as systems of ideas which provide much of
the rhetoric and rationale for social policy.[1] It should also be remembered that
popular acceptance of contraception may be influenced as much by uncontrolled
social forces – such as industrialization, urbanization, fiscal pressures on public
programs, depression, emancipation of women – as by religious or secular values
and orientations.

However, it is our purpose here to examine the religious views involved in two
of the major faiths in the Western world, namely Christianity, both Protestant
and Catholic, and Judaism. It is hard to estimate the effect religious doctrine has
had on legislation regarding birth control, including abortion and sterilization as
well as contraception. It is interesting to note that liberalization of North Ameri-

*Editor's note: The following paper deals primarily with the religious views of three major
groups. It does not attempt to examine the varied views and interpretations of the numerous religious groups and sects in Canada.

can legislation in these areas has occurred mainly in the last ten years – *after* the major Protestant sects changed quite drastically their viewpoint on contraception if not so much on abortion and sterilization. In the United States, the prevailing Puritan viewpoint found expression in the Comstock Act of 1873 which banned the dissemination of contraceptives as being articles for immoral use and the distribution of contraceptive information as obscene literature.[2] This Act remained intact for almost 50 years until the time of Margaret Sanger's successful tactic to seek medical exception to the law via judicial relief. In 1936, the medical exemption from the federal anti-contraception law was granted. It is interesting to note that this legislative change came only by defining birth control as primarily a medical matter, thus circumventing the religious issue.

A change in Protestant attitude can be seen through a few examples. In 1920, the Lambeth Conference of the Anglican Church stood firm against 'the use of unnatural means for the avoidance of conception' and stressed that 'the primary purpose of marriage was the procreation of children.' Here the Anglican Church's stand differed little from that of the Roman Catholic Church. However, by 1958, the Lambeth Conference gave unanimous approval to contraceptive practice provided it was in accord with an informed Christian conscience. In 1931, the Federal Council of Churches of Christ in America had given its approval to the use of contraceptive methods disapproved of by the Catholic Church as artificial. These examples are representative of the change in Protestant thinking on the subject as seen in statements issued at other conferences during the 1950s and onward.[3]

One Catholic perception has proved critical for liberalizing birth control law and program despite the implacable position of the Church in this area. Basically, it is the distinction between private sin and public crime. In 1959, the Reverend John Courtney Murray, a respected American theologian to whom this subtlety has been attributed, applied the distinction to the Connecticut law which classified the use of contraceptives as a criminal act. He argued that not all lapses of moral law, as defined by the Church, should merit the status of crimes under the civil law. In other words, this distinction allows for loyal Catholics holding to their religious beliefs but not seeking to impose them on the non-Catholic majority. This is intended to protect both religious and democratic principles and is seen as appropriate in a 'pluralistic society.'

This philosophy has been seen in operation on several occasions, but never, by the way, in regard to abortion law. The Catholic bishops of Canada did not oppose liberal contraceptive legislation and stated their views in terms of the loyal Catholic opposition in a pluralistic society. Cardinal Cushing employed the same rhetoric in not opposing the change in the Massachusetts law regarding contraception.

Many Catholics have feared that the non-Catholic majority might attempt to change the Catholic's private morality through its political arm, the State. In actual fact, most of these fears of 'coercion' have centred around current disputes regarding state-supported birth control programs. Catholic involvement in the formation and execution of policy has been cited as one way of avoiding coercion or fears of coercion.

Catholic doctrine does conflict with every contraceptive program aimed at reducing illegitimacy and poverty in husbandless households. On occasion, the Protestant and Catholic churches have charged welfare departments with subsidizing fornication and adultery. One Catholic clergyman, the Reverend Hanley, discussed the problem in terms of the greater or lesser moral evil. The Catholic Church rejects contraception as a moral evil, but also enjoins a moral obligation not to engage in extramarital or premarital intercourse, and certainly a moral obligation not to procreate an illegitimate child or one who cannot be born into a family. In these circumstances, whether or not contraceptives are used, a moral evil will be present, and the question then becomes one of the greater or lesser moral evil.[5]

One area in which all Christian faiths, as well as the Jewish faith, have reservations, is abortion. There is little doubt that the reticence in liberalizing the laws in this regard has been the result, at least in part, of these reservations. In order to understand the reticence of these faiths to accept wholeheartedly the use of contraceptives or to support abortion on demand it is necessary to examine the religious views of these faiths concerning marriage, sex, and procreation.

ORIGINS AND EVOLUTION OF
OFFICIAL CATHOLIC DOCTRINE

In the Gospels and Epistles of the New Testament, very little attention is devoted to the specific question of parenthood, so that answers must be sought in the broader context of the approach to marriage and family life. Jesus in his teachings on marriage and family life was not replacing Mosaic law, as has sometimes been said, but was rather dealing with the inner heart of the matter. Concerning divorce, Jesus stated 'Whoever divorces his wife and marries another, commits adultery against her; so too, if she divorces her husband and marries another, she commits adultery' (Mark 10:11-12). The 'two in one flesh' concept, which played a significant but subordinate role in the Old Testament, was moved by Jesus to the centre of Christian doctrine on marriage (Mark 10:6-9; Matthew 19: 4-6). Further, Jesus said of marriage that 'what therefore God hath joined together, let not man put asunder,' making explicit the idea that God himself is the author of marriage. This concept is the bedrock of Christian teaching on the man-woman relationship.

The idea that man should put God *ahead* of marriage and the emphasis of the claims of the Kingdom transcending those of marriage and family life are found in the Gospels. When Jesus was told that his mother and brothers were waiting outside to see him, he pointed to his disciples and said: 'Here are my mother and my brothers. Whoever does the will of God is my brother, my sister, my mother' (Mark 3:35). Similarly, when a woman cried out, 'Blessed is the womb that bare thee ...' Jesus replied, 'Yea, rather blessed are they that hear the word of God, and keep it' (Luke 11:27-28). Those who have forsaken home and family 'for my name's sake, shall receive an hundredfold, and shall inherit everlasting life' (Matthew 19:29). Also, 'He that loveth father or mother more than me is not worthy of me; and he that loveth son or daughter more than me is not worthy of me' (Matthew 10:37).

The Pauline ideal is a disciplined life of the spirit, free from the lusts of the flesh and the entanglements of marriage. For Paul, the 'flesh' was equated with the sinful element in human nature, the personality or ego of natural man. Yet it should also be said that Paul's concept of 'flesh' particularly includes the fleshly passions and desires. These should be denied, purged, and subjugated to the life of the spirit. In Paul's day the ascetic element in Christianity was emerging and celibacy was taking its place as the most sublime way to serve the Lord.

There is little in the Gospels or the Pauline Epistles directly dealing with procreation. The fact is that in the era of the New Testament, Christians were so absorbed with the imminent return of Christ and the supernatural transformation of life, that the question of the natural continuation of life was not at the forefront. It was not that there was a negative attitude toward parenthood, but rather a concentration on a different aspect of reality.[6]

A key figure in the evolution of Roman Catholic doctrine, Augustine, who was Bishop of Hippo at the turn of the fifth century, dealt at length with marriage and parenthood. Augustine was little interested in the question of populating the earth; the heathen could tend to this. Rather, he felt the proper concern for Christians in relation to procreation was in providing candidates for salvation. Further, it was for this purpose that procreation was ordained by God. Neither did procreation provide an argument against celibacy. The sexual act he saw as the mechanism by which the sin of Adam was transmitted. The sinful element in sexual intercourse was pardonable within the bond of marriage, provided it was linked to the good of procreation. Each individual act of intercourse did not have to result in conception (Augustine was too much of a realist for this), but he condemned both contraceptive method and contraceptive intent. For Augustine there was no marriage where parenthood was not in view, although he did allow for non-procreative marriage but only through complete abstinence. In other words, if both parties by mutual consent should dedicate themselves to chastity, companionship would replace offspring and the couple would be validly married. So Augustine insisted on the connection between procreation and intercourse to abolish the sin of concupiscence, and procreation remained the primary purpose of marriage.[7]

In Thomas Aquinas' two 'Summas' the main outlines of Roman Catholic doctrine on parenthood are found. Aquinas combined Augustine's thought with Aristotelian philosophy in his formulations. For the most part Augustine's stern ideas were made less rigorous and more positive. Procreation, as with Augustine, remained the primary purpose of marriage. However, it was now expressed in terms of natural law which was seen as a form of divine law, written into creation. Procreation in man and in lesser animals was the aim of mating, and thus the end which marriage must serve in order to fulfil its inherent destiny. In Aristotelian philosophy, marriage was seen as having an intrinsic goal which it was intended to serve.

Aquinas, however, added to marriage the social purpose of preservation of the species. Of course the individual need not marry, since he was still free to choose what was seen as the higher good of the celibate life for the better contemplation and worship of God. Couples were still free to take mutual vows of continence, but marriage and procreation were seen by Aquinas as essential from the perspective of the human race.

Aquinas also discussed the family in terms of natural law. The infant in the human species required the on-going care of both parents; hence, for Aquinas, procreation was linked with the education of children in the worship of God. Further, Aquinas expanded the idea of marriage from a mere remedy for immorality to a concern for mutual support. Thus companionship, a subordinate but valued motif in marriage, was emphasized by Aquinas. However, Augustine's condemnation of any form of family limitation save complete abstinence was upheld by Aquinas.[8]

Since mediaeval times, Roman Catholic thought on parenthood has moved, if slowly, in the direction of the moderation of Aquinas' thought as he modified Augustine's. Since the approach is basically historical, carrying its teaching on its back so to speak, changes in Church doctrine are slow to come about. The problem today, with our rapidly changing world, is whether the progress of doctrinal evolution in the Church can hope to keep pace.

In 1930, Pope Pius XI issued the *Casti Connubii*, an encyclical summarizing Church doctrine in the field under discussion here. Pius XI spoke of the principal ends of marriage as set forth by God in the words 'increase and multiply.' Education and training of children continued to join procreation in a two-fold primary end of marriage, its secondary end being mutual aid and the mitigation of concupiscence. Pius XI added to these subordinate ends 'the cultivating of mutual love,' reflecting the greater awareness of the valid element in the romantic ideal.[9] Pius XI also made a fuller interpretation regarding companionship in marriage. Companionship was described as a means to spiritual perfection and as such could be regarded as the primary end within the order of grace and redemption. Procreation remained the first purpose in marriage within the order of nature and creation. Pius XI's interpretation, then, could be a seed for future growth in Catholic thought.

Periodic continence became accepted in the latter part of the eighteenth century. This stand was affirmed in the *Casti Connubii* as conforming to the natural law that no direct hindrance to the possibility of conception must be present. Even onanism, the practice of 'spilling one's seed upon the ground,' was considered immoral. The matter of contraceptive intent was licit only for 'serious reasons.' It has since been over the matter of serious reasons that much debate has resulted, rather than over periodic continence itself.[10]

In July 1968, Pope Paul VI issued his long-awaited encyclical *Humanae Vitae.* It touched off reactions that ran from joyful approval to defiant rejection with all possible reactions in between – incredulity, anguish, silence, indifference, grim acceptance. Much of the reaction, at least as reported by the mass media, was highly critical. While Vatican circles had anticipated that the encyclical would not be popular, they were evidently unprepared for the storm of disapproval that arose so quickly in response to it. Interestingly, the reactions outside the Catholic Communion seem to have been milder than those within. However, it has been noted that the reactions inside the Church were so strong that Protestants had little need to over-react to it. Thus, what Pope Paul had hoped would unify the Church on an issue which seemed to be dividing its members had actually made the divergence clearer and deeper.

The timing of the encyclical did not aid in its fulfilling a unifying purpose. Four years earlier it had seemed that Pope Paul might speak on the subject of procreation and his pronouncement might have been received more readily by Catholics at that time. However, during those four years the Pope delayed his communication, and a conviction began to grow in the minds of Catholics that a state of doubt existed within the Church. An ever-growing number of Catholic theologians were finding the natural law arguments condemning the intrinsic evil of birth control increasingly difficult to maintain. Large numbers of married Catholic couples, often with the sympathy of confessors, were making their own decisions of conscience and had reached the conclusion that there were situations when intervention to prevent procreation was not only justified but the only responsible thing to do.[11]

Thus when the long period of waiting for the Church's official pronouncement on the subject was over, a large number of Catholics were unable to accept the Pope's stand or to integrate their own thinking with it. *Humanae Vitae* had in fact reiterated in strong terms the traditional position of the Church.

Of course not all the reactions to the encyclical were negative. There was some strong approval, especially in higher ecclesiastical circles. The bishops' conferences in various parts of the world expressed loyalty to the Pope and acceptance of his pronouncement, although some attached qualifications to this acceptance. Particularly, the responses of Belgian, German, Canadian, and American bishops left some room for the individual's conscience in determining the 'serious reasons' which might justify some form of contraception. These responses also made explicit the fact that while the Pope's pronouncement was authoritative, it was not made *ex cathedra* or infallibly, and therefore the faithful who, under the stern guidance of their own consciences and in the light of the Church's teaching used some form of birth control, should not be separated from the sacraments.[12]

One charge that cannot be made about the encyclical is that it ignored current issues. It called attention to the evolution that had taken place in society and the resultant changes which the Church could not ignore. Some of the changes mentioned were the population explosion and the claim of many demographers that it poses a threat to the world's future; economic and social changes; changes in the educational needs of children which have placed new burdens on parents; the changing role of women; and the deepened understanding of the importance of conjugal love in marriage.

The doctrine section of the encyclical began with the general principle that consideration of the birth control problem must go beyond partial perspectives whether these be biological, psychological, demographic, or sociological. Rather, any consideration of this problem must be within the total vision of man and his vocation. Such a vision of man in the relationship of marriage was seen as requiring a clear understanding of the meaning of conjugal love and of responsible parenthood. Conjugal love was described as human, total, faithful, exclusive, and fecund. Responsible parenthood was presented as the necessary context in which conjugal love can find its true fulfilment. The encyclical went on to say that a couple in the exercise of responsible parenthood are not free to determine 'in a wholly autonomous way the honest path to follow. ... They must conform their activity to the creative intention of God expressed in the very nature of marriage and its acts and manifested by the constant teaching of the Church' (Article 10).

Further on in the encyclical, the Pope unmistakeably reaffirmed the Church's traditional teaching when he said: 'The Church, calling men back to the observance of the norms of the natural law, as interpreted by her constant doctrine, teaches that each and every marriage act must remain open to the transmission of life' (Article 11). The Pope was not negating what he said earlier about the personal dimension of marriage, but rather asserting 'an inseparable connection, willed by God and unable to be broken by man on his own initiative, between the two meanings of the conjugal act: the unitive meaning and the procreative meaning' (Article 12). The advocates of change in the Church quarrel with the inseparable connection here and argue that conjugal love could be justification enough for the marital act, thus opening the way for birth control to be admitted into the Church's teaching.

The ensuing debate over the encyclical continues at all levels in the Church, among laity, clergy, and bishops. Many have re-examined the process of the Church's teaching in this matter, calling into question not only the issue of birth control, but also the Church's teaching authority and Papal infallibility itself. Many can no longer accept the basis of natural law for moral law. Indeed this issue has exposed the need for change within the Church in structure and process as much as in doctrine on birth control.

On abortion the basis of the Catholic position is that the fetus is a human being with a soul from the moment of conception. It is true that some theologians admit that they do not know precisely when the fetus acquires a soul, but their resultant position is the same: that under no circumstances should an abortion be carried out as the fetus is a human life and abortion is therefore homicide. Even if the life of the mother is in danger, unless both fetus and mother are going to die, the mother's life is forfeited for the child's (fetus') life. There are no exceptions in Catholic doctrine for reasons of rape, incest, eugenics, mental or physical well-being of the mother, or social and economic pressures. The sacredness of human life transcends all these.

Sterilization and the birth control pill, which are both treated in the same category, are also condemned. In both cases unnatural means are used and a mutilation of the body results, i.e., sterilization blocks ovulation and the pill prevents ovulation. The result is the frustration of a man or woman in fulfilling their intrinsic purpose of procreation in violation of the law of God. The grounds for objection here are based on concepts of natural law as derived from Aristotle, as well, of course, as all the aforementioned objections to contraception.

ORTHODOX JUDAISM

The Jewish position evolved from a basis very different from the early Christian view of marriage. Marriage was seen as a religious duty, a *mitzvah*, and a completion of the individual. It was not as in the early Christian Church a concession to man's weakness (concupiscence), with the only justification being procreation. Granted, it was also seen as entailing the procreation of children which lay at the core of the religious duty of marriage. A minimum duty in this regard was for the replacement of the couple, that is having a boy and a girl, although this was only a technical fulfilment of the duty, which was seen more in an on-going sense. Another *mitzvah* was that of the sexual responsibility of the husband to his wife with regard to her sexual needs as distinct from her procreational needs. The minimum fulfilment here was defined in terms of quantity and quality, but the husband was to use his judgment in terms of being alert to her moods and gestures in determining and fulfilling her personal needs in this area.

Thus the relational end of marriage stands with the procreational and, if the wife is endangered by pregnancy, the Jewish position is clear. The relational purpose of marriage must not be sacrificed by sexual abstinence to the procreational end, and neither should the wife's life be sacrificed in fulfilment of the procreational duty. Thus contraception is allowed in such cases. Further, non-procreative intercourse with barren, sterile, or pregnant women as well as those too young or too old for child-bearing is permissible as well.[13]

At this point one faces the problem of acceptable means of contraception. The great evil in this regard is *hash-hatat zera*, the destruction or improper emission of generative seed. The destruction of potential life (seed) has been condemned, but since intercourse with women who cannot be impregnated is permissible, then this consideration is not paramount. Rather autoerotic acts and the self-defilement of improper emission of seed (especially coitus interruptus) is condemned. What has evolved then is the belief that the seed itself has a dual purpose just as intercourse does, namely procreation and physical gratification, the latter being essential to the relational end of marriage. It was also concluded that enjoyment of the marital act could not be properly fulfilled if the device used interfered with the normal passage of the male seed to any palpable extent within the female. Thus the method of contraception chosen should be one which least interferes with the normal processes of the sex act.

The marital act then, when properly heterosexual, has its own self-sufficient value and purpose other than that of procreation. Further, it is not the 'natural law' of possible procreation that determines its integrity, but the degree of naturalness of the heterosexual act and its attendant gratifications. The Talmudic *mokh* provides most of the basis by which the legality of contraceptive measures is judged with reference to their nature and the circumstances in which they are used.[14]

Ultimately, abstinence is not an acceptable alternative to birth control or to procreation if there is hazard to the wife as related above. Celibacy was never treasured as a good by the Jewish tradition as in the Catholic faith and even rabbis were not exempt from marriage. The pill or other methods which avoid the dubious nature of *mokh* would be acceptable provided the *mitzvah* of *p'ru ur'vu* (procreation of progeny as described above) has been fulfilled.

While physical hazard to the woman is considered an acceptable reason for employing contraceptive measures, social or economic pressures are considered to be unworthy reasons for using birth control to limit births. There was concern, however, in the Talmud for the adequate nourishment of the suckling child and hence there was a call to responsible realism. Communal responsibility and the burdens and joys of responsible parenthood were not to be subordinated to material considerations. In this regard the Jewish and Roman Catholic faiths are in agreement.

In contrast to the Catholic view, the fetus is seen as potential life, and not a 'person.' Therefore, abortion is not considered homicide. However, abortion is a serious undertaking and is only justified if the mother's life is in danger or to save her 'pain.' If the mother's life is in danger, the fetus is seen as pursuer or aggressor and the mother's life takes precedence. 'Pain' here can be taken to include psychiatric indications, or even 'shame,' that is, if the child is illegitimate or the product of extramarital relations, rape, incest, or if the child is undesirable for eugenic reasons, since in this case it would cause the mother 'pain.'

Since the Jewish faith does not have the concept of original sin and the consequent need for baptism, the Catholic concern that the fetus is not only being deprived of life on earth but also of eternal life (unbaptized babies go to limbo, not heaven) does not for it become a problem.[15]

Again the Jewish and Catholic views come together when considering abortion for economic or social reasons. Apart from the social reasons described above with respect to a mother's 'pain,' economic and social reasons are simply not admissible grounds.

The basic position with regard to sterilization is that the woman may become sterilized, but the man is forbidden to do so. The reason for this distinction lies in the man's religious obligation (*p'ru ur'vu*) to have progeny. While the woman is under no direct obligation to 'be fruitful and multiply,' she does, however, have an indirect obligation to help her husband fulfil his duty, moreover, according to rabinic injunction, the woman must contribute to the world's population.

A serious reason must be present to justify sterilization on her part, and the most common one is unusual pain in childbirth. In this case, even if her husband forbids her to take this action, and if he also refuses divorce, then the woman may go ahead with sterilization *without* his permission. She is not obliged to endure unusual pain for his sake.[16]

THE PROTESTANT CHURCHES

Both Calvin and Luther regarded marriage as fundamentally equal to celibacy in status, and a preferable state except for the gifted few. In the eyes of these men, marriage was a remedy for concupiscence in man's state of sin, much as Paul had seen marital relations serving an important negative function. While procreation is a major purpose of marriage, and children are seen as a divine gift which bless the married state, procreation is not necessarily the essential or primary end of marriage.

However, for all practical purposes, the attitudes of Wittenburg, Geneva, and Canterbury were as strongly pro-fertility as that of Rome.[17] In the nineteenth century, the official Protestant opposition to the birth control movement was a close second to that of Roman Catholicism. In fact, in some American states such as Massachusetts and Connecticut, the anti-contraception laws were passed by Protestant not Roman Catholic legislators. It was also true, however, that Protestant laymen and women were active in the birth control movements. Nevertheless, up until the last forty years the churches themselves focused little attention on the birth control issue and its role in marriage and sex. Before that time, little clerical leadership could be discerned in this area.

The Lambeth Conference of the Anglican Church in 1958 proved to be a milestone in the development of a philosophy of responsible parenthood. A significant statement from this conference was: 'where there is a clearly felt moral obligation to limit or avoid parenthood [complete abstinence is the] primary and obvious method, [but if there is a morally sound reason for avoiding abstinence] the Conference agrees that other methods may be used, provided that this is done in the light of ... Christian principles.'[18]

A further contribution to a deeper understanding of marriage and parenthood can be seen in the following excerpt from the statements of the conference: 'Those relational acts of "coitus" between husband and wife which cement and deepen their love, ... have an effect which naturally overflows the bounds of one flesh, so that such "coitus" is directly beneficial to the whole family. It cannot too strongly be stressed that the well-being of the family depends to a greater extent than has perhaps been recognized hitherto, on the well-being of the one flesh – and to that well-being regular "coitus" makes a profound contribution.'[19]

The Protestant churches are not bound by natural law as is the Roman Church. Reinhold Niebuhr expounds upon man's sexual drive, setting down many of the shifts in Protestant thought in this area. According to Niebuhr, sex is not sinful in itself, but, given the freedom of the human spirit, sex can be made a vehicle for either sinful licence or a creative relationship. Niebuhr sees that in nature procreation is the prime purpose of the two sexes, but challenges the making of this natural fact into a universal law of reason, which sets bounds for the human personality. He states: 'The prohibition of birth control assumes that the sexual function in human life must be limited to its function in nature, that of procreation. But it is the very character of human life that all animal functions are touched by freedom and released into more complex relationships.'[20]

In 1956, the United Lutheran Church in the United States published a brief statement called 'Marriage and Family Life.' In essence the husband and wife are called to responsible procreation in terms of their ability to provide for their children and give them a Christian foundation in life. The health and well-being of the mother should be a major consideration. Procreation to the limit of biological capacity can be as irresponsible and selfish as limitation of family. Furthermore, the means of contraception should be decided in terms of medical advice.[21]

With the growth of personal freedom and individual responsibility which can be seen in society in the last hundred years, changing standards in the prohibition of contraceptives can be traced in the Christian churches. Some of the churches that have specifically stated their change are:

1931 Congregational Christian General Council
1936 General Convention of the United Church of Canada
1943 British Council of Churches
1951 The Bishops of the Church of Sweden (Lutheran)
1956 General Conference of the Methodist Church in the USA
1959 The World Council of Churches[22]

Some Protestant scholars of note who have taken a position against the absolute prohibition of contraception include Karl Barth, Emil Brunner, Jacques Ellul, and Helmut Thielecke.

Thus it seems that since the Reformation, Protestants have had a conception of marriage which is both broader than and fundamentally different from that of Roman Catholics. The purposes or ends of marriage allow a place for contraception in the Protestant churches and natural law does not stand in the way of a conception of responsible parenthood by means of contraception.

As with contraception, the Protestant view of abortion is based on the individual's responsibility to act in accordance with Scripture and his own conscience.

That most Protestant positions would understand abortion as cutting off human existence and therefore a form of homicide is true. However, unlike the Catholic position, abortion could sometimes be seen as the lesser of two evils. In the case of real danger to the mother's life, Protestant thinking would not forfeit her life for the child's, a position similar to the Judaic view. With regard to legislation on the subject, Protestant faiths would not feel they should impose this Christian morality on non-Christian citizens. In contrast to the absolute position of Catholicism, the judgment as to when abortion is the lesser of two evils is ultimately left to individual Christian conscience.[23]

Sterilization, while considered a serious step and not necessarily to be sought after as a good, would again be seen in terms of the circumstances or perhaps the lesser evil. Unfettered by the natural law criterion of the Catholic Church, the decision would be left to the individual's conscience guided by prayer and Christian principles.

CONCLUSION

The Roman Catholic Church's role as teacher and thinker in regard to doctrine is based on the concept of the infallibility of the Pope, a hierarchical structure, and an appeal to historical tradition. The result is that the evolution of doctrine is slow, and in fact does not seem to be keeping pace with modern change. In no matter is this seen with greater clarity than in the issue of birth control. The effects are numerous but a few are striking. Many predominantly Catholic countries are underdeveloped and have severe problems with economics and overcrowding. Birth control, however, is still illegal, and one result, in Brazil, for example, is an abortion rate which accounts for 60 per cent of the budget of maternity hospital services.[24] Another effect is a deep division within the Church over the problem of birth control, touching off doubts about the process and structure responsible for present policy.

The Protestant position is based mainly on the individual's responsibility to make his own moral decisions in the light of Christian principles. Official statements have been based on Scripture, conscience, and study but are regarded as guidelines, not law or authoritative teaching. The Protestant approach is therefore relatively flexible and can effect changes more quickly than the Catholic process.

The Orthodox Jewish position is based on Scripture, precedent, and law. More concerned with what mankind does currently, Jewish leaders interpret the law for their own day. The evolution of Jewish law is authorized by God to make possible the continuing faithfulness of the people of Israel throughout history.[25] Thus while Judaic law evolved slowly in other eras, it is capable of quite rapid growth and development in response to the contemporary rate of change in society. With regard to family planning, a very positive and realistic (i.e., less as-cetic) view of marriage in comparison with the traditional Catholic view has made possible a less negative response to modern developments in contraception, steri-lization, and abortion.

NOTES

1 Greenblatt, Bernard, 'Policy Issues in Welfare Referrals to Birth Control Pro-grams,' in Florence Haselkorn, ed., *Family Planning: Readings and Case Materials* (New York, 1971), p. 35.
2 See 19 USCA, S. 1461 for the modern version.
3 For a more detailed report on the outcomes of Protestant conferences see Fagley, Richard M., *The Population Explosion and Christian Responsibility* (New York, 1960), pp. 194-209.
4 Other examples of the use of this philosophy may be found in Greenblatt, p. 44.
5 Greenblatt, p. 43.
6 Fagley, p. 142.
7 *Ibid.*, pp. 170f.
8 *Ibid.*, p. 173.
9 *Ibid.*, p. 175.
10 *Ibid.*, pp. 182, 183.
11 Shannon, William H., *The Lively Debate, Response to Humanae Vitae* (New York, 1970), pp. vi, vii.
12 *Ibid.*, pp. 119-137.
13 Feldman, David M., *Birth Control in Jewish Law* (New York, 1968), pp. 192, 193.
14 *Ibid.*, pp. 170-75.
15 *Ibid.*, pp. 274f.
16 *Ibid.*, pp. 241f.
17 Fagley, *op. cit.*, pp. 190-92.
18 *Ibid.*, pp. 194f.
19 *Ibid.*, p. 201.
20 *Ibid.*, p. 199.
21 *Ibid.*, p. 205.
22 Spitzer, Walter O., and Carlyle L. Saylor (eds.), *Birth Control and the Christians* (Wheaton, Ill., 1969), p. 459.
23 *Ibid.*, pp. 83-86.
24 Greenblatt, p. 43.
25 Borowitz, Eugene B., *Choosing a Sex Ethic: A Jewish Enquiry* (New York, 1969), pp. 49f.

LORNA R. MARSDEN

Family planning and women's rights in Canada*

Whatever benefits family planning has for Canada in terms of happier, healthier women and children, lowered infant and maternal mortality rates, well-spaced children and dependable career strategies for women, it is quite clear that *family* planning is quite distinct from *population* planning for this country. That is, contraception, as it operates through family planning, may rationalize the plans of individual families but not necessarily those of population planners. Deciding to have twelve rather than two well-planned children makes quite a difference to school needs, manufacturers' markets, and a host of other social planning problems which are in no way directly linked to the family.[1]

But if any government decides to follow a rational planning strategy for its country, it must have some reliable predictors about population growth and age distributions. As it is now, planners attempt to double-guess by predicting future trends on the basis of past behaviour. As one might expect, this is only marginally effective. If an ecological or population crisis hits a country, the government of that country may very well be tempted to try to control family size by such means as cutting off family allowance benefits after a certain parity, taxing single people into marriage if a larger population is wanted, or taking other drastic coercive measures.[2] None of these measures is being used and certainly no such measures are contemplated in Canada. What such suggestions accomplish is to throw into dramatic relief the questions of human rights and family planning. Who has the ultimate power to decide how many children you will have? Those

*I am grateful to Trudy Don and Flora Hogarth for comments and suggestions on an earlier draft of this paper.

people who tax your income until another child is not economically feasible? Your doctor? Your spouse? Who? What are your rights as an *individual* in these matters; what are your rights as a *family*? Where father and mother differ on these matters, who has the final say?

Suppose that Canadians decided, for example, that Canada's population needed to expand dramatically and passed a law saying that every family must have at least five children (a most unlikely state of affairs). One can see that immediately there would be a great outcry. The family unit is felt to be a sacred one in Canadian society and the decision-making that goes on within the family is seen as an entirely private matter. The rights of the family are supported by the Canadian Bill of Rights as well as in various other constitutional and legal ways.[3] Thus, if government does want to influence population growth and change, it uses more indirect means: increasing or decreasing immigration is the most obvious example of control of population growth, and various subtle means are used to influence family size. For example, the age at marriage determines to some extent how many children a woman can have; the later the age at marriage, the fewer the chances are for child-bearing. The more easily divorces are obtained, the smaller the number of children born. Family size is affected by tax law to some extent. We suspect, for example, that many people would have more children if it were financially possible for them to do so.[4] The children's allowance program, while unlikely to affect the number of children a family has, reflects a pro-natalist attitude on the part of the Canadian people. Housing and building regulations have an impact on family size. Five-bedroom apartments are hard to come by in most Canadian cities and as more and more people are forced to move into apartment dwellings, so they are forced to limit their family size. The costs of education are another way of limiting family size. For most Canadians it is now imperative to consider giving their children at least some form of post-secondary education and as the costs of this education are not borne by the government but by each family directly, this may affect family size. It is clear that although the family unit is held to be an inviolable basic unit of Canadian society, the decision-making over the number of children can be *influenced* in a number of indirect ways by law.

Family planning, as the name implies, has, in the years since Margaret Sanger's death, more or less accepted the definition of the family as the basic unit of the society in which children should be reared. It is not that counselling and advice are not being given to single women but it is roughly true to say that it is not the woman that family planning has been concerned with but the woman in the context of man-woman-children situations. But reproduction is an aspect of life that is much more important to a woman than to a man. The possibilities for women in Canada are constantly and systematically affected by the fact that it is women who bear the children and, at the present time in this society, it tends to be women who rear them.

Contraception has, to a greater extent than ever before, freed a woman's sexuality from reproduction. Sexuality no longer has to take place within the context of a family group in order to legitimize it for the contingency of reproduction. But reproduction is still not possible for most women without some sort of family support or at least an income and arrangements for the socialization of the child. Outside the family few such arrangements exist. Only married couples have the legal right to children.* All other children are illegitimate.

There are three considerations here: The first is the link between population growth and family planning; the second is the link between family planning and women in families; the third is the connection between human rights and the status of women.

RIGHTS OF CANADIANS VS RIGHTS OF CANADIAN WOMEN**

Although human rights are not formally set out in Canadian law the way they are in some other countries, there is, nonetheless, a body of law stemming from the BNA Act and subject to judicial interpretation, as well as civil rights law which exemplifies the type of conflict over basic rights that is crucial for women, particularly in the area of family planning. These laws attempt to establish things in such a way as to protect the rights of the individual, the rights of the minor (the child), and the rights of the family. In 1960, Prime Minister Diefenbaker passed a bill (c44) through the House of Commons which was made law in August – his Canadian Bill of Rights. He notes at the outset that the Canadian nation is founded upon 'principles that acknowledge the supremacy of God, the dignity and worth of the human person and the position of the family in the society of free men and free institutions.' In the various sections of the Bill of Rights it states that without discrimination by reason of sex, every individual has the right to life, liberty and security, the enjoyment of property, and so on.[5] Unlike other human rights documents which have been passed in other countries, this Canadian Bill of Rights makes no recognition whatsoever of the additional rights and needs of women.[6]

---

*Various types of families exist normatively and even legally. For a developing reconceptualization of the family and individuals, see Pryor, Edward, Jr., Robert Sproule, and David Viveash, 'Rethinking Family Census Data.' Paper presented at the annual meeting of the Canadian Sociology and Anthropology Association, Kingston, May 28-31, 1973.

**It must be made quite clear that the author is not a lawyer. This is the point of view of a concerned layperson.

In 1968, Prime Minister Trudeau published a paper, *A Canadian Charter of Human Rights*.[7] In it he differs with the Canadian Bill of Rights passed in 1960 and favours the establishment of a set of rights regarding particular activities where discrimination on the basis of race, national origin, colour, religion, and sex should be explicitly forbidden, including voting, employment, admission to occupations, education, use of public facilities, and so on. Once again, no special recognition is made of the special rights of women.

FERTILITY: FAMILY'S RIGHT VS WOMAN'S RIGHT

Evidently, then, in Canada* most matters of reproduction and the socialization of children are left to the family to decide.

The rights of the family are protected in matters of family planning because it is clear that one wants to prevent governments from legally imposing upon couples what may be an arbitrary decision about family size. But it is, of course, essential to protect society from the unilateral decisions of families to have as many or as few children as they like. An absolutely crucial aspect of this situation is that in protecting the rights of the couple to decide the number of children they will have, one may very well contravene their related rights as individuals and the rights of their children.

It is not clear that the rights of women as individuals can be protected at the same time that the rights of the family are being protected.[8] It is quite clear that it is very difficult to protect the rights of children in a family while one is protecting the rights of the parents to make decisions. For example, if the individual in Canadian society is guaranteed the right to education and if, as a result of having had the decision for a large family imposed upon her, a woman is not able to exercise her rights to education in Canadian society, her individual rights are in fact contravened. If the couple have more children than they can afford to educate, are the rights of the children contravened?

The legal rights of Canadian men and women stem from the body of law which we have in Canada, but one must also consider the United Nations Declaration of Human Rights, a document which Canada signed.[9] While this is not legally binding and certainly not implemented in Canada, it represents an important international consensus in defining the major rights of human beings at the present time. Under this Declaration,[10] both men and women have the right to marry and found a family if they are of full age (Article 16); the right to legal protection against arbitrary interference with privacy in the family home (Article 12); the rights of freedom of thought, conscience and religion and the right

---

*With the notable exception of rights to abortion.

to manifest these beliefs (Article 18); the right to education and 'education ... directed to the full development of the human personality and to the strengthening of respect for human rights and fundamental freedoms' (Article 26). In addition, family planning was declared a basic human right by the United Nations at the 1968 Proclamation of Teheran. All these rights have direct bearing on both family planning and population planning at the present time. These rights mean that men and women may demand to be educated about methods of contraception; if they believe in the necessity of controlling population growth and size, they have the right to manifest these beliefs; they may decide whether or not to use contraceptive knowledge and technology made available to them; they may choose to marry or not, to have children or not, and to have their privacy as family units and as individuals respected with regard to these matters.

HUMAN RIGHTS AND THE STATUS OF WOMEN

The question now becomes: How do the rights of human beings relate to the status of women?[11] The knowledge of and access to methods of controlling their own fertility is fundamental to the exercise of human rights for women. This special concern of women is recognized in the Declaration of Human Rights of the United Nations, Article 25, Section 2, and in the Declaration of the Elimination of Discrimination Against Women, 1967, especially article 9e which protects motherhood and children, legitimate or illegitimate, and ensures access to educational information for the health and well-being of families.

There are two ways of looking at the status of women in Canadian society. One reasonably useful way is to compare the position of women to that of men in some particular aspect of their lives. For example, we find in figures from 1967 that the average earnings of men with a university degree in Canada were 84.4 per cent higher than those of similarly educated women for all age groups. Thus we can say that as far as earnings in the labour force go, the position of women is much worse than the position of men.[12] Insofar as earnings contribute to social status in Canadian society, the fact that women with similar education to men receive lower wages lowers the status of these women.[13] Another point of comparison is in political rights. Women have the right to vote federally and in every one of the Canadian provinces, but this right is a fairly recent one. Women only won the right to vote federally in 1918 and later than that in many of the provinces. Thus we can say the status of women relative to the status of men has improved since women got the vote. However, if you compare the number of women in the House of Commons with the number of men, even at the best point in time (between 1950 and 1970) there have been very, very few women. Thus, since there is no legal barrier, we can say the representation of women in the House of Commons indicates the lower status of women in Canadian society.

This first method of looking at the status of women provides a considerable amount of useful information and can be extended to such areas as life expectancy, health and other aspects of life on which both men and women can be measured.

The second approach to the study of women's rights and their status is, of necessity, historical or cross-cultural; that is, we can compare Canadian women with themselves at earlier periods in time or with women in other countries.[14] We can also show how the legal rights and the human rights available to women in this country work for or against an improvement in their status. The United Nations Commission on the Status of Women recognized that women are treated as inferior to men in most countries. It must certainly be said that Canada is one of those countries. In those areas about which people have shown any concern, such as the position of women in the labour force, at time of writing women are at a disadvantage federally where discrimination on the basis of marital status and sex is still legal, and in many provinces as well.[15] The United Nations Commission recommended that 'all appropriate measures shall be taken to educate public opinion and direct national aspirations towards the eradication of prejudice and the abolition of customary and all other practices which are based on the idea of the inferiority of women' (Article 3).

In the area of contraceptive information, Canadians fought a battle until very recently to have the illegality of contraceptive information removed from the Criminal Code. Now that it is legally available and now that the possibility of abortion exists in some cases, one can argue that women's rights have been recognized to a greater extent and that their status has improved.

PRODUCTIVE AND REPRODUCTIVE STATUS

However, women, as the bearers of children, have a special status for which there is no equivalent for men. As Juliet Mitchell points out, four major aspects of women's lives must be analysed in discussing women's status and position in any society. These are sexuality, reproduction, the socialization of children, and production.[16] Each must be considered separately. Although it is customary, there is no logical reason for women to bring up the children they bear. Although we associate sexuality and reproduction, there is no logical necessity why a woman should be the customary sexual partner of the man with whom she has children. Probably more important for the purposes of this argument is the recognition of the separateness of and important differences between reproduction and production.

Some of those who are interested in population growth and control argue that if women are given full opportunity in the labour force, this will provide alternative satisfactions and goals and turn them away from the desire to have a great many children. This is a major misinterpretation of the position of women in society. The child cannot be realistically viewed as a product nor can it be assumed that mothers (or fathers) relate to their children as people relate to forms of production for which they receive economic and psychological rewards. Both reproduction and production are important roles and rights of women (and men). It is true to say that the emphasis might well be shifted from reproduction to production for a great many reasons, including the health of the mother and the population goals of the society. It is also quite true that women have not been treated equally in the paid labour force and that they are entitled to be so treated. Fair working conditions would make production more attractive. What is not true is to argue that participation in the paid labour force will replace reproduction in the lives of women.

While many people, including many women, do want to have children,[17] it is a great imposition upon women to assume that this is somehow part of the definition of womanhood[18] and to ignore their rights as individuals by keeping contraceptive information from them, especially now that it is so easily available.[19] Contraceptive information and its use has undoubtedly lengthened the lives of women, improved their health, improved the happiness of their lives and made it more possible for them to plan with confidence other aspects of their lives such as education and participation in the labour force.

CONTRACEPTIVE INFORMATION
AND THE NEED TO CONTROL IT

There are, however, a number of ways related to reproduction and contraception in which the rights of women could be better fulfilled. It has been demonstrated quite clearly that the perfect contraceptive has not been found. The pill has many negative side effects and other means of contraception are less effective.[20] How much effort in Canada is directed toward finding a better contraceptive? Very little.

Even more crucial than basic research on contraceptives is research on how to get this information to women. This is an issue upon which women must be prepared to defend their rights. Just as we fought doctors and legislators who refused to let women have information about contraceptives, so we must fight them again if they attempt to impose contraceptives on women without adequate information about the effect a smaller family will have upon their lives.

Reproduction is one of the few aspects of life over which women have more control than previously. It may also be a very important aspect of their status.

For many groups of people, child-bearing is an important aspect of the status of women. It is within the memory of many Canadian women still living that having children was an important part of the family economy in manning the homestead or living on the Canadian frontier where many hands were needed. For Hutterite and some native women, for example, having children remains a key to their power and status in the group.[21] It is still part of the Canadian tradition to praise women for bearing many children. But times are changing and when women recognize the change which comes into their lives with contraceptive technology, they must also realize the change which that portends in our ideas of what is a family and in their relationship to the economy and to the society. To have the means of achieving recognition and status through child-bearing taken away because of the values and goals of outsiders[22] is potentially devastating.

I am not arguing that these women should not be told about contraception and family planning. Indeed, I believe it is the right of every woman of child-bearing age to know all about contraception. What I am saying is that if women are to be asked to give up their status as mothers of many children, this must be compensated for in some way. Thus, contraceptive knowledge must be accompanied by knowledge of alternatives to motherhood. The woman who loses control over her own fertility may also lose her power in her group if the status of reproduction is not replaced by alternative status possibilities.

The manner in which many women have lost their status in the community through the introduction of new technology has been documented by Ester Boserup.[23] In Uganda, for example, where women were cultivators of the land, the new agricultural technology was brought in by European settlers. These settlers, who assumed that men were the appropriate people to carry out agricultural work, taught the men how to use agricultural machinery and ignored the women who had traditionally done this work and thereby obtained a high status. The men then acquired a considerable advantage in this form of production and gained control over the economy of the entire society. This, in combination with a series of factors stemming from the introduction of the modern world into the society, led to a cycle of loss in status for these women and left them powerless to exercise their rights within the society.

POLITICAL POWER FOR
PRODUCTION AND REPRODUCTION

One can foresee comparable situations arising in connection with contraceptive technology. In itself and as an economic aspect of society, it will often be seized upon as a great advance for women. However, contraceptive technology will only be a great advance for women if women control that technology and do not necessarily give up their status as mothers in response to economic demands by those who do not have their best interests at heart.*

Although many Canadian women have been fighters for their rights for many years,[24] still at no time have the bulk of Canadian women taken part in the design and development of Canadian society in a way which is open to them now. It is by no means essential that it be exclusively men who run the Canadian economy and polity. It is quite clear that women's relationship to economic production is different from that of men. To a great extent this question circles around family planning and contraception. Are Canadian women going to see that their rights as women and as mothers as well as members of the paid labour force are protected in Canadian law? Maternity benefits are only one step in this procedure. When cities are planned with offices in one area and with residential suburbs in another, is it really feasible for mothers to work? Why not design cities so that school children and parents may be closer together physically? How should holiday schedules and hours of work be optimally designed for parent vs. non-parent workers?

A great deal of women's ability to exercise their rights depends upon their being conscious of and wary of the moves taken by governments and organizations. For example, in the area of population growth, many of the goals of those in favour of population control are in direct contradiction to the rights and improvements for which women are pressing at national and local levels. Kingsley Davis[25] has suggested that in order to slow population growth, governments might raise the age of marriage and increase economic pressures not to marry and have children. In many ways these suggestions contradict our notions of basic human rights. Some of the other suggestions put forward such as reduction in paid maternity leaves or a reduction in the family allowance stand in direct contradiction to what most women are fighting for.

On the other side of the question, however, those groups which suggest that every child who has potential for being born must be born ignore the rights of women as individuals. Some religious beliefs and practices have long overlooked completely the rights of women. Here in Canada, one might examine the goals of some of the trade unions with respect to hours of work. It is clear that if women were in control of the trade unions, they would have different ideas of what constitutes appropriate working hours for women. The cycles of women are not the same as the cycles of men and this affects their relationship to the labour force.[26] The time cycles of parents (men and women) are not the same as childless workers. Were women more involved in planning labour legislation and

---

*It has been suggested that contraceptive information be introduced to women in some developing countries in literacy programs. Thus in learning to contracept, women learn to read. Private correspondence with Dr Emily C. Moore, 1973.

labour codes, one might find more account taken of these basic facts of parents' lives in the legislation concerning hours of work and holidays.

CONCLUSION

It is being argued here that, first of all, women's rights are not recognized or respected under Canadian law to the extent that is desirable or to the extent that exists in many other countries. It is being argued further that there is a direct relationship between the rights of women as individuals and their status in the society.[27] No improvement in the status of women will come about unless women have the power to effect that improvement. A large part of that power rests upon legal protection of their special rights as women and as mothers. Finally, it is being argued that women must be cautious in their acceptance of family planning and contraceptive information. While it has the potential for bringing about an improvement in the status of women that is greater than anything that has happened before, it is imperative that this technology be in the hands of women; that it not be tied to the family unit which has rights which contradict the rights of women as individuals; and that where a loss of status is to be incurred through limiting family size, women press their demands for some improvement in other aspects of their status.

At the present time the federal government provides opportunities for the provinces to establish family planning clinics. I would urge that these family planning clinics and that health workers of various kinds who furnish education for women in these areas not confine themselves to a discussion of contraception alone but extend this to the meaning of limiting family size and to other aspects of the life of women – sexuality, production, and the socialization of children. I would urge further that anyone involved in family planning or the distribution of birth control information take the broad view of the status of women in this society. This would involve studying cultural differences and the meaning of motherhood among many groups of women in Canada.[28] It is true that contraception has positive effects on the health of the woman and her children. It is true that contraception improves her chances of a successful work life in the paid labour force. It is true that family planning has many other beneficial effects. But it is equally true that not having large numbers of children can have a negative effect on the status of the woman within certain cultural groups. It is also true that some cultural patterns may enable them to see the positive effects of family planning in their lives.[29] If women want more serious effort spent in this country on the improvement of contraceptives, the improvement of medical research on women's reproductive lives in general, and improvement in the status of women, then they must fight for it.

NOTES

1 Marsden, Lorna R., *Population Probe: Canada* (Toronto, 1972).
2 See, for example, Chasteen, Edgar R., *The Case for Compulsory Birth Control* (Englewood Cliffs, NJ, 1971), and Berelson, Bernard, 'Beyond Family Planning,' *Science* 163 (1969), pp. 533–43.
3 See the *Report* of the Royal Commission on the Status of Women in Canada, Chapter 4, Part A, for a discussion. See also Cleverdon, C.L., *The Woman Suffrage Movement in Canada* (Toronto, 1950), and MacLellan, Margaret E., 'History of Women's Rights in Canada,' in *Cultural Tradition and Political History of Women in Canada,* Report no. 8, Study for the Royal Commission on the Status of Women in Canada.
4 See, for example, Marsden, Lorna R., 'Family Formation in a New Land,' unpublished report to the Planning and Research Branch, Ministry of Community and Social Services, 1973. For a general discussion see Easterlin, Richard A., 'Towards a Socioeconomic Theory of Fertility: A Survey of Recent Research in Economic Factors in American Fertility,' in Behrman, S.J., Leslie Corsa, and Ronald Freedman, eds., *Fertility and Family Planning, A World View* (Ann Arbor, 1970) and the critical literature which surrounds this debate.
5 See Brownlie, Ian, ed., *Basic Documents on Human Rights* (Oxford, 1972).
6 Cf. German Federal Republic: Basic Law, 1949, Article 6; USSR: Constitution, 1936, Article 122; Republic of India: Constitution, 1949, Article 42; People's Republic of China: Constitution, 1954, Article 96; Venezuela: Constitution, 1961, Chapters 3 and 6 (II).
7 (Ottawa, 1968.)
8 Insofar as abortion is legal if it endangers the life or health of the woman, her rights are protected over that of the foetus or, in some senses, the family.
9 For a valuable résumé of Canadian ratification of United Nations Documents and Declarations see Labour Canada, Women's Bureau, *Women in the Labour Force, 1971, Facts and Figures*, Part V, 1973. Note especially in this section that Canada has *not* ratified the International Covenant on Civil and Political Rights, Convention on Consent to Marriage, Minimum Age of Marriage and Registration of Marriages, the Convention against Discrimination in Education among others.
10 See Brownlie, *Basic Documents,* pp. 106–12 and 183–87.
11 For an excellent general discussion of female sex-linked statuses and salient statuses see Epstein, Cynthia Fuchs, *Woman's Place: Options and Limits in Professional Careers* (Berkeley, 1970), Chapter 3.
12 *Women in the Labour Force, 1971, Facts and Figures,* pp. 78–79.

13 One implication is that because they have lower status, women can be paid lower wages which perpetuates that low status. Wage differentials are used as an indicator of, not an explanation of, status in this context.

14 See, for example, Safilios-Rothschild, Constantina, 'A Cross-Cultural Examination of Women's Marital, Educational and Occupational Options,' *Acta Sociologica* 14 (1971), pp. 1-2.

15 Amendments to the Canada Labour Code Bill C206 have been introduced by Mr Munro but are not yet passed through the House.

16 Mitchell, Juliet, *Women's Estate* (Penguin, 1971).

17 Bearing a child, which is described as a 'natural' event by non-feminists, has been described in this way by feminists: 'It is claimed that women enjoy having or at least wish to have children. The evidence is against this too. A) Does anyone wish to hold that the blood-curdling screams that can be heard from delivery rooms are really cries of joy? B) How are you going to account for the fact that as much as two-thirds of the women bearing children suffer post-partum blues and that these depressions are expressed in large numbers by these women killing their infants, or deserting them, of internalizing their hostility to such an extent that the women must be confined in mental hospitals for "severe depression" (often a euphemism for attempted murder).' Ti-Grace Atkinson, 'The Institution of Sexual Intercourse,' in *Notes from the Second Year: Women's Liberation* (New York, 1970), pp. 42-46.

18 See Marsden, Lorna R., 'Human Rights and Population Growth – a Feminist Perspective,' *International Journal of Health Services,* June 1973, for a fuller discussion of this issue.

19 See *Report* of the Royal Commission on the Status of Women in Canada, Chapter 4, Section 208.

20 Vaughn, Paul, *The Pill on Trial* (Penguin, 1970).

21 See, for example, Ishwaran, K., ed., *The Canadian Family* (Toronto, 1971), articles in Chapters 2 and 6. See also Henripin, Jacques, *Trends and Factors of Fertility in Canada,* 1961 Census Monograph, Statistics Canada, 1972, esp. Chapter 6; Cruickshank, J.M., 'Role of Northern Canadian Indian Women in Social Change,' University of British Columbia PHD thesis, 1969, p. 61; Landes, Ruth, *The Ojibwa Woman* (New York, 1971).

22 See, for example, Thomas, W.D.S., 'Maternal Mortality in Native British Columbia Indians, a High-Risk Group' in Gendstaff, Carl F., Craig L. Boydell, and Paul C. Whitehead, *Population Issues in Canada* (Toronto, 1972), p. 58.

23 Boserup, Ester, *Woman's Role in Economic Development* (London, 1970), p. 53.

24 Cleverdon.

25 Davis, Kingsley, 'Population Policy: Will Current Programs Succeed?' *Science* 158 (1967), pp. 730-39.

26 Dalton, Kathrina, in her book *The Menstrual Cycle* (Penguin, 1969), documents the effect of menstrual cycle on women at work, on accidents, and on the men in their lives.
27 See Moore, Emily C., 'Population Problems from a Woman's Perspective (1970),' in Pohlman, Edward, ed., *Population: A Clash of Prophets* (Scarborough, Ontario, 1973).
28 United Nations Commission on the Status of Women, *Participation of Women in the Economic and Social Development of their Countries,* Report of the Secretary-General, 1970.
29 For a discussion of the women's movement in Canada over the recent past see Canadian Women's Educational Press, *Women Unite!* (Toronto, 1972), esp. the Introduction.

PART TWO

PROFESSIONALS AND VOLUNTEERS

LISE FORTIER

The role of doctors in

family planning in Canada

Doctors may be proud of the progress they have made in the technical area, but in the area of ideas they have not evolved so quickly and for years they have fought ferociously against the advent of contraception. In England, at the end of the nineteenth century, in spite of increasing concern over the high morbidity and mortality rates of mothers and babies, phenomena very often related to fertility disorders, the medical profession continued to ignore the causes of the problem for over forty years. Around 1860, when ignorance was no longer possible, it was replaced by violent opposition. Lord Amberley, the father of Bertrand Russell, was accused of scandalously insulting the medical profession when he suggested that contraception be investigated. In 1887, a doctor by the name of Allbutt was banned from the profession for having published a manual that had a chapter on contraception in it. For years the term contraception was never printed without a whole train of adjectives along with it such as 'egoistic,' 'immoral,' 'libidinous'; it was claimed to cause cancer, sterility, nymphomania, suicide, and amnesia. On the other hand, it was easy to see, by the size of their families, that doctors were the first ones to practise birth control. As recently as 1905, the British Medical Association condemned the use of contraceptives. It was not until after the First World War that doctors slowly and reluctantly began to change their minds. Later, out came the oral contraceptive requiring a doctor's prescription, medicine became prevention-oriented rather than cure-oriented, and doctors really had to commit themselves.

Sex and religious taboos would explain such behaviour which did not disappear with the Victorian era. To give just one example, the term *family* planning implies that only those persons who legally and religiously constitute a family are permitted to use contraception. But, under the cloak of such an uncompromising term as family planning, we shall really discuss here birth control and, in an even broader sense, contraception. All family planning requires contraception, but all contraception is not necessarily family planning. Prostitutes need contraception, but it would be pure hypocrisy to call this family planning. This is also true of adolescents who experiment with sex, as well as couples who have no desire to procreate and are living together without being married. Family, if I am not mistaken, means people of the same blood or a unit made up of the father, the mother, and the children. But make no mistake; if I prefer to discuss contraception rather than family planning, it is not because I am considering only the technical aspects of the problem. To me, contraception is first of all a matter of education and the need to use it or the ways it is used often indicate problems of social behaviour and psychological problems.

Resistance to words, furthermore, indicates a resistance to the concept of contraception, and such resistance is seen just as much in doctors as in other people. Doctors, in general, know few contraceptive methods and are often poorly informed on their effectiveness or their indications. How many of them are still 'anti-pill,' inventing old wives' tales for their patients, making them stop using the pill arbitrarily without offering them any dependable alternative contraceptive?

Another way of resisting contraception is trying to convince women that pregnancy is a 'normal,' 'desirable' condition from the physiological and social points of view and that they are failures if they are not or do not become pregnant. For this purpose the real hazards of pregnancy are minimized: as, for example, the fact that its mortality rate, which used to be 45/1000, only dropped when, in the light of knowledge of the important changes of the organism due to pregnancy, it was considered an illness requiring intensive care. Obstetricians in particular would profit from defining pregnancy as being the most desirable state of health for women. When half the children died before reaching adult age, it was normal that pregnancy should be considered a way of survival for society. This is less understandable now that we are threatened with overpopulation and when, in terms of individual survival, pregnancy can be a menace to women. Women asking for abortion define pregnancy as a disease for which they are seeking a cure and it has been proven that for these women abortion is truly therapeutic: physically, the symptoms of fatigue, nausea, and general malaise go away; psychologically, the pathological symptoms disappear.

All this has been denied by doctors who have gone on preaching that it is not pregnancy that is the disease, but rather the desire to seek abortion, and who claim that abortion causes severe psychological disturbances, when in actual fact the majority of women aborted feel a great relief. When do we see newspaper articles exposing the risks of pregnancy and, in particular, that the risk is higher than illegal abortion which is a consequence of restrictive abortion laws?

Reticence in the information sector is even more evident in the services sector. Outside of the large cities, contraceptive services are practically non-existent. Only 23 out of the 900 general hospitals in Canada had a family planning clinic in 1971, whereas if one were provided for every 30,000 citizens, there should be 700 clinics. In this field, resistance is not so much at the governmental level as at the hospital level, as hospital administrations and their medical bureaus are often made up of the most conservative people. Finally, preventive medicine, of which birth control is one of the most effective forms, is not considered interesting for hospitals because it lacks prestige. It is not the number of intrauterine devices a hospital fits but the surgical acts of bravery such as heart transplants or big cancer operations in which the patient is almost carved in two, that are believed to make its reputation glitter. To me, this type of snobbery is intolerable.

This passive resistance becomes much more violent when it concerns sterilization or abortion. One of the main objections of hospital administrations is that their hospitals will become abortion mills or sterilization factories, and that this would be detrimental to the training of young doctors. But about ten years ago when effective contraceptive methods were not widely used, nobody complained about the residents spending a third of their time doing curettages for (usually induced) miscarriages, or else observing normal deliveries. As long as such a role was imposed on them by nature (or so they thought) and not by women, doctors had no objection to being mere technicians.

With regard to sterilization, it is known that the government, at least in the Province of Quebec, bears the cost of sterilization, whether medically indicated or not. But the majority of Catholic hospitals have continued to refuse to perform these operations and the others stick strictly to the medical indications. This attitude is certainly not due to economic concern although it must be admitted that under a health insurance system sterilization is a very costly contraceptive method. Canada is the one country in the world in which medical care is the most costly sector, taking up 5.2 per cent of the gross national product, compared with 4.7 per cent in Australia and 3.2 per cent in Norway. Consequently, I think the people should be educated to use a contraceptive method requiring some effort on their part, instead of encouraging them to demand that the problem be permanently solved for them. The patients should also be made to accept the fact that if they are ready to tolerate a certain degree of uncertainty in all other aspects of life, the same should go for contraception. If they will not do this, it is probably because they are not offered the alternative of abortion in case of failure. Nevertheless, C. Tietze has shown that the least harmful contraceptive methods are those which do not have a 100 per cent efficiency rate but in which failures can be righted by abortion.

This brings me to point out that those who think they can practise contraception without being concerned with abortion are not realistic. Before contraception becomes available to all, abortion will become more and more in demand because sex mores are changing, because youth is rebelling against anything that hampers their freedom, and women against the traditional mores that force them to submit to their biological destiny; because there is an increasingly high proportion of youths who will have the right to vote; because the Judaeo-Christian culture is questioning its values; and finally because of the enormous growth of the mass media. The demand for abortion will increase because it is the result of the absence or failure of contraception. Information alone is not sufficient, either. The proof of this is that in the colleges and universities, where there is now plenty of information on contraceptive methods, the frequency of sexual relations without protection is not decreasing. One may always claim that society is not responsible for the pregnancies that result. It would be just as logical to say that society does not have to bother about treating venereal disease in prostitutes because they have voluntarily exposed themselves to it, forgetting that such a punitive attitude will backlash from the prostitutes to the people they infect.

The American Public Health Association said in an official statement: 'Abortion is an important way of ensuring the right to space and choose the number of children wanted.' As physicians, we cannot but be concerned over the ravage caused by illegal abortion, which is partly measured by maternal mortality rate. Whereas from 1958 to 1964 the maternal mortality rate in the United States declined from 3.8 to 3.5 per 10,000 births, the number of deaths attributed to illegal abortions rose from 16 to 21 per cent. The liberalization of the abortion laws will only reduce this rate, if the psychosocial indications are accepted.

The present Canadian law on abortion is a monstrous inequity which results in bringing about different medical practices for Canadian women, i.e., for those who are French- or English-speaking, have access to a Catholic or a non-confessional hospital, live in a large centre or a small village, have or do not have the financial means to go to New York State. Only repeal of the law, giving the doctor and his patient the sole responsibility for the decision, can eliminate such injustices. We can bring a woman to conceive by force and this is rape. We can also force a woman by arguments from civil or religious authority to carry a child against her will, which would be rape on another level.

This description of what the doctor has not been and has not done in birth control clearly spells out what he should be and what he should do. He should be free of male and religious prejudices which make the practice of sound medicine impossible. He should acquire adequate knowledge on contraception which he will pass on to his patients. He should co-operate enthusiastically in team work in which the nurse and social worker will have leading roles in motivating and educating. He should cease to regard himself as the one and only leader, giving over more responsibility to the paramedical personnel, and in particular to the nurse who should be entrusted with the task of educating the patients, advising them on the choice of a contraceptive, fitting intra-uterine devices and distributing oral contraceptives. Also, birth control clinics should be set up in local health centres, as designated by the Castonguay-Nepveu Report, and the university hospitals should limit themselves only to research and staff training.

Thus, it is in this perspective of freedom of progress and co-operation that we may provide the population with the contraceptive services to which it has the right.

W.J. HANNAH

The family doctor's role in

preventing unwanted pregnancies*

Never a day goes by that we are not reminded of the pressing human problems that confront us all – pollution of the environment, economic disparity, foreign domination of our economy, to name a few. As citizens of this country we must be intensely concerned about these matters, but as physicians there are rather serious limitations to our ability to deal effectively with them.

There is one problem, however, about which we can do a great deal – both as citizens and physicians – and that is the unwanted pregnancy. Despite the fact that this has been an age-old problem and not one simply of our own time, it now ranks among one of the most serious unresolved social issues of our day, and for a variety of reasons.

First of all, there is justifiably growing concern about the world's over-population, with serious doubts being expressed in many quarters about our ability to cope with a global population that threatens to double in the next 37 years. Moving closer to home, we must be imaginative enough to consider a question to which most of us have probably paid little or no attention – what is the optimum population for this country? Because of Canada's vast size, I suppose most of us have assumed that there was virtually no limit to the number of people this country could accommodate. A realistic look at all the social, economic and political forces which shape Canadian life compels us to re-assess our thinking and consider carefully what our population growth rate should be and what final level we should try to maintain.

*Reprinted from the *Canadian Family Physician*, August 1972.

To narrow the problem to the community level, and to our own practices, doesn't decrease its importance. In 1970, the first full year of the amended legislation permitting abortion on the grounds of a threat to the health as well as life of the mother, 11,000 abortions were reported in Canada. In 1971, this number had jumped to 31,000 and there is no evidence yet of any levelling off. Although I do not have any breakdown of these statistics into the percentages of those patients who were married and those who were not, I can say from our own experience that this is by no means a problem of the single woman.

WHY SO MANY ABORTIONS?

Why are so many abortions being done? Why are so many unwanted pregnancies taking place? After all, we consider the majority of people in this country to be reasonably literate and informed, and combined with this we now have available to us a variety of the most effective contraceptive techniques ever created. One could perhaps be forgiven for assuming that an unplanned, unwanted pregnancy should almost be a thing of the past. Since this is obviously not the case, it might be worthwhile to consider for a moment what I believe are some of the reasons why we have this problem on our hands.

First of all, we must look at the question of 'changing moral values.' How often has it been said that this is the age of permissiveness, where freedom to pursue one's pleasures should be regarded as a right, regardless of the consequences? How difficult it is to know to what extent the hedonist philosophy which prevails among many of the young today contributes to the problem under discussion. Naturally, there are no data to enlighten us, but I have a strong hunch it's greater than we think. The sexual urge in all of us a generation or two ago was certainly no less strong than it is in the youth of today, but perhaps there was more restraint and self-discipline then than there is now. The young bucks of today seem to complain less of the acute gonadal discomfort which was almost endemic in the youth of yesterday. It is debatable whether such prolonged sexual restraint was desirable on physiologic grounds, but the avoidance of an ill-advised conception was certainly one of its tangible rewards.

But although sexual freedom among our young is greater than it used to be, there is a strange attitude on the part of many teenagers toward contraception. We have encountered repeatedly among such patients in our own clinic a refusal to consider any form of planned, effective birth control on the grounds that it is premeditated, and interferes with the spontaneity of a sexual relationship. This quaint but appallingly irresponsible attitude does not, however, discourage these individuals from seeking an abortion soon after the likely pregnancy results. Part of this philosophy is unfortunately related to the growing idea among many that abortion is an entirely satisfactory substitute for responsible contraception, and the increasing availability of abortions for social reasons lends substance to this belief.

It would be undesirable for our society to return to a rigidly Puritan moral code, but I would be intellectually dishonest if I failed to state, in the strongest possible terms, that what is required here is a return to a sense of responsibility to our fellow human beings, and in the sexual sphere this means that the beautiful physical and emotional relationships between two people should not be marred by leaving an unwanted pregnancy in its wake. Just as we would consider it shocking to expose a sexual partner to an untreated venereal disease, so should we consider it equally selfish to risk an unwanted conception. This is a dual responsibility and, somehow or other, this idea should become an integral part of our moral code.

BIRTH CONTROL TECHNOLOGY

Next, we should consider the birth control technology now available to us. The wide variety of contraceptive measures in existence, are at best totally effective, and at worst, reasonably effective. Have we made the best possible use of contraceptive methods? The answer has to be an unequivocal no.

Several reasons for this are clear. To begin with, assuming that the majority of Canadian women are informed about and have access to one or more methods of birth control, there is still a substantial percentage of these who are uneasy and uncertain about the alleged risks of these measures, either on a short-term or long-term basis. The most obvious case in point is the oral contraceptive. Here is a substance which has been in continuous clinical use for over 15 years. The effects of these agents on human metabolic and physiologic activities have been studied perhaps more extensively than any other drug in medical history. Their chemical composition has been continually modified in an effort to reduce side effects to a minimum, and although we have not yet achieved the ideal, we still have a totally effective, highly safe product. Despite all this, virtually every side effect the pill has ever produced (and a great many it has never produced) has been headlined in the press and the women's magazines in what is far too often the most unfavourable and sinister light. Of course the pill is not without its problems - no drug is - but let's put these problems in proper perspective.

The serious side effects - thrombo-embolic hazards, liver damage, serious emotional side effects, hypertension - still affect only a small percentage of its users. These problems can be sorted out by taking a careful history; patients subject to such hazards should be taken off the pill and another method substituted. That is simple enough.

The nuisance problems – weight gain, fluid retention, break-through bleeding, hypomenorrhea – are not serious and simple reassurance and time serve to minimize these effects.

Despite the logic of such an approach, a large number of women still refuse to consider the pill, or persevere with it, and they continue to be aided and abetted in this course of action by the media, by their neighbours – and by their physicians. I wish I could tell you the number of women who have been referred for abortion because they were advised by their doctor to discontinue the pill for 'two or three months,' simply because they had been taking it for one or two years. Although there is not a shred of scientific evidence to support this advice, it is still being proffered by a large number of physicians, often with the substitution of a much less effective contraceptive method, or simply the admonition to 'be careful while you're not taking the pill.' One can perhaps understand the natural caution which prompts physicians to give such counsel, but it hardly seems necessary and the results can be disastrous.

MDS ENCOURAGE UNWANTED PREGNANCIES

This brings me next to the physician's role, unwitting or not, in encouraging unwanted pregnancies. There are basically three ways in which we can be derelict in our duties and responsibilities in providing optimum contraceptive advice to our patient.

First of all, through ignorance or inertia we may fail to acquaint ourselves with the technical knowledge about the various forms of contraceptive techniques, and in so doing may fall far short of providing our patients with the most highly effective and suitable method for each individualized case. I have already cited one example where physicians may not be serving the best interests of the patients by advising them to use the pill on an intermittent rather than a continuous basis. Numerous other examples can be suggested, but I suppose the most frequent is the advice to patients not to use the pill, advice often given for no very good reason, or alternatively recommending that they discontinue the pill because of trivial side effects.

I have already made my position clear about the over-all safety of the pill, and its total effectiveness matched only by surgical sterilizations, makes it the first choice of reversible contraceptive measures. There should be an extremely sound reason for not prescribing it. In this event, an alternative method of only slightly less effectiveness should be substituted. The intra-uterine device, diaphragm and jelly (properly fitted and with detailed instructions about its use), vaginal foam, and condoms – in roughly that order – are the methods we should offer, bearing in mind the patient's own particular situation, her motivation and so forth.

STERILIZATION

Individualization is the key, and in this regard an important word still needs to be said about sterilization. Until a very short time ago, surgical sterilization was reserved for patients for whom another pregnancy would constitute a serious threat to life or health, as for example patients with rheumatic heart disease, or diabetes of long standing. We then went through a stage of what I can only describe as hypocrisy when a medical condition (and varicose veins was the most common example) was listed in the hospital chart as the indication when in fact the sole reason for performing the operation was to prevent any further pregnancies which the patient didn't want. In other words, we recognized the right of persons to limit their reproductive potential to suit their own particular needs, and on a permanent basis, but we were not honest enough to state it publicly. At long last, like a breath of fresh air, we faced this situation realistically and in the last five years we have seen a growing acceptance of sterilization, for husband or wife, on request. This has been a giant step forward, and very neatly solves the problem of avoiding the prolonged use of any contraceptive method about which the doctor or patient has serious reservations.

Another shortcoming we must face is our failure, far too often, to ensure that our patients are using some form of contraception when they are at risk (and the most realistic assumption we can make these days is that every woman in the reproductive years is now, or soon will be, at risk), even though that is not the purpose of their visit to their doctor. Inquiry about a woman's birth control program should be part of every medical history; it should never be taken for granted. Many patients are still reluctant to bring the subject up.

JUDGMENTAL ATTITUDES

This naturally leads to the third and final criticism I must direct to many members of my profession. I refer here to the rigid, intolerant, and judgmental attitude assumed by some physicians when confronted with a request for contraceptive advice from the unmarried teenager. I am the first to support the principle of restraint and self-discipline as an integral part of civilized human behaviour. But we must recognize and live with certain realities. When a teenage girl takes the sometimes difficult initiative of seeking medical advice on contraception, it nearly always means she has made a conscious decision to begin her sexual career, and in fact has very likely already done so. It is perfectly true that some girls in this situation may be dissuaded from this course of action by kindly, thoughtful counsel from a physician whose judgment they respect, but I'm afraid they are a minority. Most such patients have already made an irrevocable decision and at least they have demonstrated a laudable measure of responsibility in seeking proper professional advice. They do not respond well to preaching or moralizing on our part; perhaps it is regrettable that this is so, but it *is* so, and we must face this reality. I recognize the difficulties faced by many physicians in accepting this, especially those who may have teenage daughters of their own, but if they can't accept it I believe they should be sensitive enough to refer these patients to physicians who can.

PUBLIC EDUCATION

Finally, we come to the area where perhaps our greatest hope lies in solving the problem of the unwanted pregnancy – public education. Most of us have long since come to appreciate the necessity for an intelligently and sensitively graded program of sex education, or family life education, for our children. Most progressive boards of education have incorporated such programs in the primary and secondary schools, supplemented of course by discussion at home. It is a matter for some regret that not all schools, or all homes, have adopted such programs, and much needs to be done here. No such program, however, can be considered complete without the incorporation in it of birth control instruction. By this, I don't mean simply instruction in the techniques of contraception; important as this is, it is not enough. Our young children, from an early age, should be encouraged to accept their sexuality as something precious and beautiful, not to be exploited selfishly and irresponsibly. They should learn that it involves a sense of commitment to another human being and such commitment must necessarily be reflected in responsibility to avoid the damaging sequelae of venereal disease or an unwanted pregnancy. They must understand that abortion may solve this problem in the short run, but that the long-term effects of this may be more serious than any of us realize.

Hand in hand with the education of our young is a program of public education at all ages, and at all levels of society. Just as we are trying to publicize the benefits of adopting programs against poverty, war, and pollution, so should we pursue, with equal vigour, the cause of responsible family planning. It is not nearly enough to state this as a desirable goal. It must be reinforced by something far more tangible, and this must include the provision of family planning facilities in communities of every size right across the land. These should be established not just in hospitals but in accessible and well-advertised locations outside the hospital. I have little doubt that no serious difficulty will be encountered in finding the necessary skilled personnel, full-time and voluntary, to staff such facilities. The federal government has already declared in principle its intention to support such a venture, though unquestionably more financial assistance than has been projected to date will ultimately be required. There are many thousands of Canadians in possession of a social conscience who would respond enthusiastically to requests for help. Physicians have, it seems to me, a special responsibility to demonstrate leadership here, not just as skilled technical personnel but as part of their role as responsible members of our society. The problem of preventing unwanted pregnancies is not insoluble. By solving it we can ultimately reduce the necessity for the distasteful alternative of abortion to an absolute minimum, and thereby achieve a maturity in our approach to this important social problem which has so far eluded us.

CHERYL ARGUE AND BENJAMIN SCHLESINGER

Family planning and social work practice

INTRODUCTION

Before looking at why social work has taken such a passive role in this area, it is wise to clarify the terms we are using. Birth control or family planning are terms used 'to describe the means whereby couples are able voluntarily to determine the number and spacing of their children through prevention or postponement of conception.'[1] For the purposes of this paper, we see contraception as one method of birth control. (Others include abortion, abstinence, and sterilization.) Present methods of contraception are based either on placing a barrier between the sperm and the egg, thereby preventing possible union, or on preventing the initial production of the egg. Certainly the most effective methods are those which require a medical examination and prescription, such as the oral contraceptive, the diaphragm, and the intra-uterine devices. Other methods, if utilized correctly and consistently, can also be relatively effective. These include the use of condoms, foams, jellies and creams, withdrawal, or rhythm.

Since social workers have, for some time, been concerned with the relationship between unwanted children and disturbed parent-child relationships, as well as the relationship between family size and poverty, it is difficult to understand why they have taken such a passive role in this very vital area. Family planning has, of late, received wide sanction and legitimation through changing public opinion and legislative changes. Indeed, family planning is a part of national policy, regarded as a basic right of the individual and as a basic health measure. Canada decided to enter the twentieth century in the area of family planning in April 1971 when the Department of Health and Welfare worked out some objectives.

Their purpose is to ensure, in co-operation with provincial health and welfare departments, professional organizations, universities, and voluntary organizations, the availability of family planning services and facilities to those who need and desire them. These objectives are as follows:

1 To inform Canadians about the purpose and methods of family planning so that the exercise of free individual choice will be based on adequate knowledge.

2 To promote the training of health and welfare professional and other staff involved in family planning services.

3 To promote relevant research in family planning, including population studies and research in human behaviour and reproductive physiology.

4 To support public or private family planning programs through federal grants-in-aid and joint federal-provincial shared-cost programs.

The value base of family planning and social work is the same: both value the right to self-realization and self-determination regarding one's fate. In spite of this, there have been few policy shifts in social agencies, or few social workers actively involved in this area in our country. Perhaps the passivity on the part of social workers may be explained by the fact that traditionally we have been more concerned with secondary and tertiary prevention. Thus, our efforts tend to be remedial or rehabilitative rather than in the field of primary prevention with healthy populations in need of services. Workers fall back on their own values and beliefs, which usually give rise to either rigid and moralistic views or feelings of discomfort with the whole subject. Hence, contraception is usually dealt with, if at all, as separate from sexual behaviour.

INDICATIONS FOR FAMILY PLANNING

The need for family planning services is indicated by several factors. Manisoff[2] outlines the major indications for family planning as being either medical, social, economic, cultural, religious, or emotional, all having implications for social work practice. (We might add ecological and political factors.)

Medical indications
Family planning as a health measure may be appreciated in the fact that having too many children and close intervals between births are directly associated with poor health in mothers and children. This relationship is even more compounded when one considers those already impoverished women who suffer the effects of poor living conditions, inadequate health care, and malnutrition. Statistics reveal that the age of the mother is a determining factor for family planning from a medical standpoint. Mothers who are under the age of eighteen show a higher

rate of premature births, toxemia, and nervous system defects in the child. Those mothers over the age of thirty-five have a higher risk of giving birth to a mongoloid child.[3] The length of intervals between babies is also significant. When births are one year apart, the death rate for the child is 50 per cent higher than when the interval is two years.[4] Family planning is necessary to avoid aggravation of illness or disease in the mother. Pregnancy can mean a high risk to a woman suffering from heart or kidney diseases.

Family planning seen as a health measure can have direct implications for social work. Concern from the social worker regarding the mother's health may be used to initiate discussion and encourage the use of family planning services. This is certainly appropriate after the birth of a child or when there have been short intervals between the client's last few children. If the mother is physically or emotionally overburdened with her present situation or suffers a persistent or chronic disability, it is the social worker's responsibility to offer much needed family planning services.

Social indications

Social indications for family planning often come to light during the initial intake and assessment process, or during the process of ongoing treatment. A desire for family limitation (that is, want no more children) or family spacing (that is, want longer intervals between) may be seen in numerous presenting problems. The mother who cannot cope with the children she has or who cannot provide for another is certainly in need of family planning counselling. Spouses in the throes of marital conflict must realize that another child will not solve existing problems. Adolescent sexual activity is another area of social concern for both parents, social workers, and the teenagers themselves. Since social work has traditionally held as its goal the improvement and enhancement of social functioning, surely family planning should be its legitimate concern.

Economic indications

Unwanted pregnancy intensifies family poverty. Unless income rises, the degree of poverty rises with increased family size. Births coming while parents are young limit the parents' opportunities for education and the ability to accumulate financial resources. Without family planning it is difficult, if not impossible, to break this poverty cycle. Unwanted children are children at risk. They are found not only in poverty statistics but also in the battered children or delinquency statistics. These situations pose grave social problems which are not only difficult to deal with but also represent a large public expenditure in providing services.

Family planning as an anti-poverty measure poses some controversial issues. Is poverty caused by too large families, lack of financial resources, or both? Our own opinion is that family planning can only help on an individual basis but that poverty must be fought with social and economic means. The poor have traditionally been seen as unmotivated, apathetic, present-oriented, and totally incapable of planning. We question whether it is that they are unable to use family planning services, or whether that until very recently such services have rarely been available or accessible. Lydia Rapoport elucidates two approaches to family planning in this regard: the cultural approach and the environmental approach.[5] In the former, the recipient is regarded as inadequate to utilize family planning services. The 'culturalists,' therefore, advocate counselling in family life and sex education as an attempt to restructure values and strengthen motivation towards family planning. The environmental approach sees inadequacies in terms of services. They advocate broader family planning services which would promote greater availability and accessibility.

Cultural factors
Cultural values may either promote or impede family planning services. If a large family is seen as a sign of future security or a show of masculinity, acceptance of contraception will be difficult to achieve. Sometimes these cultural values are so strong that even the hardships of poverty are not sufficient to sanction the use of birth control. The social worker must appreciate and understand these cultural values if he is to have any success in an educative role. It is only with such an awareness that he can empathically confront a couple with the predictable consequences of having more children.

Religious factors
The influence of religion on family planning has been the subject of numerous articles, books, conferences, and debates. It may be said that, without exception, religious organizations are moving toward broader support of birth control rather than away from it. Though there is still disagreement among the various religious groups as to which contraceptive techniques are morally acceptable, all of the major faiths currently approve of family planning and all approve of some birth control method to accomplish it.[6] This means simply that there is a permissible method of birth control available for every couple who want to plan their family, regardless of their religious beliefs. It is interesting to note that although the traditional Roman Catholic view gives sanction only to the rhythm method of birth control, a number of studies have shown that a high percentage of Roman Catholic couples are, in fact, using other methods of birth control.[7] The implication for social work suggests that it is the social worker's obligation to respect and acknowledge the couple's religious values and beliefs in an attempt to help them select a method which is morally acceptable and agreeable.

Emotional needs and fears
The emotional needs and fears of clients may act as a support to family planning services. If fear of pregnancy impedes the sexual relationship between spouses, contraception counselling will be welcomed. However, there are numerous client needs which actually interfere with services offered. Some women seem to have a need to have someone totally dependent upon them – for instance, a baby. If it is felt that pregnancy will patch up a marriage, hold on to a boyfriend, or achieve for the mother a kind of status, contraception will not be used. Often one finds among impoverished communities the need to prove one's ability through pro-creation when one has failed in all other areas.

Sometimes a desire for contraception counselling remains hidden behind the fear of discussing a subject which has been considered, up to this point, taboo. Clients are often embarrassed by their ignorance of sexual matters and shy away further because of fear of the cost involved. Distortions, such as 'contraception causes disease,' are also responsible for clients' failure to use available services.

THE ROLE OF THE SOCIAL WORKER

It is apparent from the above discussion that the social worker must be prepared to initiate discussion of contraception and family planning. It is the social worker's responsibility to enable people to realize how birth control can enhance family life and help prevent family problems. When offered information through discussion and recommended reading material, the client is afforded the opportunity to become aware of and to understand the alternatives available. A decision can then be made on an informed basis. Family size is not dictated by the worker but rather decided upon by the couple in light of the new information received and in accordance with their right to self-determination. As Burnstein points out: 'Educational techniques in the sexual area serve not only to provide information but in effect, to sanction sexual activity and pleasure.'[8]

We would suggest that if we are to achieve our goals in family planning, routine intake questions should include some exploration in the area of family planning. If the client requires and is interested in obtaining family planning services, the social worker should ascertain what knowledge the client has regarding contraception and how accurate it is. For example, if the couple are using a contraceptive, how satisfactory is it? Are there any religious, cultural, or emotional factors impeding the use of contraception? Contraception has sometimes been found to affect role performance of one of the spouses. For instance, a change in contraceptive practice may have changed the dominant-submissive role relationship between husband and wife, which may in turn account for marital difficulties.

If a referral is indicated, it should be thoroughly discussed with the couple. Too often the husband is not involved, which only perpetuates the erroneous view that contraception is something separate and apart from sexual behaviour between man and woman. The husband who is not involved in family planning may perceive contraception as a threat to his masculinity or as a sign of his wife's infidelity. Referral is crucial for a client to obtain medical supervision for birth control and should always be followed up by the social worker. Often couples may be more able to speak freely with the social worker about how satisfied they are with their chosen method of contraception.

CONTRACEPTION COUNSELLING AND ADOLESCENTS

A special problem area in offering family planning services arises when one begins to consider adolescent sexuality. Rightly or wrongly, teenagers are having intercourse and are getting pregnant or contracting venereal disease. If we are compelled to accept this as a fact of life, with its possibilities of accelerating rates of pregnancies, what is being done about giving contraceptives and family planning counselling to the teenager or single person? How do we react to the 16-year-old who tells us, 'I'm sleeping with my boyfriend and want some means of birth control'? In some clinics a girl must 'prove' her 'promiscuity' by already having an illegitimate child before she is given any advice regarding contraception. Our own stand on this issue is that rather than holding to an outmoded value of sexual abstinence, we must accept reality and rather promote responsibility in sexual relations. Teenagers are hardly ready for this kind of investment, but being ignorant of what is involved in nurturing a child, frequently find themselves in the unhappy and often impossible position of trying to 'play at being parents.' Just handing teenagers contraceptives with the admonition not to get pregnant is only part of an effective family planning program. The other part comes in a sex education program which includes a real understanding of responsible parenthood.

There have been some questions regarding the legality of providing such services to minors. Contraception is considered to be 'medical treatment' and, therefore, must be done with the consent of parent or guardian. However, most doctors and social workers working in the field of family planning will provide family planning services if the adolescent in question is considered to be emancipated (that is, married, self-supporting, or in the armed services) or if the situation is deemed to be an emergency. The National Advisory Council considers pregnancy in the unwed minor to be a health hazard and for that reason advocates that 'minors with a history of sexual activity who have been exposed to the risk of pregnancy should be considered for contraceptive advice.[9] We would take this one step further and advocate that if a teenager is responsible enough to seek contraceptive counselling we, as professional social workers, should be responsible enough to provide it.

FACTORS IN SOCIAL WORK PRACTICE

Social work responsibility in family planning would be more assured if it were clear and explicit in agency policy. As Haselkorn points out: 'The presence of policy does not insure that workers will operate on other than that which they are comfortable. The absence of policy, however, compounds the problem and either blocks the worker from family planning activity or leaves him free to function in accordance with personal beliefs and values.'[10] The absence of birth control policy in some agencies, especially those agencies who operate under religious auspices, has become a very live issue of late. For example, the Catholic Children's Aid Society of Metropolitan Toronto has recently set up a Moral Issues Committee to look at this whole area.

Social work practice is also influenced by the knowledge and skill of individual workers. The paucity of courses in sexuality within professional education is astounding. In Schools of Social Work, family planning and human sexuality could be included in the major methodology classes, as well as in the social policy sequence and the human behaviour and social environment electives.[11]

Attitudes of individual social workers can and often do impede family planning services. Discomfort and embarrassment due to personal inhibitions in areas of sex in one's own life experience will determine the amount of family planning activity. Judgmental, moralistic attitudes cause the client to be regarded in very punitive terms. For instance, rather than receiving contraception counselling, another out-of-wedlock child may be regarded as due punishment for the promiscuous girl. Effective family planning services are realized only when the client's life situation is accepted realistically and aid is given in helping her plan to prevent the conception of unwanted children. Conflicts with personal religious values and conscience pose problems for some social workers. We feel that agency policy regarding family planning services should be explicit enough that a worker would know and understand the expectations prior to accepting a position of employment. If a worker is already an employee before policy is established and is then unable to accept the policy position, we feel it is the agency's responsibility and obligation to transfer the worker to another area of service. One must also caution social workers not to give unconditional acceptance to such stereotype and myths as: 'The poor are irresponsible and want large families.'

CONCLUSION

In our opinion social workers have a responsibility – indeed, an obligation – to become involved in offering family planning services. Unplanned and unwanted pregnancies take a heavy toll in human suffering and social consequences. If social work is committed to advocacy, prevention, and need fulfilment, contraception counselling is certainly a priority.

NOTES

1 Manisoff, Miriam T., *Family Planning Training for Social Service* (New York, 1970), p. 10.
2 *Ibid.*, pp. 21-31.
3 *Ibid.*, p. 22.
4 McCary, James L., *Human Sexuality* (New York, 1967), p. 132.
5 Rapoport, Lydia, 'The Social Work Role in Family Planning: A Summation,' in Haselkorn, Florence, ed., *Family Planning: The Role of Social Work* (Garden City, Long Island, NY, 1968).
6 Guttmacher, Alan F., *Birth Control and Love* (New York, 1969). See Chapter 13, pp. 119-34.
7 Manisoff, p. 29.
8 Burnstein, in Haselkorn, ed., *Family Planning*, p. 139.
9 As quoted by Savel, Lewis E., 'Medical Aspects of Family Planning,' in Varela, Alice M., ed., *Family Planning* (New Brunswick, NJ, 1968), p. 15.
10 Haselkorn, Florence, 'Value Issues for Social Work in Family Planning,' in *Family Planning*, p. 14.
11 A course entitled 'Sexuality and Social Work' was started during the 1970-71 academic year at the School of Social Work, University of Toronto.

MARY F. BISHOP

Voluntarism in family planning in Canada

A government program in a field related to health, welfare, or education is often brought about by the efforts of volunteers who see a need, form an organization, develop a service, and demonstrate its value and acceptability. In the process, professionals aspiring to qualification in the new program often give time to the voluntary agency to acquire it. In other words, volunteers and voluntary agencies are frequently key factors in developing government services and in training personnel to provide them.

Therefore, when a government agrees to take over delivery of the service, the next step, ideally, is to establish whether the voluntary agency has a continuing role, and if so, what it should be, either in filling existing unmet needs or in developing innovative projects.

If the agency is to have ongoing responsibilities, it must have funding either from government or a combination of government and private sources; and its programs must be organized so that neither consumer group, government, nor volunteer is exploited.

Assuming a continuing need for the voluntary agency, the philosophy is best expressed in a statement made several years ago by a member of the Philadelphia Health and Welfare Council: 'We can no longer have the kind of voluntarism which is unrelated to government policy and action. We can no longer walk alone, nor can we behave as rivals and survive. We must travel the road together, as partners, with each influencing the other while in the process of making the journey. We need government and the government needs us in making this long and arduous trip to a better society.'

Family planning is a case in point. A co-ordinated plan is sure to be needed in Canada very soon. The volunteers have pioneered the program, expertise has been developed, acceptability has been established, and the federal government has announced support for public information, research, and training. It has offered a cost-sharing arrangement to the provinces for the delivery of services, and it has also given support to the Family Planning Federation of Canada (FPFC) to assist the development of voluntary agencies. Several provincial governments have begun to give the services and/or to help the volunteers as well.

Numerous new and enthusiastic voluntary family planning organizations are springing up across Canada, some are running birth control clinics, and others are giving advice and referrals to private physicians or local public health facilities. Some are also working in fields of motivation, notably public education for parents and in the school system, training for related professions and home visiting. Some have applied for federal government grants, some are receiving support through the FPFC. Other private agencies are also entering the field, as are universities. So a hodge-podge is developing both in activities and financing, and there is a need for consultation and planning before the situation becomes further complicated. Since public funds are playing an ever-increasing role, it is logical that governments should take the lead in co-ordinating programs.

Before listing several ways in which effective programs in Canada may be developed, it is useful to review briefly the history of voluntarism in this field, and to describe needs and difficulties which have arisen in other countries and which are sure to arise here unless evasive action is taken.

There is nothing new about individual attempts to control fertility or about group efforts to control population size. There are records of both at least as far back as 1850 BC in ancient Egypt, Greece, Israel, and Rome. In each case, the degree of support or opposition has been governed by the needs of the society and the strength of the social, economic, and political interest groups with the most to gain or lose by birth control.

What has been distinctive, however, is the rise of the birth control movement, started by volunteers and dating back about 200 years in western countries, and about 60 years in South Asia as the first of the developing regions in which it was introduced. In both cases it was led by people who were concerned with social reform and also with the possibility that population growth could threaten both the family and the nation.

Early folk methods of birth control varied from induced abortion and infanticide to more genteel, but ineffective, solutions such as eating bees or spitting three times into the mouth of a frog. The better informed and more prosperous segments of the population had knowledge of more effective methods – pessaries made of crocodile or elephant dung, or barriers of grasses or sponge soaked in protective solutions such as honey or gum arabic. Over the years more reliable methods were invented – the diaphragm, the IUD, the contraceptive pill, foam, and sterilization, for example – but all were for use by women. Men, in some societies, including our own, used coitus interruptus (or withdrawal) but it was not a universally popular method because of male dislike or female distrust. The other male method, the condom, was intended primarily as a prophylactic, and its acceptance as a contraceptive has been comparatively recent. Male steriliza- tion has only become popular in recent years and that popularity seems to be limited largely to the upper socio-economic group.

The reformers who led the birth control movement believed that if the work- ing classes could limit their fertility, wages would rise. (They also supported such 'radical' causes as compulsory education, universal adult franchise, free speech, the separation of church and state, and land reform!) Women's rights were added justification, as were maternal and child health and genetics. Family welfare and national and international prosperity and peace were logical extensions of their aims; and the impact of population growth on resources was a concern even as early as the late eighteenth century. Recently the environmental aspect has been added, but the other ideas are by no means new. From the beginning, therefore, the birth controllers – both men and women – were not only social reformers, but were concerned for the effect of population growth on human progress.

Their opponents fell into four main categories: government leaders who saw international power in large armies; business interests who saw profits in low wages and high rates of consumption; church leaders of all denominations who saw birth control as a threat to their authority as purveyors of education and arbiters of moral standards. The industrial revolution brought the emergence of a new professional class which included doctors, lawyers, school teachers, and others, most of whom also opposed birth control in public but practised it in private.

Depending on particular biases, all sorts of arguments against it were advanced: It would mean the suicide of the white races, the end of their empires, and the twilight of genius and virility. Birth control was tantamount to castration, mas- turbation, and infanticide. It would cause lunacy and sterility. Women, being in- capable of independent thought on any subject, had better find virtue in endur- ing without complaint whatever life might hold for them (and indeed most of them did). If they used birth control they would become degenerate, adulterous, and they might even develop an obscure ailment known as *Malthusian Uterus* – the external manifestations of which were a pale face and a worried expression!

It is of passing interest to note that, although opposition to contraception is almost gone today in Canada, the same arguments have been revived and refur- bished by the modern opponents of induced abortion. Once again we hear warnings of race suicide, are told that population density is somehow good, that technology can feed the world, that the poor should not be allowed to outnumber the rich, and that old people will be murdered next. They insist that Canada *needs* people, that life should be enjoyed now, and that posterity can worry about the future. Situation ethics are smothered in a sea of dogma, none of which will affect the fact that abortion always has and always will be practised, legally or illegally, and that other alternatives should be pursued.

The old-time advocates of contraception as a means of social reform used a combination of aggressive and defensive tactics. They sought confrontation with the law as a means of publicizing the fact that people could decide for themselves about their own fertility. The case of the Queen *vs.* Charles Bradlaugh and Annie Besant in 1876 in England was an example. Margaret Sanger's confrontations with the law in the United States before and after the First World War were others. These stalwarts urged contraception as the logical alternative to illegal abortion. Defensive tactics were also apparent in the 1920s and 1930s when declining birth rates in Europe were thought to augur population shrinkage, and pro-natalist policies were attempted by some governments. John Stuart Mill's concept of 'quality – not quantity' was revived; and the idea of spacing – not limiting – pregnancies was introduced. The diagnosis and treatment of infertility was stressed. The term 'birth control' which had been coined to replace the Malthusian term 'preventive checks,' gave place to the more euphemistic 'planned parenthood' or 'family planning.' That the term 'birth control' is now being advocated again by some people is indicative of another swing in public attitudes.

As a note to the abortion controversy, it should be recalled that it was confrontation which drew attention to the inadequacies of the 1969 amendment of the Criminal Code of Canada and loosened up the medical profession, to some extent at least, in the application of the law. Today it is a coalition of women's and mixed groups – radical and moderate – which is pressing for repeal, not because the members advocate wholesale abortion, but because the principle of individual responsibility should be involved, and because the law discriminates against the poor.

On the question of population policy, we all know that death control and migration control have contributed to the crises in the poor countries since they began to achieve independence after the Second World War – a time span of about 25 years. But some of us, at least, are not aware of the fact that through growing capacity to control epidemic diseases a population explosion would have occurred in Europe too beginning 200 years ago, had it not been for the increasing use of contraception and the migration of surplus population to other temperate regions in the world – to North and South America, to Australia, to New Zealand, and to South Africa. The industrial revolution introduced such further incentives to fertility limitation as the use of capital-intensive instead of labour-intensive methods of production, and a growing need for education.

The only real difference today is that the rich countries, with no further lands to conquer, are only now having to face up to the same problem as the poor; and we have the classic example of India as a poor country on the one hand, and the United States of America as a rich country on the other, both caught in the grip of population pressures.

Does Canada need a population policy? Does she have a population problem already – or will she face a crisis at some future date? No one knows, but *examination*, at least, of the question should begin. We do know that continuation of *ad hoc* measures will no longer suffice, even in this country.

To get back to family planning and some of the practical difficulties that always seem to face every country which is moving toward a government-sponsored program, one of the problems which arises is time lag between the announcement of policy and its implementation. Delays occur while training, financing, and logistical difficulties are worked out. They seem to occur also in inverse proportion to the degree of government commitment and leadership; and thoughtful analysts such as Bernard Berelson of the Population Council are forced to conclude that, in many countries, voluntary family planning has failed because it has never really been tried.

Yet another unfortunate and unnecessary development sometimes takes place in the growth of strained relations between the volunteers and the new professionals and therefore between volunteers and the governments who hire the latter to advise them. Universities get into the training field and are eager to undertake research, some of which may already be under way, and relatively successfully, by voluntary agencies. Power struggles can develop among the various branches of the medical profession for precedence in delivery of family planning services, and among *all* the related professions for a corner on the right to 'counsel.' A sudden fascination with special premarital and marital counselling also develops; and next, there is a conflict between those who advocate individual counselling as opposed to group counselling. Finally an argument arises over who shall teach 'family life education' either in whole or in part – the teacher, the clergyman, the school counsellor, the social worker, the home economist, the doctor, or the nurse. In the meantime, the health and well-being of many individuals is forgotten.

A final question is sometimes asked: Is a family planning program necessary in this country? It is said that, after all, the crude birth rate is declining steadily, and everyone who wants birth control can get it now. Both are dangerous generalizations. Little research on the subject has been done in Canada, but enough KAP studies have been done in other countries to indicate that crude birth rates are in no way indicative of problems, and the availability of services does not mean that they will be used. As there is no *basic* difference among people throughout the world, except for the accident of geography, and as much American data is borrowed by Canadians to prove their points, we can also borrow the findings of the 1965 *National Fertility Study* by Ryder and Westoff. Therefore in Canada only about 26 per cent of contraceptors are entirely successful, and nearly 20 per cent of all pregnancies are unwanted at the time of conception. Other reliable studies have also shown that although family size is not necessarily the cause of poverty, the poor tend to have more unwanted children than the rich; that higher parity and inadequate education go together; and that poverty increases in proportion to both.

We all know that even among the educated and the prosperous there is still considerable ignorance about human sexuality and human reproduction. The advertising industry and the information media continue to promote feminine submission and male virility. The result of both ignorance and exploitation is that one-third of first children are conceived before marriage. Illegitimacy rates are still rising in most parts of the country, the demand for induced abortion is rising, the incidence of battered babies and infanticide continues as usual, the emotional problems of 'unwantedness' increase, and venereal disease continues to spread. Birth control services and education are not the only answers to these problems, but they are essential ingredients of any proposed solution, and I am thankful that the fact is beginning to be recognized and admitted. So the need for a family planning program is as urgent in Canada as in any other country.

To sum up, the history of family planning and the universality of problems related to fertility indicate that we, too, need a two-fold program: first, to provide services and motivation so that individuals can make a voluntary choice concerning their fertility; and, second, to lay the groundwork for a population policy which all Canadians can understand and support. Volunteers have demonstrated the need and acceptability, and have developed some expertise, at least, in the former. If they have further roles to play in either, these should be delineated and all should be adequately financed. Representative advisory and coordinating committees could be set up to assess needs, and keep voluntary agency, university, and government activity at a high level of efficiency, in which the interests of the patient will come first.

The following well-known points concerning volunteers should be restated:

1 More often than not, volunteers are professionally or otherwise qualified, and are seldom fumbling amateurs.

2 Being detached in their attitudes, volunteers can help define over-all objectives and anticipate future needs.

3 Volunteers can influence bureaucratic inflexibility if it occurs.

4 In support of a needed service, especially if it is controversial, volunteers can be a powerful force for social progress.

5 To be really effective today, volunteers must be supported by paid staff.

6 Volunteers can fill supportive roles in public programs: *a* provided they are trained and properly placed; and *b* provided it is recognized that some volunteers are program-oriented, whereas others are administration-oriented.

7 Volunteers should be recruited from all age and income groups.

8 Volunteers should receive expenses.

9 Because they fill non-threatening roles, volunteers can be very useful in building motivation.

Tasks which can be undertaken by voluntary agencies include: promotion of medical services for all who want them; institution of specially designed programs to serve the poor, the handicapped, and ethnic groups; public, parent, and school education; training of clinic counsellors (including peer group representatives); co-ordination and presentation of basic information for professionals in related, non-medical fields; an ombudsman service to track down and defuse rumoured cases of coercion before they become partisan issues; and the study of population policy for Canada. But in all cases, they require adequate funding.

The following are alternative over-all plans for the use of volunteers:

1 Voluntary agencies can continue as they are, independent of government, but with some government funding, fighting a losing battle against growing demands on their time and energies.

2 Governments can accept responsibility for the delivery of services, and voluntary agencies can be assigned educational and motivational roles and be given sufficient funding to train their personnel and to maintain an efficient administration.

3 Voluntary agencies can be dissolved as soon as possible, leaving responsibility for both services and motivation in family planning: *a* wholly in the hands of government, public servants and the professions, or *b* shared with volunteers trained as supporting staff.

REFERENCES

1 Berelson, Bernard, 'The Present State of Family Planning Programs,' *Studies in Family Planning,* no. 57, The Population Council, New York, September 1970, p. 3.

2 Bishop, Mary F., 'From Left to Right: The Role of the Volunteers in Family Planning in the West and South Asia,' MA thesis, University of British Columbia, 1971.

3 Harp, John, and John R. Hofley, eds., *Poverty in Canada* (Scarborough, Ontario, 1971), p. 133.

4 Jaffe, Frederick S., 'Toward the Reduction of Unwanted Pregnancy: An Assessment of Current Public and Private Programs,' *Science* 74 (October 8, 1971), pp. 119-26.

5 Naylor, Harriet H., *Volunteers Today: Finding, Training and Working With Them* (New York, 1967), pp. 28-29.

6 Notestein, Frank W., 'A Critical Evaluation of National Family Planning Programmes,' *Proc. 8th International Conference of the International Planned Parenthood Federation* (London 1967), pp. 223-27.

7 *Poverty in Canada*. A report of the Special Senate Committee, Information Canada (Ottawa, 1971), pp. 14, 18.

8 *Report of the Royal Commission on the Status of Women in Canada* (Information Canada, Ottawa, 1970), pp. 313-14.

9 Westoff, Leslie Aldridge, and Charles F. Westoff, *From Now to Zero: Fertility, Contraception and Abortion in America* (Toronto, 1971), pp. 284-305.

10 Morris, Mary, *Volunteer Work in the Welfare State* (London, 1969).

PART THREE

GOVERNMENT REPORTS

CENOVIA ADDY

The federal family planning program:

Some implications for social work

As a potential resource to the field, the federal family planning program has implications for social work at several levels. Assistance to schools of social work in curriculum development is but one example. The federal program also has implications at the policy and practice levels. Furthermore, as family planning services become more available, social workers may find changing expectations from clients, particularly in the area of counselling.

Any discussion of the federal family planning program would be incomplete without reference to its philosophic base and at least a cursory examination of some of the current issues which could influence its future direction. The federal philosophy and the national issues may in the long run prove to be just as significant to social work as the present federal program.

In a democracy, legislation is regarded as a reflection of the will of the people, or at least as a response to what is perceived to be the wishes of a majority of the country's voters. Perhaps, then, it is valid to conclude that the 1892 federal legislation which prohibited the dissemination of information about birth control and the sale of contraceptives was a reflection of the prevailing attitudes and values of Canadian society at that time. The philosophy of the government of the day must have been based on the premise that it was in the public interest to deny access to contraceptives, and even to information that might enable persons to exercise a measure of control over their own fertility. The purpose of marriage was considered to be procreation; a large family was regarded as an asset. If this philosophy were not shared by such a large segment of the population, it is doubtful that such a law could have been passed or would have endured for so long. The climate in which such legislation was considered necessary was probably shaped by many factors, including social and economic conditions, the state of knowledge about human reproduction, and the morality of the times as well.

With changing societal values and attitudes, and with scientific and technological advances which brought reliable methods of birth control, the restrictive law of 1892 gradually fell into disuse. Progress was slow though, since as late as the 1930s the few birth control clinics that existed tended to be underground operations, in many instances providing service at considerable risk to the operators. But by the early 1960s effective contraceptives, though still illegal, were widely available in many parts of Canada, at least to the middle-class married woman who was willing to search for a co-operative physician. Public opinion had swung over to a much more liberal stance vis-à-vis birth control. The use of contraceptives to limit family size had become acceptable. Voluntary family planning associations were emerging.

Where was social work during this time? For the most part, social workers were silent. Although individual social workers became involved in the family planning movement, the profession was not among those pressing for change.

The next mile-stone was the 1969 Amendment to the Criminal Code which reversed certain aspects of the 1892 legislation. After 77 years of prohibition, the dissemination of information about birth control and the sale of contraceptives were once again legal. This amendment cleared the way for federal activity in family planning.

In 1970, in response to public demand, and in particular to the recommendations of the Royal Commission on the Status of Women in Canada, the government announced a program of public information, training, and research in family planning. Then in January 1972, the Family Planning Division was created to provide a centre of responsibility for federal activities in this field. It is headed by a physician and is located in the Social Allowances and Services Branch on the Welfare side of the Department of National Health and Welfare.

The philosophy on which the current federal program is based involves a recognition of (1) the rights of the individuals to control their own fertility, and (2) the responsibility of the federal government, in co-operation with provincial and municipal governments and voluntary agencies, to ensure that all Canadians have access to the knowledge and means that will enable them to exercise free choice in determining the number and spacing of their children. This is not to say that the social, economic, and health benefits of family planning for individual families are ignored, but rather to point out that from its inception the federal program has emphasized the right of the individual to make his own decisions in these matters.

The current program could be said to be a reflection of the prevailing values and attitudes of Canadian society and is indicative of the magnitude of the shift which has occurred since 1892.

There is evidence that an increasing number of social workers have come to the conclusion that the philosophy of the federal program, i.e., the recognition of the rights of individuals to control their own fertility, is compatible with the social work principle of the clients' rights to self-determination, and have decided that social work has a legitimate interest in family planning.

The objective of the federal family planning program is to ensure the accessibility and availability of family planning services to all Canadians who want them:

a By informing Canadians about the purpose and methods of family planning so that the exercise of free individual choice in this area will be based on adequate knowledge.

b By promoting the training of health and welfare professional and other staff involved in family planning services.

c By promoting relevant research in family planning.

d By aiding family planning programs operating under public or voluntary auspices through federal grants-in-aid and joint federal-provincial shared-cost programs.

It is important to note that the federal program does not have demographic objectives, that is, it does not aim to influence family size or population growth rates.

It might also be noted that the promotion of sex education which emphasizes responsible parenthood is regarded as an important component of the federal program on the basis that the acquisition of knowledge in this area is essential and that the process needs to begin long before an individual reaches adulthood.

Since, under the constitution of Canada, responsibility for the provision of health and welfare services, except to some native peoples who come within federal jurisdiction, rests with the provincial governments, the federal role is to stimulate, encourage and assist the provinces to provide family planning services.

The activities of the Family Planning Division include the purchase, preparation, and free distribution of family planning and sex education publications and audio-visual materials; the provision of consultation to government and non-government organizations; the provision of assistance in the education and training of health, welfare, and education personnel in those aspects of their jobs that are related to family planning or sex education; and the administration of the Family Planning Grants Program.

There appears to be a veritable explosion of interest in family planning and sex education throughout the country. During the past year, approximately one million pieces of literature on these subjects were distributed to individuals and organizations, including many social agencies, in response to specific requests. The purchase and distribution of foreign publications is regarded as an interim measure to fill a gap arising from a scarcity of Canadian literature on these subjects. That such a gap exists is understandable in light of the legal restrictions in effect prior to 1969. The division is currently developing a number of its own materials which are being produced in both official languages. Already available is a pamphlet on birth control facts for teenagers. In preparation are handbooks for nurses, for teachers, and for social workers. A publication on pastoral counselling in family planning is under consideration.

Consultation on matters related to family planning is provided on request to provincial, territorial, and municipal governments, including departments of health, welfare, and education, and also to a broad range of non-government organizations such as local family planning associations, child welfare agencies, YWCAS and YMCAS, family service agencies, social planning councils, clergyman's groups, and universities.

The division's consultants are available to assist in training and educational activities in health and welfare agencies and educational institutions. The extent to which this resource is being used by the social welfare field provides evidence of a recent but rapidly growing interest in family planning and related questions on the part of social workers, administrators, agency boards, and schools of social work.

As the division's social service consultant, the author has responded to numerous requests from public welfare departments and voluntary social agencies for advice and guidance in the formulation of policy statements and in the creation of opportunities for staff members to examine their attitudes toward family planning and sexuality and to become more knowledgeable about and comfortable with the subject matter. Assistance has been given in planning, organizing, and conducting staff development programs which focus on the social worker's role in meeting client's needs in the area of family planning.

As well, consultation on questions of curriculum development in family planning and sexuality, and other assistance, such as textbooks and guest lecturers, have been provided to schools of social work. In response to requests for information about courses and institutes for social workers, the social services consultant has compiled an inventory of learning opportunities in this area.

The Family Planning Grants Program provides short-term financial support for services and for demonstration, training, and research projects. Provincial and municipal departments, voluntary organizations, and universities are eligible to apply for grants. During the fiscal year that ended March 31, 1973, a total of $1,150,000 was awarded to 45 family planning projects.

Family planning grants were received by the following social welfare organizations: the Canadian Association of Schools of Social Work, for a seminar on family planning and sex education; the Nova Scotia Department of Social Services, to design a training program for social welfare staff; the University of Toronto Faculty of Social Work, to produce a book of readings in family planning; the McMaster University School of Social Work, to design a multi-disciplinary course in family planning; the British Columbia Department of Human Resources, to conduct a staff seminar in family planning.

At first glance one might conclude that family planning is not an issue in Canada. No major church group is opposed to the concept of permitting couples to plan the number and spacing of their children, although differences exist regarding the means by which this should be achieved. There also appears to be broad acceptance of the federal program and of its objectives. Critics of the program tend to suggest that the federal government is not doing enough in this field. In other words, there appears to be no real opposition to family planning. But on closer examination, one finds that what is generally accepted by Canadians is family planning for married couples. Those who disapprove of sexual activity outside marriage tend to disapprove of providing birth control services for single persons – particularly for unmarried, widowed, or divorced females.

The question of contraceptives for single parents is an issue in some social assistance agencies because of a belief that the provision of contraceptives to these clients is equivalent to sanctioning immoral behaviour, and further that such behaviour is often associated with child neglect. The unmarried mother presents a dilemma for some child welfare agencies.

One of the most controversial issues centres on whether contraceptives should be available to sexually active minors without parental consent. Those opposed claim that parents have the right to be consulted in advance of any 'treatment,' advice, or guidance provided to their children. Some also argue that the availability of contraceptives to minors is tantamount to condoning, if not encouraging, sexual activity. These persons feel that doctors or family planning counsellors who provide such service to minors without parental consent ought to be liable to charges of contributing to juvenile delinquency. Those on the other side of this issue argue that most minors who seek out birth control information are already sexually active, and that the withholding of information about, or access to, contraceptives will not ensure abstinence but may result in an unwanted pregnancy. Social agencies whose clients include adolescents or parents of adolescents are increasingly finding themselves facing this issue. Many child welfare agencies have developed policies in relation to contraceptives for their wards. Retarded adolescents present particular problems for the social agency.

A widely debated issue is the question of whether abortion should be considered an acceptable method of family planning. The federal government does not regard it as such, since abortion is legal only under certain prescribed conditions. On the other hand, the government does recognize the importance of abortion counselling and believes that a woman faced with a problem pregnancy should have an opportunity to examine all the alternatives open to her; should herself choose from among these options, with no pressure from the counsellor; and, further, should be eligible for post-abortion counselling which includes information about contraception. As family planning services become universally available and accessible, it is hoped that the incidence of abortion will be reduced.

Social agencies are grappling with the abortion issue as it affects individual clients, especially in relation to counselling. Child welfare agencies in particular have felt the impact of the more liberal legislation because of their responsibility for the medical care of their wards.

The question of sex education in the schools is an issue in many parts of the country. There is no real consensus among Canadians regarding an acceptable definition of sex education, its objectives, desirable content, or its place in the school curriculum. A number of communities have developed good programs, but this is not the case throughout the country.

Many of those who oppose incorporating sex education into the school curriculum do so on the grounds that it would encourage sexual activity among children. On the other hand, most of the leading authorities in the family planning field regard a comprehensive sex education program emphasizing responsible parenthood as crucial to the effectiveness of a family planning program. As we indicated above, the federal government supports the concept of sex education in the schools.

If a child welfare agency has responsibility for the total care of its permanent wards, does this responsibility include sex education? Some agencies have decided that it does and are finding ways of meeting this responsibility including educational programs for staff and foster parents.

Questions related to population growth are beginning to emerge in Canada, some of which have implications for the federal family planning program. People who advocate a national policy aimed at curbing the rate of population growth tend to believe that the federal government should be attempting to persuade Canadians to have fewer children. They believe that motivation for controlling fertility should include consideration of the future well-being of the nation, and of the whole world, not just that of the individual family. It is interesting to note, though, that those who favour continued population growth have not recommended the curtailment of family planning services. Obviously, the development of a population policy would require an examination of the possible impact on population growth of a large amount of existing social legislation and a broad range of social and economic programs, and would need to take into account the views of the majority of Canadians. An examination of the implications for social work of a possible population policy is beyond the scope of this paper.

Another issue worth noting involves oral contraceptives. Some physicians are advocating that they be made available without prescription, on the grounds that experience has shown that they are as safe as many non-prescription drugs. The importance of this issue lies in the fact that, not counting sterilization, the two most effective methods of contraception, i.e., oral contraceptives and the IUD, presently require medical intervention which some regard as a barrier to their ready accessibility. The removal of restrictions would most certainly have immediate implications for many social agencies, particularly those in the child welfare field.

If the resolution of most, if not all, social issues entails value judgments, then the answer to the question of what constitutes responsible sexual behaviour is perhaps basic to the resolution of many of the current family planning issues. It is probably safe to say that most Canadians are in favour of responsible sexual behaviour. It is not uncommon to see the acquisition of this attribute listed as one of the objectives of sex education. But an individual's definition of responsible sexual behaviour, for himself and/or for others, may depend to a large extent on his own value system.

During discussions with social work students, practising social workers, administrators, and agency board members in many parts of the country, the author has found wide variations in the definition of responsible sexual behaviour. For many it means that sexual intercourse should occur only between two people who are married to each other. Others are less concerned about the marital status of the persons involved, but will say that it simply means not exploiting a sexual partner. Or, for some, it may mean taking steps to ensure against conception, unless both partners, married or unmarried, actually want a child at that particular time and are willing and able to care for it. To those who are concerned about population issues, responsible sexual behaviour may mean not contributing to what they believe is an already existing problem of over-population. The significance of the definition of this term for individual social workers lies in the influence which their attitudes exert in their relationships with colleagues, clients, patients, or students; and also in the formulation of agency policy or the planning of agency programs related to family planning.

As current issues are resolved, new ones will surely emerge. Most will reflect changing values, which in turn may be influenced by scientific and technological advances, and by prevailing socio-economic conditions and many will have implications for social work. One might hope that, regardless of changing circumstances, the rights of the individuals to control their own fertility will remain the guiding principle of legislation enacted by some future generation of law-makers. One might also hope that a majority of social workers would concur with this philosophic concept.

FROM *THE STATUS OF WOMEN*

Responsible parenthood

From the Report of the Royal Commission on the Status of Women in Canada, *published by Information Canada at the end of 1970. The following sections relate to family planning in Canada.*

The scientific control of the human reproductive function is one of the most important developments of this century. Conception can be circumvented temporarily by a variety of birth control methods or permanently by sterilization; it can be induced by artificial insemination or inovulation; a precarious pregnancy can be maintained by drugs or techniques preventing spontaneous miscarriage; pregnancy can be safely terminated; a precise date for delivery can be planned. Further research is opening prospects of even more exact control.

Control of human reproduction has far-reaching consequences. It enables parents to plan the size of their families and the spacing of their children. It helps individuals and couples to reach a better sexual adjustment. Like many forms of scientific progress, it reduces the tyranny of natural forces over human beings; it makes possible more intelligent control of events; it increases personal freedom. All this requires readjustments in the law, and reshaping of social customs and attitudes. Women, as the child-bearers, will be most affected by this new freedom and responsibility.

In one sense, birth control is a social problem in Canada. Families with higher education and in higher income brackets have had easy access to birth control methods; the poor and less well-educated have not. The size of families has changed considerably in this century. In 1961 a married woman of 45 in Canada had had on the average about three live births, compared to six for a woman of the same age in 1900.

Nine major methods of birth control in order of relative effectiveness

Method	No. of likely pregnancies per 100 women using this method for one year
Sterilization	0.003
Pill	0.3
Intra-uterine devices	5.
Diaphragm or cervical cap (with jelly)	12.
Condom	14.
Withdrawal	18.
Chemical barriers	20.
Rhythm	24.
Douche	31.

SOURCE: Havemann, Ernest, and The Editors of Time-Life Books, *Birth Control* (New York, 1967), p. 59.

Today women want to take advantage of the increasing control over birth. They want sexual fulfilment as well as the right to plan a family. But no totally reliable method of contraception has yet been developed, and some methods still widely used are comparatively ineffective. The above figures indicate the relative degrees of effectiveness of the nine major methods in use today, by giving the number of likely pregnancies among 100 women using one of the methods for a year. Although measurement of the effectiveness of different birth control techniques varies according to the method of analysis, two techniques are usually considered most effective: the contraceptive pill and sterilization.

When properly used, the pill provides almost 100 per cent protection, but it is not medically recommended for all women. The possibly dangerous side effects of some contraceptive pills for some women are being studied. Health investigation committees in several countries have come to different conclusions. Since the first contraceptive pill was licensed for use in 1960, a large variety of pills, some with a lower percentage of hormones, have come on the market and research to improve their efficiency is continuing. Also being tested are other contraceptives, including kinds to be taken once a month or every six months, to be taken the day after sexual intercourse, or to be taken by men. Research may soon render today's contraceptives outdated.

Further research to develop a safe and reliable contraceptive is highly important, but more than research is needed. The safest and most sophisticated techniques are useless to women who do not know they exist or are afraid to use them. Accurate information about birth control must be more widely circulated, and better understanding and acceptance must be promoted by public debate. The acceptance of birth control has been hindered by general ignorance, by lack of specific information, by some religious beliefs, and by the law. The Roman Catholic Church, for instance, has not lifted its ban on the use of contraceptives, and church policy was restated in the encyclical *Humanae Vitae* (1968). This policy may inhibit the use of family planning programs by some Roman Catholic agencies.

The legal ban on the sale and advertisement of contraceptives and on the dissemination of information ended in Canada on August 18, 1969, when the Act amending section 150(2)(c) of the Criminal Code became law.[1] Since its introduction in 1892, few attempts were made to enforce the ban. Birth control drugs and devices have been available at pharmacies all over Canada for years and some doctors have been prescribing the pill for control of procreation since it was first marketed in 1961. One birth control device (condom) has always been sold openly as a prophylactic against venereal disease.

Under the new legislation, the advertisement of contraceptives is controlled by the Food and Drug Directorate. The first regulation[2] banned all advertisements for commercial purposes. Representations from various concerned people brought about the adoption of new regulations authorizing the commercial advertisement in the mass media of contraceptives except for the pill and the intrauterine devices (IUD).[3]

This regulation excludes the advertisement of what are at present two of the most effective methods of birth control. Although they are available only on prescription because they require medical supervision, we believe women should not be prevented from knowing about them. In fact, the diaphragm, which may be advertised, also needs medical supervision to be effective since it must be fitted properly by a physician. Equally important, there is at present no requirement that advertising carry information about the limited effectiveness of the other methods of birth control. Women should be informed of the limitations of each birth control method in advertisements on the label.

For 40 years before the law was amended, a few people dared to operate birth control centres in spite of the risk of being prosecuted. Since the ban was lifted a number of centres are being planned, but there are still relatively few in Canada. In 1969 it was estimated that there were approximately 38 centres, including seven Family Planning clinics (under the Family Planning Federation of Canada), eight public health clinics and 23 hospital clinics. The need for more facilities is obvious; in 1968 there were 4,378,100 women of child-bearing age (15 to 45 years) in Canada.[4] Yet, according to their own estimate, one of the Family Planning clinics in Toronto could process only 1250 calls in one year.[5]

Case histories[6] convinced the commission of the human distress caused by the lack of birth control information and medical advice in regard to family planning.

The commission strongly believes that information and medical assistance on contraceptives should be made available to Canadian women in all walks of life. The same services should be available for men. The right to these services has been recognized by the United Nations in the 1968 Proclamation of Teheran, which declared family planning to be a basic human right.

The use of contraceptives cannot be isolated from the complete sexual life and the quality of relations with the other sex. These questions are critically important for young people, particularly young girls, because of the effect that information, or lack of it, may have on their future. Since many teenagers do have sexual intercourse, they also need the means to avoid conception and should therefore receive appropriate advice and have access to the most effective birth control information and advice. Social workers report that some young unmarried girls involved in sexual relationships neglect to use contraceptives through sheer ignorance. These are the girls who subsequently become child mothers.

The commission believes that young girls should be informed and advised about birth control and given access to contraceptives. It is important that adequate knowledge of the reproductive function of the body and of human sexual behaviour be taught at primary and secondary school. The commission endorsed the principle of sex education in schools in the chapter dealing with education.

The commission recognizes the excellent work initiated by the Family Planning Federation of Canada and endorses its request for a much wider family planning program in Canada. The principal responsibility for the dissemination of information on birth control methods rests with the health and welfare authorities. The main question is how to reach women. According to recent estimates, only about 23 of the 948 general hospitals in Canada had family planning clinics. Clearly more of these clinics should be organized and widely publicized. As a policy, federal and provincial governments should print and distribute birth control information to hospitals, teachers, doctors, public health nurses, social workers, and the public.

Imaginative programs can be developed. Hospitals now give maternity patients information on the care and upbringing of their babies. At this time they could also give them information about family planning, methods of birth control, and services available in the community. As an example of initiative, we note that the Health Department of London, Ontario, recently included a circular on birth control with the hydro bills sent to London households. The circular listed family planning clinics and other family health services provided by the department and said, in part: 'If you wish assistance with spacing your children and planning your next pregnancy, or help if you have been unable to have children, you may ask your district Public Health Nurse, inquire at the Child Health Centre in your district, or telephone the London Health Department at the Family Planning Clinic.' This practice could well be adopted by other departments of health.

Making people aware of the facts does not necessarily mean that they will be able to get the medical assistance and advice they need to put the information into practice. Many women do not have a family doctor; they do not know where to go or even what questions to ask. Every provincial health department should organize family planning clinics within the existing provincial public health units, to provide relevant information, medical examination, and birth control devices and drugs to anyone who wants them. The clinics should be open not only during the day but also in the evenings and on weekends. Such clinics would need trained personnel; public health nurses and social workers should be trained for this additional function.

Therefore, *we recommend that birth control information be available to everyone.*

Further, *we recommend that the Department of National Health and Welfare (a) prepare and offer birth control information free of charge to provincial and territorial authorities, associations, organizations, and individuals and (b) give financial assistance through National Health grants and National Welfare grants to train health and welfare workers in family planning techniques.*

Furthermore, *we recommend that provincial departments of health (a) organize family planning clinics in each public health unit to ensure that everyone has access to information, medical assistance, and birth control devices and drugs as needed, and (b) provide mobile clinics where they are needed, particularly in remote areas.*

The use of sterilization as a birth control method has been limited by the fear of unknown effects, by linking it with the eugenics movement, and by the attitude of medical authorities who consider it dubious practice to sterilize patients for birth control reasons. The only laws dealing with the subject in Canada were adopted in the 1920s by Alberta and British Columbia; they prohibit compulsory eugenic sterilization. There is a great misunderstanding about the effects of sterilization. The operation does not remove any organ, nor does it interfere with sexual desire or performance. It does not create a hormone imbalance. New surgical techniques make the operation much easier for the surgeon and less painful for the patient. The vasectomy is a minor operation performed in less than 20 minutes in the doctor's office.[7] For a woman, sterilization requires hospitalization.

No law in Canada expressly prohibits a physician from sterilizing an individual on request for contraceptive purposes only and there is no case law to that effect in Canada. The only two Canadian legal cases on sterilization[8] deal with the question of the consent of the patient to the operation. However, sterilization is usually carried out for medical reasons only, and doctors do not ordinarily perform the operation simply on request.[9] At stake for the physician is the question of his criminal or civil liability. He might be found criminally liable if a Canadian court of law were to rule that sterilization entails bodily harm or maiming as defined by section 216 of the Criminal Code. So far no Canadian court has done so. Civil liability of the physician might arise if the operation were carried out without the consent of the patient and the patient's spouse, unless it were performed because of medical necessity under emergency conditions. The law is not clear as to liability if the consent of the spouse is not obtained.

The commission believes this situation should be clarified by declaratory legislation to make sterilization available to everyone for non-clinical reasons. The law should specify that non-therapeutic or elective sterilization performed by a qualified medical practitioner, upon the written request of a patient, will not create criminal or civil liability for the practitioner if the patient is informed of its consequences in advance, and the operation is performed with due care. The consent of the spouse should not be required.

Therefore, *we recommend that the criminal law be clarified so that sterilization performed by a qualified medical practitioner at the request of his patient shall not engage the criminal responsibility of the practitioner.*

Further, *we recommend that the provinces and territories adopt legislation to authorize medical practitioners to perform non-therapeutic sterilization at the request of the patient free from any civil liabilities toward the patient or the spouse except liability for negligence.*

We have been discussing only the legal relationship between patient and doctor. In the relationship between husband and wife, other considerations arise, including their concept of marriage.

We can expect that birth control will be practised by Canadian women through increasingly reliable and readily available methods. This may in time lead to a reduction in the incidence of abortion. We doubt that abortion can be eliminated entirely. We must therefore consider abortion and the laws that apply to it. At one time abortion was a serious threat to the life of a woman. Today, owing to improved surgical techniques, it is safer during the first 12 weeks of pregnancy to undergo an abortion than to continue the pregnancy. It is possible that new methods of abortion may be even safer. Abortion is permissible in some states and countries for pregnancies ranging from 12 weeks to 26 weeks – by which time the foetus is generally considered to be viable. A few countries set no time limit on abortion at the woman's request ...

The amendment of the Canadian Criminal Code in 1969 adapted the law to current medical practice by allowing, under section 237(4) of the Criminal Code,[10] a qualified medical practitioner in an accredited or approved hospital to procure a miscarriage if the hospital's therapeutic abortion committee, by a majority of its members, has certified in writing that the continuation of the pregnancy would endanger the life or health of the woman. This formal procedure may make it even more difficult for some women to obtain a therapeutic abortion than it was in the past. The principal benefactor of this law is the medical profession which will know exactly under what conditions a therapeutic abortion can be performed and criminal responsibility avoided. It can even be argued, and illustrated by the experience of other countries, that a therapeutic abortion committee has the effect of reducing the number of therapeutic abortions performed by a hospital.[11] The current law cannot be relied upon to reduce the number of illegal abortions or the maternal deaths and injuries that follow the improper medical practices used in many illegal abortions. The first report issued by the Dominion Bureau of Statistics since the Code was amended shows that only 235 legal abortions were performed over a three-month period in six provinces: Prince Edward Island, Nova Scotia, New Brunswick, Saskatchewan, Alberta, and British Columbia.

Requiring the approval of a hospital therapeutic abortion committee has the effect of limiting the possibility of obtaining legal abortion.[12] Approval is not easily obtained and involves delay. For many women in remote areas there is no nearby hospital, accredited, approved, or otherwise. Under the present law, they cannot get legal abortions even though qualified medical practitioners may be at hand, unless the life of the mother is endangered.

Is there a case, then, to broaden the grounds for abortion in Canada? It is common knowledge that illegal abortions are taking place. The number cannot be accurately known; estimates range from 30,000 to 300,000 a year. Dr Serge Mongeau[13] gives an estimate for Quebec of from 10,000 to 25,000 annually; for Canada the figure would be 40,000 to 100,000. If the estimate of 100,000 were accurate, it would mean that one pregnancy in five is being aborted by illegal means. Prosecution is not an indication of the number of illegal abortions, since an average of only 30 persons are convicted each year. Law enforcement is nonexistent except in a few cases where the woman's life has been seriously endangered.

Who are the women who seek abortions? Most national statistics indicate that the majority are married and already have two or three children.[14] For example, a study made in Sweden of women who had abortions showed that 66 per cent were married. In Czechoslovakia, the proportion of married women among those seeking legal abortions was 82 per cent in 1962. In the United States, the Kinsey Report, in 1953, indicated that of 5293 women interviewed, 1044 admitted having had abortions; of these, 11 out of 20 were married; the great majority had been aborted by a doctor.

Fifteen years ago there was no public demand for legalized abortion. However, in a national opinion survey released on March 7, 1970, a Gallup Poll of Canada showed that 43 per cent of the adult population favoured legislation that would permit a woman to terminate pregnancy at any time during the first three months. Another type of survey carried by the French and English editions of *Chatelaine* in January 1968 indicated that the respondents were certainly in favour of liberalizing the abortion laws. Fifty-six per cent and 54 per cent of the respondents of the English and French versions, respectively, felt that the law on legal abortions should copy Britain's new law, while (respectively) 32 per cent and 25 per cent believed that it should be granted at the request of the women. Combining these two groups would show that more than three-quarters of *Chatelaine's* respondent, both English and French, favoured abortion on request or close to it.

During the public hearings of this commission many organizations and individuals urged the liberalization or the repeal of all abortion laws. We also heard eloquent appeals to retain them. Some people consider the foetus as being a human life and for them abortion amounts to murder. Others believe that the foetus, though having the potentiality of human life, is not yet a human being, and consequently these people do not regard abortion as harming any existing person. The conviction that women have the right to make their own decisions about abortion was often expressed in the formula: 'A woman should have control of her own body.' Three excerpts from briefs illustrate this point of view: 'This is a problem for which only the woman involved can answer. She knows her circumstances and her emotional limitations. She alone should be allowed to make the decision. We cannot and dare not stand in judgment. This one additional pregnancy may be the "final straw" to break one otherwise reasonably stable home ... who then cares for any other children? ... who then cares and pays for her broken health, physical and mental?'[15] 'The law should be amended to permit abortion at the mother's request after she has received the best medical advice available. Such legislative reform would then allow the Canadian woman complete dignity as a person with full rights, no longer subject to a discrimination imposed in a different century by an altogether different society.'[16] 'We do not feel that the proposed changes in abortion legislation go far enough in giving women control over their own bodies.'[17]

It is not the function of this commission to give preference to one trend of religious opinion over another. Moral judgments change with time or when seen in other and wider perspectives.

A law that has more bad effects than good ones is a bad law. We believe the present abortion law should be amended. As long as it exists in its present form thousands of women will break it. Breaking the law forces them to resort to methods that seriously endanger their physical and emotional health. The present law also discriminates against the poor, who do not have the means to get an abortion, for example, by going outside the country.

We have come to the conclusion that each woman should have the right to decide if she will terminate pregnancy. We believe that a woman who has been the victim of rape or incest should not be forced to bear a child. We propose that the approval of a hospital abortion committee no longer be required and that the decision be made by the woman after consultation with her physician. Anytime during the first 12 weeks of pregnancy is considered to be a relatively safe period in which to perform an abortion.

Therefore, *we recommend that the Criminal Code be amended to permit abortion by a qualified medical practitioner on the sole request of any woman who has been pregnant for 12 weeks or less.*

Further, *we recommend that the Criminal Code be amended to permit abortion by a qualified practitioner at the request of a woman pregnant for more than 12 weeks if the doctor is convinced that the continuation of the pregnancy would endanger the physical or mental health of the woman, or if there is a substantial risk that if the child were born, it would be greatly handicapped, either mentally or physically.*

NOTES

1 An Act to amend the Food and Drugs Act and the Narcotic Control Act and to make a consequential amendment to the Criminal Code. *Statutes of Canada.* 1968-69, C. 41.

2 *The Canada Gazette,* Part II, Statutory Orders and Regulations 1969, SOR/69-417, vol. 103, no. 16, Ottawa, Queen's Printer, August 27, 1969, p. 1169.

3 *The Canada Gazette,* Part II, Statutory Orders and Regulations 1970, SOR/70-29, vol. 104, no. 2, January 28, 1970, p. 80.

4 Dominion Bureau of Statistics. *Vital Statistics Preliminary Annual Report.* Cat. no. 84-201 (Ottawa, 1968), table I, p. 5.

5 One clinic in Vancouver, BC was reported to receive an average of 45 patients each week (the clinic was open only three nights a week). The two clinics in that city received a total of 500 patients in 1967. The total case-load of the two clinics is 7000. In Hamilton, Ont., the oldest family planning clinic in Canada has served 6418 patients in its 36 years of operation.

6 Brief No. 5.

7 The Ontario Health Services Insurance Plan lists the cost of a vasectomy at $50.

8 Murray *v.* Murray, 1949, 2 Dominion Law Report, p. 492; and Chivers and Chivers *v.* Weaver and McIntyre, unreported case of the Ontario Supreme Court.

9 The College of Physicians and Surgeons of Ontario has said: 'The Council views the performance of vasectomy on the same basis as any other surgical procedure which should only be performed in the best interests of the patient, and with the consent of the patient and his spouse. The decision to perform vasectomy is a judgment to be made by the medical practitioner in the individual case; and the procedure should be done only after the results of the operation have been clearly explained to the patient prior to the operation.' *Canadian Medical Association Journal* 102 (January 31, 1970), p. 211.

    The position of the Canadian Medical Association was reviewed at a meeting of its General Council on June 15, 1970, when it passed a resolution which stated: 'That any procedure for the purpose of producing sterilization of either male or female is acceptable in the following circumstances: When it is performed by a duly qualified medical practitioner; and if performed in an active treatment public hospital or other location with adequate facilities; and if performed with the written permission of the patient and after the patient has signed a statement to the effect that he or she understands that the sterility will in all likelihood be permanent, similar consent of the spouse, or guardian, if applicable, to be obtained when possible.'

10 Criminal Law Amendment Act, 1968–69. *Statutes of Canada*. 1968–69, Chapter 38.

11 In New York where formerly therapeutic abortions had to be reported to the Health Service, there was a decrease of 65 per cent of such abortions from 1943 to 1962, following the appointment of hospital abortion committees. Another factor could be the reduction of clinical indications calling for such an operation, as a result of medical development in this field.

12 Abortions may be performed only in accredited or approved hospitals. A hospital is accredited by the Canadian Council on Hospital Accreditation if it provides certain facilities: in January 1970 of the 948 general hospitals in Canada only 450 were accredited. Hospitals may be approved by the provincial ministers of health: it is not known how many fall within this category.

13 Mongeau, Dr Serge, and Renée Cloutier, *L'Avortement* (Montreal, 1968).

14 Potts, Malcolm, 'Legal Abortion in Eastern Europe,' *The Eugenics Review* 59 (1967), 232, and Mongeau and Cloutier, p. 76.

15 Brief No. 250.

16 Brief No. 29.

17 Brief No. 437.

FROM *POVERTY IN CANADA*

Poverty and family planning

In 1971, the report Poverty in Canada *was published by Information Canada. This book contained the final report of the Special Senate Committee on Poverty, chaired by Senator David A. Croll. Among the 209 briefs submitted to the hearings of this committee was the following statement from the Family Planning Federation of Canada.*

The Family Planning Federation points to family size as a cause of, and to family planning as one approach to the reduction of, poverty in Canada. The poor in Canada have more children than the non-poor, and many of these babies are unwanted. Recommendations centre on the need to democratize family planning in Canada, through the federal government's leadership in information, research, training, and financial aid to the provinces, and through provincial governments' initiatives in the delivery of family planning services and in family life education.

FAMILY SIZE AND POVERTY

The FPFC wishes to make a self-evident point. However large the material resources available to a family unit, the more members there are of that family, the less of these resources there are available to each dependent individual. The knowledge of, and means to practise, family planning put one of the two major parts of this equation into the hands of the parents, and give them some measure of control over many important aspects of their future family life. The effect of this control is not of course confined to the simple numerical equation between numbers of children and material resources, but has wider effects in the non-material aspects of family life.

The impact of family size obviously varies at different income levels and increases in severity at lower levels. The larger the family at lower income levels the greater the effect of poverty on the individual family member. To limit family size therefore mitigates poverty.

Unfortunately the effect of family size on the impact of poverty is not confined to a single generation, but is a further factor in the incidence of what is known as 'hereditary poverty,' where the children of poverty become the parents of poverty in their turn. A large family limits the possibility of parents' investing in each child as much as they would like to do, whether in schooling or training or whether in land, farm machinery, tools for a trade, or even adequate personal equipment like clothing. These children of poverty are therefore handicapped, as others are not, by the lack of investment in their lives and in their turn cannot as easily provide for their children as they might have done. To break out of this chain of 'hereditary poverty' they too need to know how to limit their family size.

POVERTY: DEFINITION

1 It is a negative commentary on our society that we lack a total definition of poverty in theory. It is a positive commentary on our society that we now know we cannot accept poverty in practice. The conviction that poverty can be eliminated is now very high on our scale of beliefs. In earlier times that scale maintained that poverty was inevitable for some people. Industrialization is marked by fundamental alteration in the rank of poverty in our value system. Where earlier there was passive acceptance, today there is universal hostility to its toleration.

2 This hostility has been translated – notably in North America in the 1960s – into vigorous efforts to dissect, define, and defeat poverty. A very important output of these efforts has been the realization that a total definition of poverty cannot rest solely on economic indices. We now speak of a 'culture' of poverty; we divide poverty into material and non-material aspects. We attempt to balance economic indicators with social indicators and social systems accounting.

3 This federation approaches the definition of poverty with the use of a traditional unit of analysis, the family. The family is our basic unit of social learning and social organization. As goes the health of the family, we reason, so goes the health of our Canadian community. The identification of poor families then hinges on answering the question: 'Does the family possess a matrix of material and non-material resources adequate to cope fulfillingly with its environment?' From the material side then, we look at both income and number of people in the family; from the non-material side we look at the socio-cultural aspects which we know contribute to, and follow from, the material situation.

4 In defining poverty therefore, we cite the family that *does not* possess a matrix of material and non-material resources adequate to cope fulfillingly with its environment.

FAMILY PLANNING: DEFINITION

1 Our dilemma with poverty in theory and practice is just the reverse when we consider family planning. We know a lot about family planning in theory, but – especially in Canada, a developing country in family planning – we have not yet fully made up our minds about family planning in practice.

2 In earlier times, large families were necessary for man's survival as a species. A large number of children had to be born every year to replace the many people who died. With industrialization came the possibility of providing for man's minimal needs for food, clothing, and shelter, and the diminished economic utility of children. The desire to limit family size came to be a common characteristic of all societies. But only in recent times have we had adequate technological answers to meet this common desire.

3 In defining family planning and its role in our society we know a common desire for it exists. We know that the aspiration 'Every child a wanted child ...' is a hope we all share. We know that family planning is *one* of those resources crucial to the ability of a family to cope fulfillingly with its environment. If every child is a wanted child, children are better cared for, both physically and emotionally. Mothers are subjected to lower health risks if births are spaced carefully. The assurance that another child won't come before it's wanted helps couples plan other material and non-material aspects of their lives with more confidence. And we know family planning – in the wide sense in which it must be defined – can assist some of the childless to bear normal, healthy babies. Family planning is not simply the insertion of an IUD. It embodies a careful calculation of family needs balanced against family resources with the aim of happy, healthy, responsible family life.

4 Reviewing the definitions of poverty and family planning, we see clearly that family planning is not only a means of helping people who are already poor, but also of helping people avoid poverty.

FAMILY PLANNING AND THE
REDUCTION OF POVERTY IN CANADA

1 The Economic Council of Canada identified one in five Canadians as living in poverty. We have evidence that these poor have more children than the non-poor.

2 In 1961, families with a university-educated head in the 35 to 40 age group averaged 2.6 children and earnings of $8610 annually; family heads in the same

age group with less than five years of schooling averaged 4.2 children and an annual income of $2467.

3 An on-going study of Vancouver multi-problem poor families gives us a slightly wider picture of the number of children and poverty situation. It found that such families were larger than the Canadian average by 1.1 person, and more significantly, that one-third of the families had one or more children over 15 years of age living apart from the family for reasons of adoption, placement, emotional treatment, or delinquency.

4 It is not very useful, therefore, to look just at crude birth rate figures* for Canada and conclude that all families desiring to plan are doing so. We must look at the relationship between socio-economic status and use of the resource family planning. Our conclusion is that the non-poor are using family planning as one way of avoiding poverty – but the poor are not. We know that the practice of family planning declines rapidly from the top to the bottom of Canada's socio-economic ladder. The poor are still having the babies, many of them unwanted.

5 This last bit of evidence, that Canada's poor are having unwanted children, is most important when we consider government efforts to reduce poverty. The federation is not making an arbitrary judgment of the desires of Canada's poor – the desire is daily expressed to us through our work. We are merely passing it on. And in doing so, *we are suggesting a goal for government efforts: To democratize family planning as one way of reducing poverty in Canada, to offer to our poor the resources already available to the non-poor from private sources.*

FAMILY PLANNING FOR CANADA'S POOR: GUIDELINES

1 The Federation commends the following guidelines to the consideration of government.

a The purpose of family planning programs is to offer services, not impose them.

b Information about family planning should be offered to mothers confined for delivery in public hospitals and during post-partum care.

c Family planning services should be available to all regardless of income.

d Eligibility requirements for family planning services should be liberal in regard to marital status.

These guidelines are by no means exhaustive, but they provide orientation points for the development and extension of family planning services of public sponsorship in Canada.

---

*Rate per 1000 population: 27.2 (1946); 27.2 (1951); 28.0 (1956); 26.1 (1961); 19.4 (1966).

FAMILY PLANNING FOR
CANADA'S POOR: RECOMMENDATIONS

From the perspective of public involvement and leadership in family planning, Canada started off 1969 as an underdeveloped country – and ended as a developing country. The long-standing Criminal Code prohibition on the sale of or the dissemination of information on contraceptive materials was removed. The Food and Drug Directorate issued a regulation allowing public advertisement of some contraceptives. The Canadian International Development Agency took the initiative of preparing for requests for family planning aid from developing countries. The federal and provincial governments began to study in earnest the implications of public involvement in family planning.

2 These are encouraging developments. But since the previous prohibition of the Criminal Code prevented public and publicly-funded agencies from offering family planning to the poor, much remains to be done.

3 With the above guidelines in mind the FPFC urges the committee to recommend the following:

a That all governments in Canada adopt the policy of *democratization* of family planning, within their particular constitutional jurisdictions.

b That the federal government assume responsibility for leadership: (*i*) in the *training* of health and welfare workers, both through the National Health Grants and the National Welfare Grants, and through the proposed Canadian Centres for Population Studies; (*ii*) in the family planning *research* area, both through the National Health Grants and the National Welfare Grants, and through the creation of at least one English- and one French-speaking centre for population studies; (*iii*) in the provision of *funds for provincial delivery* of family planning services, initially guided by a national conference on family planning, and through the existing provisions of the Canada Assistance Plan; (*iv*) in the family planning *information* area, through a national public information campaign.

c That the federal government assume full responsibility for leadership in the delivery of family planning services to Indians and Eskimos wherever such services are welcome and wanted.

d That the federal government extend the existing regulations on public advertisement of all contraceptives approved by the Food and Drug Directorate.

e That the provincial governments: (*i*) assume full responsibility for the delivery of family planning *services* within their existing primary constitutional jurisdiction over health and welfare; (*ii*) assume full responsibility for family life *education* including advice on contraceptives in the schools, through their exclusive constitutional jurisdiction over education.

THE FIRST NATIONAL CONFERENCE

Recommendations of the

First National Conference on Family Planning

FEBRUARY 28 TO MARCH 2, 1972
OTTAWA, ONTARIO

The First National Conference on Family Planning was convened by the Department of National Health and Welfare to assess progress in the development of family planning services and to consider how public and voluntary organizations could co-operate effectively to improve services. Attended by 310 delegates, the conference brought together for the first time, from all parts of Canada, a broad cross-section of people interested in family planning. Included among the participants were legislators, public officials, physicians, nurses, social workers, educators, researchers, and consumers.

The agenda covered a wide range of topics related to family planning, with particular reference to information programs, services, teaching and training of service providers, and research. The format combined plenary sessions, where a number of papers were presented; small heterogeneous discussion groups; and somewhat larger, self-selected, special interest groups.

In addressing the conference, the Minister of National Health and Welfare, the Honourable John Munro, said that he hoped that the deliberations would produce recommendations which could be translated into action. Accordingly, the 15 discussion groups directed some of their attention to the formulation of recommendations. A drafting committee, consisting of three non-governmental conference participants, then summarized in one document the recommendations of all of the discussion groups. The committee report, which includes a preamble of general principles, was revised by the participants at the final plenary session of the conference and forms the major portion of the contents of this pamphlet. The recommendations of two of the special interest groups have been included, although they were not considered by the entire conference.

Following the conference, the Department of National Health and Welfare appointed a task force to examine the recommendations in terms of their feasibility for implementation. The task force's comments on federal programs and policies as they apply to specific recommendations also appear in the pamphlet.

It should be noted that the conference recommendations and findings represent the views of the majority of the participants and do not necessarily reflect the existing policy of the federal government. Copies of the recommendations have been sent to the appropriate provincial, territorial, and municipal jurisdictions and to many non-governmental agencies and organizations for their information. Additional copies of this pamphlet may be obtained from the Family Planning Division, Social Allowances and Services Branch, Department of National Health and Welfare, Ottawa, Ontario, K1A 1B5.

The conference proceedings have been printed separately for distribution to the conference participants.

FINDINGS AND RECOMMENDATIONS
AS AMENDED AT FINAL PLENARY SESSION

General principles
Delegates to the First National Conference on Family Planning, meeting in fifteen discussion groups,
Recognized and Emphasized That, freedom of choice being understood,
1 The right of all Canadians to family planning services involves an obligation on the part of individuals and families to determine, responsibly and realistically, the number and spacing of their children; and

2 Informed judgment and action by individuals and families require not only availability of the full spectrum of birth control information and services, but knowledge and understanding concerning *inter alia* human growth and development, human sexuality and psycho-social relationships, the privileges and demands of parenthood, and the relationships among population growth and density, production and consumption of resources, and natural and man-made environments; and

3 Family life education and family planning involve responsibilities and opportunities not only for the individual and the family but also for religious institutions and other voluntary and community groups, the educational system, health and welfare agencies and professions, commercial enterprises, the media of communication, and governments at all levels; and

4 Family planning information and services as an essential part of a system of health and social services are a necessary but not a sufficient approach to public family and social policy (by way of example, family and social policy also includes migration and settlement, housing, taxation, social security, environmental protection, etc.); and

5 Co-ordination will therefore be essential at all levels in policy development, program planning, and organization and delivery of information and services.

CONFERENCE RECOMMENDATIONS AND TASK FORCE COMMENTS*

1 Family planning policy, programs and services should encompass the full range of birth control methods, sterilization (vasectomy, and tubal ligation), abortion, fertility and genetics, as well as marriage and family (including adoption) counselling, and assessment, diagnostic, referral, and follow-up functions.

(Although the federal government does not regard abortion as an acceptable method of primary birth control, it recognizes that, since no contraceptive method now available is completely reliable, and since contraception is often used ineffectively or not at all, unplanned pregnancies are inevitable. Provincial and municipal governments and voluntary agencies providing family planning services may consequently consider that there is a place for post-conception fertility control within the limits currently imposed by the Criminal Code, and that their programs should include abortion counselling services.)

2 Family planning information and services should be available to any individual in Canada:

a Without economic, geographic or other barriers to access.

b Without reference to age or marital status.

c Without legal liability (apart from negligence) to the provider of the service.

(The federal government agrees, with the proviso that, in their own interest, providers of family planning services may wish to take into account the relevant legal age of consent.)

3 *a* Family planning services should become an integral component of all community-based health and/or social (personal) services.

(The federal government agrees.)

b Appropriate representation should be made to the governmental task force on community health centres, reporting to the federal and provincial cabinet ministers, to include family planning in the functions and services of such centres.

*Comments by Department of National Health and Welfare Task Force appear in parenthesis after the recommendations.

(This recommendation has been forwarded by the Department of National Health and Welfare to the Chairman of the Community Health Centre Project for consideration.)

c The further development of family planning clinics, mobile units, 'storefront' services, youth service centres and similar programs, public and voluntary, should be encouraged and assisted to meet the needs of individuals and groups who are unable or unwilling to seek information and/or services in other ways.

(Support for a number of innovative and demonstration family planning projects has been, and is being, provided by the federal government under the Local Initiatives Program and Opportunities for Youth.)

d A family planning clinic or equivalent service should be made a prerequisite for the accreditation of all general hospitals.

(The federal government has brought this recommendation to the attention of the Canadian Council on Hospital Accreditation.)

4 The federal government should develop, review continuously, and keep the public informed concerning a national population policy; the policy should take careful account of such variables as fertility and mortality rates, immigration and emigration, and internal migration.

(The Department of National Health and Welfare believes that the first step should be an examination of the need for a national population policy, and that one starting point for such a review would be a national fertility survey as recommended by the special interest group on research. Examination of the need for, and development of, a national population policy is complex and would involve many government departments and non-government agencies, co-ordinated at the highest political level.)

5 a Provincial and territorial governments should develop clear family life education and family planning policies, program priorities, and, where relevant, standards, in the relevant areas of information and education, services, research, and teaching, and training.

(The Conference Recommendations have been sent to all provincial ministers of health, welfare and education, and to the territorial governments.)

b Through earmarking a percentage of their health and welfare budgets, or in some other identifiable fashion, provincial governments should provide expanded financial and staff support for family life education and family planning services public and voluntary.

(See comment 5a above.)

6 High priority should be given in all Canadian provinces and territories to the provision of family life education programs, family planning information, and health and social services (including family planning) to relatively 'isolated' communities and groups, including, for example, people in remote rural and

northern areas, native peoples living in self-contained settlements, and adolescents living away from home.

(The Department of Indian Affairs and Northern Development has a responsibility, which is exercised in co-operation with the government of the Yukon Territory, for the development of family life education programs for native peoples. Courses in family life education offered by the department are based on similar courses offered in the respective provincial schools. This recommendation has been noted by the Department of National Health and Welfare. As well, copies have been forwarded to the Department of the Secretary of State, to provincial and territorial departments of health, welfare, and education and to a number of municipal governments and voluntary organizations for their information.)

7 Provincial, territorial, and municipal governments should develop as rapidly as possible a network of community health or personal service centres, designed to ensure maximum participation of people from the local community in policy development and program and service planning and evaluation.

(See comment on Recommendation 5a above.)

8 Provincial, territorial, and municipal governments should employ social workers and others in their health units to complement the family planning services provided by health professionals.

(See comment on Recommendation 5a above.)

9 The proceedings and recommendations of the First National Conference on Family Planning should be on the agenda in the immediate future of meetings of Ministers of Health, Social Welfare and Education, and various government departments, for discussion and co-ordinated planning and action.

(See comment on Recommendation 5a above.)

10 *a* Federal funds should be earmarked to encourage and assist conferences or workshops on family planning in the territories, the provinces, and the metropolitan centres.

(Assistance towards family planning conferences, seminars, and workshops is included in the scope of the Family Planning Grants. During the fiscal year 1972-73 priority will be given to the support of broadly based conferences concerned with provincial or regional needs and priorities in family planning.)

b The planning and development of regional conferences or workshops should be a responsibility and an opportunity for interested individuals, groups, and organizations in the particular area, especially for those from the areas attending this conference.

c The planners of these conferences should aim for an equal balance in their conference participants between laymen and professionals.

(The federal government agrees that these conferences should be broadly

based and should include representation from a wide range of citizen groups and from potential users of family planning services.)

11 Through delegates to this conference, voluntary organizations and other appropriate channels, provincial and/or municipal governments should be pressed to take initiative in and responsibility for the establishment of planning and development bodies (where they do not already exist), concerned with family planning and family life education, and involving representatives of health, welfare, and education, voluntary agencies, and consumer groups or others.

12 Recognizing that language, ethnic, religious, and similar differences frequently impede the availability of family planning information and services:

a Indigenous people should be trained and used to provide information, referral when requested, and follow-up activity concerning family planning for their particular groups or communities.

(The Department of National Health and Welfare has already taken positive steps to train native health workers to provide public health services in Indian reserves. Within the limits of departmental policy, these services could include family planning counselling.)

b Indigenous people should also be involved in the planning and preparation of family planning information and educational material appropriate to their particular groups or communities.

(The Department of National Health and Welfare is currently involving indigenous groups in the preparation of family planning informational and educational materials.)

c Family planning publications and audio-visual and other resource materials should be made available in a variety of forms and languages, understandable to all sections of the population.

(A grant recently made by the Department of National Health and Welfare to the Yellowknife Family Planning Clinic is intended, in part, to support the development of family planning educational material in Eskimo.)

d The federal Department of Manpower and Immigration should make available on arrival to new Canadians, in their mother tongue, information on Canadian health and social welfare programs, including family planning services.

(Future immigrants are now receiving booklets containing information on health and welfare services in Canada. These pamphlets are given out by the Department of Manpower and Immigration and are available in six languages. The Department is prepared to include information on family planning services in the future editions of booklets or publications of this kind.)

13 Since a significant increase in information and education on family life and family planning is clearly required and acceptable, the federal government and provincial and territorial governments should earmark substantial funds for

the production of resource materials appropriate to particular provinces, regions or groups, and for their dissemination through the media of communication.

(Funds are earmarked in the operating budget of the Family Planning Division of the Department of National Health and Welfare for resource materials for particular groups. Materials will be developed in consultation with their potential users. With the aid of a federal grant, the Family Planning Federation of Canada is disseminating information about family planning services through newspaper ads and radio announcements.)

14 Federal consultative services and financial assistance should be continued and expanded for experimental research and demonstration projects in both family life education and family planning services, especially for adolescents and young adults.

(Limited federal consultative services for research and demonstration projects in family life education and family planning services are available. An increase in the number of consultants in the Family Planning Division is planned, and the quality of consultation offered may be expected to improve as experience is gained. Projects of this type are eligible for consideration under the Family Planning Grants.)

15 Federal financial assistance should be assured to foster required expansion of research in all aspects of family planning; for example, research on attitudes toward family planning, on psychological aspects of sterilization and of abortion, on the effectiveness of different methods of birth control and of organization and delivery of family planning services, on the socio-ecònomic determinants and consequences of fertility, mortality, and migration in Canada, and on the consequences for population size and distribution of existing or projected socio-economic policies and programs.

(Federal funds for the support of research projects in the areas given as examples are available from a number of sources including the Family Planning Grants, the Medical Research Council, and the Canada Council.)

16 *a* Through separate courses, through the systematic and co-ordinated introduction of material in established curricula, or through a combination of the two, education in human development, human sexuality and relationships, parenthood, family planning, and demography (sometimes encompassed iń the term 'family life education') should be included in all school curricula from kindergarten through secondary school.

b Parents, students, teachers, and specialists from all relevant disciplines and professions should be involved in the planning, delivery, and evaluation of family life education programs and content in primary and secondary schools.

17 Governments at all levels should provide encouragement and financial assistance for the planning and development of family life education programs

for adults by voluntary organizations, schools, colleges, universities, and other appropriate bodies.

(See Recommendation 14. The comments concerning the federal government's role in family life programs for schools apply equally to those aimed at adults.)

18 Federal and provincial encouragement and assistance, financial and otherwise, should be provided to ensure the planning and development of:

a Training programs for specialists in the planning of family life education programs, and in the related education of teachers, social workers, and health and other professionals in this area.

b Curricula, materials, and courses in family planning and family life education, in education, social work, health, and other university faculties or departments.

(The federal government is prepared to provide, free of charge, informational materials on sex education and family planning to any institution requesting them. Limitation of available funds, and jurisdictional considerations, restrict Family Planning Grant support of training programs for specialists in family life education in schools to a few demonstration projects. The support of selected training courses in family planning at various locations falls within the scope of the Family Planning Grants.)

19 The federal government should establish a professional training program on birth control for all relevant professions and disciplines, including medicine, social work, nursing, sexology, psychology, etc.

(This recommendation would be feasible and acceptable if it were amended to read 'The federal government should promote and support professional training programs etc.' Funds for support of selected training projects are available under the Family Planning Grants.)

20 The federal government should amend the Food and Drug Act and any other relevant legislation to eliminate restrictions preventing the advertisement of effective birth control devices and family planning pills on the same basis as other (advertised) prescribed drugs or products.

(Existing legislation already places the advertising of birth control devices and oral contraceptives on the same basis as other prescribed drugs or products. Any contraceptive device or product obtainable without prescription can be advertized to the general public. Any device or drug, including oral contraceptives, which can be sold only by prescription cannot be advertized to the general public.)

21 The federal government, with the co-operation of the provincial governments and other relevant bodies, should develop a directory of organizations and other resources active in family planning.

(The Family Planning Resource Guide, prepared by the Department of Na-

tional Health and Welfare and available on request, contains much of this information, and will be updated from time to time.)

22 A representative of Metis associations and others should be invited to attend all future conferences on family planning, national, provincial, territorial, and local.

(The federal government agrees.)

RECOMMENDATIONS OF THE SPECIAL INTEREST GROUP ON DEVELOPMENT OF FAMILY PLANNING SERVICES*

1 We recommend that provincial and territorial governments ensure that public hospitals provide family planning services including surgical procedures and counselling in accord with the principles of universality of services and freedom of choice by patients.

(Provincial and territorial governments have received copies of this recommendation.)

2 That this conference most strongly urges on the governments of the provinces and territories the desirability of establishing inter-departmental family planning committees at an early date; these committees to consist of representatives of all departments involved with the family and to be charged with the responsibility for planning and implementing integrated family planning services appropriate to the province or territory. Copies of this recommendation should be forwarded to the voluntary family planning associations.

(Copies of this recommendation have been sent to Serena Inc. and to member associations of the Family Planning Federation of Canada.)

3 We further recommend that these provincial family planning committees be assisted by advisory committees representing interested voluntary citizen groups as well as local health, education and welfare agencies to advise on policies and services.

4 A plan for funding family planning services be developed by the federal government in co-operation with provincial governments to ensure that financial barriers do not prevent the development of provincially and locally co-ordinated comprehensive family planning services.

(Federal-provincial shared cost health programs assure virtually all Canadian residents access on a prepaid basis to family planning procedures for which the services of medical practitioners, and/or hospital care, are medically required. Eight of the ten provinces participating in the federal Hospital Insurance and Diagnostic Services Program and Medical Care Program, and the two northern

*Not discussed in final plenary session of Conference. Comments by the Department of National Health and Welfare Task Force appear in parenthesis after the recommendations.

territories, have so defined the medical requirements for these procedures that they are generally considered medically necessary by their actual provision. The spectrum of family planning services for which federal sharing is available to the provinces is further expanded through the Canada Assistance Plan which can share in family planning services additional to ones covered by the Medical Care and Hospital Insurance and Diagnostic Services Programs provided to those in need or those who would be in need were such services not available.

Certain proposals are presently being discussed which would provide greater flexibility to the provinces in the use of the federal contribution while trying the federal contribution to changes in the economy. Should this new approach come about, it is conceivable that some of the fallout from the ensuing new methods of health care delivery, for which the federal financial contribution would then be available to the provinces, could favourably affect family planning services within a province.)

RECOMMENDATIONS OF THE SPECIAL INTEREST
GROUP ON RESEARCH IN FAMILY PLANNING*

It is recommended that urgent priority be given to the following research areas:

1 A national fertility study, to examine the attitudes and behaviour of Canadians regarding fertility and family planning.

(The federal government is examining the need for the aims of, and the means of financing a national fertility study.)

2 Operational research on the provision of family planning information and services is urgently required. Demonstration projects should be undertaken under a wide variety of conditions to examine different approaches to groups of different age, sex, socio-economic level, and ethnic character. These demonstration projects should be concerned with different uses of manpower and methods and should evaluate results and measure the relative cost-effectiveness of various approaches.

(The federal government agrees, and is prepared to consider support of worthwhile projects within the limits of available funds.)

3 The relationship of family planning to social and health indicators.

(The federal government is prepared to support well designed projects of this type.)

4 On-going evaluation of family planning activities across Canada is urgently required.

(See comments on 3 above.)

*Not discussed in final plenary session of Conference. Task Force comments appear in parenthesis after the recommendations.

MARGARET WHITRIDGE

Venereal disease in Canada*

THE FACTS

Venereal disease is on the increase – in Canada, as in most other countries. There were 34,405 reported cases of gonorrhea in Canada in 1971 – more than in any year since 1945. About 57 per cent of these cases were young people between the ages of 15 and 24. More than 6000 Canadian teenagers were reported to have contracted either gonorrhea or syphilis.

But these reported cases don't begin to tell the story. Public health officials believe that, at the most, only one in three cases is reported. They estimate that between 150,000 and 200,000 cases of gonorrhea and up to 7500 cases of syphilis are contracted each year in Canada.

While syphilis may not be as prevalent, it is more serious and, left untreated, can lead to blindness, paralysis, heart disease, insanity, and death. Gonorrhea has reached epidemic proportions. Although most people have no ill effects if they seek treatment promptly, it can, in a small percentage of both men and women, spread to the reproductive organs and cause sterility. Crippling gonococcal arthritis and endocarditis are other possible aftermaths of this disease.

Venereal disease is Canada's most urgent communicable disease problem. The vast spread of these diseases is taking its toll in its effects on a predominantly young population.

THE FACTORS

Ignorance is one of the chief factors in the spread of venereal disease. People, and especially young people, do not know even the most elementary facts about VD.

*Reprinted from *Living*, Winter 1973.

Without a knowledge of the high risks and the effects of VD, people are unable to act intelligently if they become infected.

There is still a social stigma attached to VD. Explicit information and broad public education are needed to tell people, especially young people, the facts. There must be more adequate treatment services, including street clinics and community health programs, to help control the spread of infection. Public health nurses and doctors, school counsellors and health personnel, street clinic and hospital outpatient department staff all require frank, accurate information and suitable audio-visual materials to help them fight VD.

Another factor in the increase of VD is urbanization. Young people in particular are leaving the small towns and rural areas for city life. And the population of Canada is growing all the time, especially in the young, sexually active age groups. At the same time, people have a longer span of sexual life, as a result of earlier maturity, better health, changing social attitudes, and deferred effects of aging.

THE FALLACIES

Many people still believe that you can catch VD from toilet seats, doorknobs, money, or shaking hands with an infected person. If you can, the chances are one in a million.

So let's face facts. VD is spread through sexual contact. And the more sexual partners you have, the greater the chance of contracting VD – and the greater the chance of giving it to someone else.

THE FIGHT

Individual cases of syphilis or gonorrhea can be diagnosed and treated. It's harder to prevent the spread of these diseases because of the complex interaction of the medical and social factors involved.

Gonorrhea is particularly difficult to control. Up to 80 per cent of infected women have no symptoms and can unwittingly continue to spread the disease. In fact, there is increasing evidence that some men don't have any symptoms either. (The usual symptoms are a burning sensation when urinating and a discharge of pus. They appear within six days of infection. If you have them or if you find unexplained sores on your body in 2 to 12 weeks after intercourse, assume that you have VD and go for the tests.) Then, too, the incubation period is so short – about three to six days – that it is impossible for even the most efficient health authorities to find and treat all infected persons before they, in turn, spread the disease to others.

Of course, contacts can't be located at all if their identities are kept secret. Everyone who has VD caught it from someone else and has, perhaps, passed it on.

Public health officials must know the names of all contacts in order to trace them and offer them treatment, if necessary.

Treatment and the checking of contacts are done in strict confidence. The spread of VD can't be checked unless all infected contacts are found and treated.

Venereal disease is a growing epidemic, and health, educational, and other agencies must co-operate to fight it. All vestiges of social stigma must be erased. Above all, people must be informed about VD. Recent studies indicate that venereal disease educational programs in high schools can lead to a dramatic decrease in incidence in adolescents and young adults. But people of all ages must become familiar with the symptoms and possible complications of both syphilis and gonorrhea.

A World Symposium on Venereal Disease, held in Tel Aviv in July 1972, outlined a plan for combatting the VD epidemic. It includes education through all available media, training teachers and health professionals to instruct those in their care, routine screening for venereal diseases as part of general health examinations, the establishment of free evening clinics accessible to young people, and the enactment of legislation to permit treatment of adolescents without parental knowledge. A concerted effort must be made to control this epidemic effectively.

PART FOUR

CONTRACEPTION

ELAINE DAWSON

Conception control in family planning*

When planning a family, a couple should consider many factors: their expected economic status which will determine how they can best feed, clothe, house, and educate their children; the spacing of each child; the stability of their marriage; and their own emotional and physical health. Being well-informed about contraception could be an integral part of their family planning so that their children, when born, are there through choice and not through chance.

While many nurses may never recommend any means of birth control, one of the first steps to becoming comfortable with the subject is to be knowledgeable about the various methods available.

PREGNANCY RATES

The normal pregnancy rate is estimated as 60-80. This means that with 100 fertile women using no method of contraception for one full year, we could expect 60-80 pregnancies to occur in that group. From these figures it is plain to see that uncontrolled fertility can be disastrous, whether on the family or the national level.

Since the dawn of history, man has shown concern in regulating the size of his family. Many ideas were developed in an effort to find drugs or devices which would inhibit fecundity. It is interesting to note that the rationale for all so-called modern methods is ages old; only the materials that are used today are really new.[1]

*Reprinted from *The Canadian Nurse* 63, no. 12 (December 1967).

ORAL CONTRACEPTIVES

The search for an effective and safe oral contraceptive was carried on for centuries, but it was not until the 1950s that such a drug was developed. After considerable research and countless field trials involving thousands of women, the 'combination' products and then the 'sequentials' were made available.

Mode of action
The ovulatory cycle is controlled through a complicated hormonal interaction of the gonadotropins from the anterior lobe of the pituitary gland and the estrogen and progesterone from the ovary. These two hormones, when given to the non-gravid woman, act to prevent ovulation by inhibiting the secretion of the pituitary gonadotropins. The ingestion of these hormones also results in endometrial changes and a thickening of the cervical mucus.[2] It is thought that these additional two factors may play a role in the effectiveness of the method.

Combination oral contraceptives
The 'combinations' contains synthetic estrogen and progesterone (progestin). Doses of 10 mg were introduced some 10 years ago. Since then doses as low as 1 mg have been developed, and are still virtually 100 per cent effective.

Starting on the fifth day after the first day of the menstrual flow, one tablet is taken, preferably at the same time each day. The tablets are taken for about 21 days, depending on the product. A menstrual period will usually commence two to five days after the last tablet has been taken. Each new tablet-taking cycle is started approximately one week after the last cycle is complete whether or not menstruation has occurred or is finished.

One of the pleasant effects of combination oral contraceptives is the scantier flow and shorter periods that a great many women experience.[3] Pre-menstrual tension and dysmenorrhea are frequently relieved. A regular cycle length of 27 or 28 days is established.[4]

Sequential oral contraceptives
The sequential oral contraceptives, while slightly less effective with regular use than the 'combinations,' are the tablets of medical choice for some women. These, too, are taken on a 20- or 21-day regimen. With this type of contraceptive, estrogen alone is taken for the first 14-16 days followed by a tablet containing estrogen and progestin combined for the remainder of the days. As with the 'combinations,' menstrual flow usually starts two to five days after the tablet-taking cycle is stopped.

Because the sequentials tend to simulate the pattern of the normal menstrual cycle, that is, estrogen early in the cycle followed by progesterone, the duration and volume of the menstrual flow tends to remain unchanged.

Side effects of oral contraceptives

A small percentage of women experience side effects with both the combination and sequential products. The most common side effects appear to be break-through (intermenstrual) bleeding, nausea, slight breast tenderness, and weight change.[5] It is interesting to note that while some women gain weight, some appear to experience weight loss, particularly with the sequential products.[6] Depression, irritability, and headaches are some subjective complaints.

For the most part these side effects tend to lessen or disappear after the first few cycles of tablet use. In some cases they are severe enough to warrant discontinuance of the method.

Precautions

Although no causal relationship has been proven between the use of progestin-estrogen compounds and the development of thrombophlebitis, doctors use caution when prescribing oral contraceptives for patients with thromboembolic disease or a history of thrombophlebitis.

Patients with pre-existing fibroids, epilepsy, migraine, asthma, or a history of psychic depression should be carefully observed. Pre-therapy examination should include a Papanicolaou smear.

Contraindications

Oral contraceptives should not be taken: in the presence of malignant tumors of the breast or genital tract; in the presence of significant liver dysfunction or disease; in the presence of cardiac or renal disorders which might be adversely affected by some degree of fluid retention; or during the period a mother is breastfeeding an infant.

Pregnancy

Patients are sometimes concerned about planned pregnancies after the medication is discontinued. It has been found that fertility is not impaired nor are there changes in the expected rate of fetal abnormalities.[7,8,9,10]

Acceptability

Because of extreme effectiveness and the fact that they are taken separately from the act of coitus, oral contraceptives are highly acceptable as a method of conception control. A study of 2040 women over 22,948 treatment cycles showed that 'oral contraception in terms of effectiveness and acceptability appears to be far superior to any other available method.'[11]

INTRAUTERINE CONTRACEPTIVE DEVICES

There are many different shapes and sizes of intrauterine contraceptive devices. The Lippes Loop and the Gynekoil (coil) are made of polyethylene. Each has a transcervical appendage; the loop has two monofilament polyethylene threads, and the coil has a stem with seven beads. These extrusions are clipped after the device has been inserted into the uterus. The bow (made of polyethylene) and the stainless steel ring do not have the transcervical appendages. These latter two are seldom used in Canada. The polyethylene is impregnated with barium salt to permit visualization by x-ray.

Insertion

The sterile device is inserted during or immediately after a menstrual period. Insertion is easier during these days and the post-insertion spotting, which occurs in a significant number of cases, is less disturbing to the patient. Also, the possibility of an existing pregnancy is ruled out.

The polyethylene devices have a 'memory capability,' that is, they can be straightened out for introduction by means of a tube-like inserter and plunger. In the uterus, the device returns to its pre-insertion shape.

The beads or threads, which extrude from the cervix, are clipped short enough to avoid penile discomfort for the husband, but long enough to permit the patient to carry out digital examination to determine the continuing presence of the device.

Mechanism of action

These devices do not act by any blockage of the cervix. Sperm are found in the uterus and tubes, ovulation and menstruation continue as normal. It is not fully understood how the devices prevent pregnancy but to the best of our present knowledge they may act by increasing the speed of transmission of the ovum from the ovary, through the tubes, to the uterus.[12]

Complications and side effects

In about 10 per cent of cases, expulsion of the device occurs.[13] These expulsions most often take place in the first two or three months of use and frequently occur at the time of menses. Patients should be advised to check pads and tampons and to examine themselves after each period to confirm that the device is in position. Unnoticed expulsions are often followed by an unplanned pregnancy.[14]

Some post-insertion spotting occurs in a high percentage of patients. Intermenstrual bleeding and/or menorrhagia is common during the first two or three menstrual cycles. Persistent and/or heavy bleeding is the most common reason for removal of the device by the physician.[15]

Slight cramping is sometimes felt at the time of insertion but this usually subsequently subsides. Some patients, however, experience cramping during the first few menstrual periods.

Pregnancies have occurred with the device *in situ*. In these cases the device is usually left in place. It remains outside the fetal sac and is often delivered with the placenta at term.

Perkin, reporting on the data of 11,222 first insertions from 43 contributing institutions, states that the pregnancy rate per 100 women at the end of the first year was 2.4 per cent for the loop, 1.8 per cent for the coil, 5.7 per cent for the bow, and 7.5 per cent for the stainless steel ring.[16]

Contraindications

Reasons for not using intrauterine devices include: pregnancy, genital malignancy, acute or subacute pelvic inflammatory disease, history of menorrhagia or metrorrhagia (these should be treated prior to insertion), fibroids, and bicornuate or septate uterus.

Acceptability

Perkin also states '... the intrauterine devices offer the following advantages as a method of contraception: a) Sustained patient motivation is not required. b) They are highly effective. c) Fertility following removal of the device is unaffected. d) The method is independent of coitus. e) They are inexpensive. The loop is well tolerated by at least 75 per cent of women in whom it is inserted.'[17]

As a rule intrauterine devices are not inserted in a nulliparous patient. The incidence of cramping, bleeding, and expulsions is much higher for this group. By and large, these patients are not considered to be good candidates for this type of contraception.

DIAPHRAGM WITH SPERMICIDAL JELLY

The diaphragm is a dome-shaped device made of latex rubber over a flexible metal rim. It must be fitted by a physician. When correctly in place, it rests: anteriorly, against the soft tissues posterior to the symphysis pubis; posteriorly, within the posterior vaginal fornix; and circumferentially, against the vaginal walls. Whether the diaphragm is inserted dome up or dome down, the spermicidal jelly used with the diaphragm must be between the diaphragm and the cervix. The diaphragm and jelly must remain in place for at least six hours following the last coitus. Douching within that period of time may dilute or remove the spermicidal jelly, so should not be recommended.

This method offers the motivated patient a fairly high level of protection. Displacement of the diaphragm during coitus and improper or inconsistent use usually accounts for the failure of this method. The pregnancy rate has been reported as low as five[18] and as high as twelve.[19]

Some women find this method a nuisance or complain that it interferes with the spontaneity of the sex act. For the woman who cannot or does not wish to use the oral contraceptive or the intrauterine devices, the diaphragm with a good spermicidal agent offers a reasonable alternative.

SPERMICIDAL AGENTS – JELLY, CREAM, FOAM

Spermicidal chemicals in a non-reactive base of jelly, cream, or foam are yet another method of contraception. These agents are placed by means of an applicator well back in the vagina, just prior to sexual intercourse. Certain jellies and creams, as well as being spermicidal, also provide somewhat of a barrier to sperm. However, some women find the jellies and creams 'messy' and prefer the more esthetically pleasing foam.[20]

Patients who wish a simple, easy-to-use method that does not require a prescription readily accept this method. The pregnancy rate for the vaginal foams ranges from 2.7 to about 10 and for the creams and jellies from about 3.5 to 15.

CONDOM

The condom is still the most widely used of the mechanical methods. When used with care and consistency, it offers a fair degree of protection. One study lists the pregnancy rate as six to sixteen.[21] The main disadvantage of this method is that its use interrupts the sex act and often prevents complete sexual satisfaction for one or both partners. When the husband feels that contraception is his responsibility, the condom may be the method of choice.[22]

COITUS INTERRUPTUS (WITHDRAWAL)

This method of contraception, surely the oldest in the world, is described as the withdrawal of the penis from the vagina just prior to ejaculation so that the semen is not deposited in or near the vagina. Conscious control by the husband is imperative if the method is to be successful. Sperm found in the urethral secretions prior to ejaculation could theoretically cause a pregnancy.

This method is often not considered satisfying to either the husband or the wife.[23] It carries an estimated pregnancy rate of 35.

RHYTHM METHOD

The rhythm method is based on identification of the time of ovulation and then abstinence from sexual intercourse around this time. The ovum is fertilizable for about 12 to 24 hours only, but sperm have been found to be viable in the female genital tract for up to five days.[24] It becomes imperative, therefore, that the couple be able to avoid coitus well in advance of the time of ovulation if this method is to prove successful.

EFFECTIVENESS RATINGS

Arithmetical calculations, involving the recording of the shortest and longest menstrual cycles over a minimum period of six months, are used. Ovulation is also calculated by plotting the basal body temperature. In one particular study where women were selected for their menstrual regularity, the pregnancy rate was found to be about 14.[25] Menstrual irregularity and febrile conditions can affect calculations of the time of ovulation. The pregnancy rate for the general population using the rhythm method is estimated at 35.

NON-ACCEPTABLE METHODS

Because sperm have been found in the uterus and tubes very shortly after ejaculation (two to three minutes), douching is considered to be a very poor method of contraception. Non-spermicidal suppositories, too, offer little or no protection. It should be noted that lactation, contrary to what some patients may think, does not really provide protection against conception.

GROUP I Most effective	Oral contraceptives Intrauterine contraceptive devices
GROUP II Very effective	Diaphragm with spermicidal jelly Aerosol vaginal foam Jelly or cream alone Condom
GROUP III Less effective	Rhythm method Coitus interruptus

GROUP IV   Vaginal douche – plain or with chemicals added
Least effective   Breastfeeding
                  Non-spermicidal suppositories

PERMANENT (SURGICAL) METHODS

Vas resection or vasectomy is a relatively permanent method of family limitation, although surgical reversibility is sometimes possible. In this simple opera-
tive procedure, spermatozoa are mechanically prevented from traversing the
length of the vas deferens by severing the vas and ligating the cut ends. Libido
and potency are not impaired.[26]

The surgical removal of sections from both Fallopian tubes is the method of
choice for female sterilization. In appropriate situations this may be done as a
postpartum procedure or as an elective operation in the non-pregnant woman.[27]

CONCLUSION

It is important to remember that there is not yet one perfect method of contraception. The method most acceptable to the couple is the one that will be used
most consistently, and hence, is the most effective for them. The full range
of methods – oral contraceptives, intrauterine devices, diaphragms, spermicidal
agents, condom, coitus interruptus, and rhythm – offer the couple a selection
from which they can choose the one best suited to their family planning needs.

Non-directive counselling, which counselling in family planning should be,
does not attempt to impose any set of values or beliefs on the patient. It respects
the right of the individual to make her own decision.[28]

Many nurses in Canada are finding that patients are looking to them for guidance and information in this field. A broad, precise knowledge of conception
control is necessary to enable the nurse to counsel comfortably and confidently.
Traditionally, there has been in the nursing profession a deep commitment to the
strengthening of the integrity of the family and the development of the individual. We must seek to assure that each child born will be, not a burden, but a
blessing – a welcome, wanted addition to the family and to the community.

NOTES

1 Finch, B.E., and H. Green, *Contraception Through the Ages* (London, 1963).
2 Rice-Wray, Edris *et al.*, 'Oral Progestins in Fertility Control: A Comparative
  Study,' *Fertil. Steril.* 14, no. 4 (July–August 1963), 402-9.
3 Mears, Eleanor, 'Oral Contraceptives,' in Pollock, Mary, *Family Planning*
  (London, 1966), pp. 25-31.

4 Goldzieher, Joseph W., 'Newer Drugs in Oral Contraception,' *Med. Clin. N. Amer.* 48, no. 2 (March 1964), 529-45.

5 Tyler, Edward T., 'Current Status of Oral Contraception,' *JAMA* (Feb. 22, 1964), pp. 562-65.

6 Newland, Donald A. *et al.*, 'Effectiveness of a Sequential Oral Contraceptive Tablet,' *Obstet. Gynec.* 28, no. 4 (October 1966), 516-20.

7 Tyler, Edward T., *et al.*, 'Long Term Usage of Norethindrone with Mestranol Preparations in the Control of Human Fertility,' *Clin. Med.* 71, no. 6 (June 1964), 997-1024.

8 *Clinical Aspects of Oral Gestogens.* World Health Organization Technical Report Series, no. 326, 1966.

9 Rovinsky, Joseph J., 'Clinical Effectiveness of a Low Dosage Progestin-Estrogen Combination,' *Obstet. Gynec.* 23, no. 1 (January 1964), 125-31.

10 Rice-Wray, Edris, *et al.*, 'The Acceptability of Oral Progestins in Fertility Control,' *Metabolism* 14, no. 3, Part 2 (March 1965), 451-56.

11 *Ibid.*

12 Perkin, Gordon, 'Intrauterine Contraception,' *CMAJ* (February 26, 1966), pp. 431-36.

13 *Ibid.*

14 Tietze, Christopher, and Sarah Lewit, 'Intrauterine Contraception: Effectiveness and Acceptability,' *Excerpta Med.* International Congress Series no. 86, October 1964, pp. 98-110.

15 Perkin.

16 Perkin.

17 Perkin.

18 Dubrow, Hilliard, and Alan F. Gutmacher, 'The Present Status of Contraception,' *J. Mount Sinai Hosp.* (NY), 26 no. 2 (March-April 1959), 118-24.

19 Wiseman, Aviva, 'Oral Contraceptives in Family Planning,' *College of General Practice of Canada, Journal* 12, no. 9 (June 1966), 15-21.

20 Kleppinger, Richard K., 'A Vaginal Contraceptive Foam,' *Penn. Med. J.* (April 1965), pp. 31-34.

21 Dubrow.

22 Tietze, Christopher, 'The Condom,' in Calderone, M.S. ed., *Manual of Contraceptive Practice* (London, 1964), pp. 181-87.

23 Sjövall, Elisabet, 'Coitus Interruptus,' in Calderone, ed., pp. 202-6.

24 Jeffcoate, T.N., *Principles of Gynecology* (London, 1957).

25 Dubrow.

26 Ferber, William L., 'Male Sterilization,' in Calderone, ed., pp. 246-49.

27 Wood, H. Curtis, Jr., 'Female Sterilization,' in Calderone, pp. 233-41.

28 Chesterman, H., 'Public Health Nurse and Family Planning,' *Nurs. Outlook* (September 1964), pp. 32-4.

NANCY GARRETT

Choosing contraceptives according to need*

For centuries, people have tried to limit their fertility in one way or another for
various reasons. Our North American attitudes toward fertility (having children)
closely approximate those of the ancient Jews and Egyptians, whose basis for
contraceptive or abortifacient use was the health and welfare of the couple and
of the children already born.

The first written reference to contraception is in the Ebers Papyrus (1550 BC),
where a pessary with lactic acid as a spermicidal agent is described. There is no
further reference to this pessary until the nineteenth century, when the spermicidal qualities of lactic acid were rediscovered.

In the interim, the ancient Greeks developed, among various sophisticated barrier methods, what might have been the precursor for the intrauterine contraceptive device (IUD): A hollow lead tube filled with mutton fat was passed partially
through the cervix into the uterus, leaving the cervix open.[1] Probably the device
was a fertility aid, intended to open the cervix to permit easier passage of sperm;
but Greek physicians and midwives undoubtedly knew that conception would
not occur as long as it was in place. This device, out of use during the middle
ages, reappeared in Europe during the fifteenth and sixteenth centuries, and,
after many modifications, became a contraceptive.

Although most of the magical amulets, potions, dung diaphragms, calisthenics,
vaginal fumigations, and so on were relatively harmless, they were not particularly pleasant or practical. The search continued. Today, we still have only a
dozen different methods of contraception. Researchers continue to try to find
the effective, safe, and acceptable method.

*Reprinted from *The Canadian Nurse* 68, no. 9 (September 1972).

Unfortunately, we often forget that the efficacy of the method usually depends more on its suitability for the individual and/or couple than on the infallibility of the method itself. Nurses are forever asking, 'What is the per cent failure for that method?' Knowing the technical effectiveness of various methods and teaching their use and side effects does not ensure usage.

The choice of a method is influenced by the following factors, with all their vagaries, variations, combinations, and problems: health status – physical, mental, socioeconomic; age, parity, and coital frequency; attitudes toward sex and sexual roles; and religion.

HEALTH STATUS

The usual contraindications or precautions in prescribing oral contraceptives are well-known. They include: a history of thromboembolic phenomena, migraine headaches, liver disease, illness involving water retention (cardiac or renal), metabolic dysfunctions, and epilepsy. There are logical contraindications to others, such as anatomical irregularities that prevent the effective use of diaphragms, and allergies to creams, jellies, and foams. Also, excessive bleeding caused by IUDs prevents use in very anemic women and may require removal to prevent severe anemia in other women.

If a young nulliparous woman with heart disease is allergic to the creams and jellies and retains too much fluid to permit her to take the pill, an IUD would appear to be the answer. It certainly should be tried. But many nulliparous women are unable to retain these devices or cannot tolerate the bleeding or pain of the initial months. Newer IUDs, such as the copper T, which seems to have few side effects, are still in the experimental stage in Canada. So little remains for this woman.

If she does not want any children, she may succeed in convincing a surgeon to sterilize her because of her heart disease. But she will likely have to see more than one doctor to find one who does not decide it is his moral obligation to get her through a pregnancy and it is her moral obligation to have a child because she is female.

If she wants a child eventually, she may be able to use aerosol foam with a diaphragm. Though similar to the other spermicides, foam has been found to cause no irritation, and possibly may be used by women who cannot tolerate jellies or creams. However, if she cannot tolerate foam, the condom is the only device left. This may appear to be a simple solution. But for those who consciously or unconsciously see it as a device for illicit affairs, it may inhibit the spontaneity of a happy relationship.

Sometimes the opportunity to identify and talk about their feelings to a nurse or doctor will help the couple resolve or mitigate the problem. For example, the health worker might suggest that the woman put the condom on the man's penis herself, as a part of foreplay before intercourse; negative feelings about the condom will often disappear.

Apparently Japanese women have been encouraged to help their husbands use condoms. In Japan, one of the world's largest suppliers of condoms, abortion has been overtaken by contraception as a means of birth control, essentially without benefit of the pill.

This love-play incentive might prove to be an effective means of persuading young, single people to use condoms, thereby protecting them from pregnancy and venereal disease. Too often, persons who have VD are not even asked about their contraceptive needs.

For the women's liberation enthusiast who objects to women helping with a condom and asks, 'Do men insert diaphragms in women?' it may be of interest to know that some men do provide such a service of love. If people have to put up with these devices, they may as well get some pleasure out of them.

The forgotten patients in family planning are the mentally ill. Clearly, if people are already losing the struggle to cope with daily demands made upon them, another child is not going to ease their burden. They are often too weary to take prophylactic measures, even if their illness has not prevented them from learning about contraceptives.

When the individual with mental illness is hospitalized, hospital staff rarely think of the sexual aspects of care and the possible results of a weekend pass or discharge from the hospital. The added worry of taking the responsibility for seeking contraceptive help makes the patient's adjustment much more difficult. It may be too difficult.

Oral contraceptives are not always given to persons with emotional problems, especially those with affective disorders, because of the increased risk of depressive symptomatology.[2] The stress of adjusting to an IUD is often best avoided or deferred, and sterilization is generally contraindicated because the person's emotional reactions could be disastrous. Other devices are closely associated with the time of coitus, require strong motivation and control, and therefore may add to anxiety and stress.

Hence, the male partner's co-operation is essential and usually not difficult to get, if one thinks of seeking it. Too often the woman's response – 'My husband won't use a rubber, I *know* he won't' – is accepted. The major problem is usually not his lack of responsibility for contraception, but rather the lack of communication between man and woman, and the tendency of most people, including health workers, to see contraception as the responsibility of the woman. Both partners should be given the opportunity, separately and together, to discuss the sex situation with a health worker. Attempts can then be made to promote understanding and communication.

When patients are admitted to hospital, a sexual and contraceptive history should be taken when possible. If this is not feasible, the nurse should obtain this history and determine the patient's need before he or she leaves hospital. All patients have enough to contend with when leaving the hospital without having to worry about a possible unwanted pregnancy. How much greater is the need of the emotionally disturbed person. This unmet need may contribute to her illness or impede her convalescence. If nurses and doctors omit the sexual and contraceptive aspects of care, they may be contributing to poor health. Worse, they may be contributing to the poor health of subsequent children. Anyone who has seen a rejected or battered child will try to prevent the potential tragedy of producing an unwanted child in a stressful environment.

AGE, PARITY, COITAL FREQUENCY

Age, as a factor in the choice of contraceptive, seems obvious. It is so great a factor that we often consider *only* age and the horrors of pregnancy for the very young, without considering the actual risk of conception. Is the young girl frequently exposed to risk, or only sporadically, as are most of the younger teenagers who are exposed at all?

For young teenagers who are only sporadically exposed to the risk of pregnancy, the pill is not usually justified; even so, oral contraceptives are invariably prescribed for them. What would be more appropriate is a handy condom-dispensing machine in high school lavatories, away from the prying eyes of adults. Until they are installed, use of those in service stations and public places should be encouraged.

Virtually nothing is known about the effects of steroids on the systems of these young people. Some physicians will not prescribe oral contraceptives for girls under 16 years of age. Others believe that once menses are firmly established, the danger of permanently suppressing ovulation is no greater than usual as long as the customary 'rest' from oral contraception is taken every one to two years. (The time span varies, depending on the physician.)

Certainly a full history of the girl's past and present sexual activity should be considered and the girl taught the advantages and disadvantages of different methods, depending on her age, history, and current plans. She should be encouraged to talk about her feelings toward contraception in general, and various methods in particular, before *any* method is prescribed.

If the girl is too young or immature to accept full responsibility for her sexual activities and does not have a steady boyfriend or husband who will, she will not likely adhere to the routine of taking a pill daily or to any other method that requires motivation. In such cases, even 13-year-old girls have been fitted with IUDs that have been retained successfully.

What is more probable is that young teenagers will be treated as if they were sexually inactive. Actually, so great is our denial of sex that we assume everyone is sexually inactive – that all children are conceived asexually. As Mary Jane Whipple quipped, when speaking at Canada's first national conference on family planning this year, 'People don't have intercourse, they just have children.'

Thus we refuse our youngest and neediest the opportunity to learn about family planning and sexual responsibility. How often is a girl's sexual and contraceptive health assessed when she sees the school nurse for menstrual cramps? When she is admitted for an appendectomy? These may be the only opportunities available to a nurse to teach preventive health care, but they usually are not taken.

In Canada, the lack of prevention resulted in more than 35,000 illegitimacies in 1970, and 31,000 abortions in 1971. If US statistics are representative, one-third of Canada's legitimate first-born were premaritally conceived.

Although as many as 48 per cent of births are unplanned, according to a recent New York survey,[3] the contraceptive knowledge and needs of a post-partum woman are rarely questioned. Older women are assumed to have all the information they need on family planning methods. This is a fallacy, as many older women of child-bearing age, particularly those in the lower income groups, do not know that the IUD exists. Yet this device is usually suitable for older women and is preferred by women in low-income groups. Once in place, the IUD requires no motivation, no storage, and no memory.

On the average, older women retain the IUD longer than younger women because they are usually of higher parity and, therefore, tend to have weaker uterine contractions; thus, there is less pain during the initial months. Older women are also more willing to put up with the usually longer, heavier, and initially more frequent menstrual periods. (Some women actually have shorter menstrual periods while wearing the IUD.)

A woman's motivation is higher if she has three children, rather than one. Also, the interference of bleeding with sexual activities is less a problem because coital frequency is usually lower than it would be for a woman in her twenties. For the same reason, the risk of pregnancy is lower.

Sterilization for either partner should be considered if the family is complete. Health personnel generally believe men should have the operation because it is easier. Actually, laparoscopy has made salpingectomy almost as easy as vasectomy. And, if the man is not convinced he wants the surgery, it should not be done, even though he is willing to undergo this procedure for his wife's sake.

Dr Edward Shapiro, a surgeon at Ottawa's Riverside Hospital, has performed over 800 vasectomies. He recommends that the couple be seen together to make sure they both understand the procedure and its implications. After their husbands have had a vasectomy, uninformed women have been known to say, in a moment of anger, 'You're not even a *man* any more!' The woman may feel she would be castrated by salpingectomy. Even if she knows rationally that this is not so, she should not undergo the procedure.

ATTITUDE TOWARD SEX AND SEXUAL ROLES

Several million additional words will probably be written on this subject without much more light being shed on the reasons why people behave as they do in respect to reproduction, sexuality, and contraception. The sexual revolution was expected to liberate women from their sexual inhibitions. With women in control of the pill, sexual status was to be equalized. The only problem is that either the sexual revolution is a myth or women are not really in control. Otherwise, why do we have family planning clinic workers searching for abortions for themselves? Why, at the end of a week's orientation program for family planning personnel, does a nurse, married one year, say: 'I'll have to be honest with a patient who comes to me in the clinic and asks about the pill. I don't believe in it. It just doesn't seem natural. I know people should limit their families, but my husband and I don't use anything.'

Bardwick did a study involving 107 young women using oral contraceptives.[4] Their ages ranged from 17 to 35, with a mean of 20. Fifteen were married. All were emotionally committed to their partners. The young women were asked to report their body changes three months after starting on oral contraceptives. (Pre-experiment testing of passivity, masculinity/feminity characteristics was done.) Depending on their attitudes toward sex and their own roles, responses ranged from pleasantly bizarre to hostile.

An additional 100 unselected women, most of whom were university students, participated because the clinicians evaluating the responses thought that the first sample of 100 must have been biased to have such high levels of hostility and anxiety as indicated by their psychological responses to body changes. The second 100 described similar responses.

All these women were resentful and hostile toward men at times for being absolved of the responsibility for contraception; but the sexually well-adjusted women were able to talk about their feelings with their partners. Those overly dependent on others for their self-esteem claimed they had more energy, increased sexual desire, lost weight and were prettier, more desirable, and so on, after taking oral contraceptives.

Bardwick's study showed that women who were passive and unable to express anger directly, projected their ills to make their partner feel guilty about 'what-I-suffer-because-of-you.' They reported such unlikely body responses as: smaller breasts, increased menstrual flow and pain (therefore less availability for sex), and acne.

Apparently the decision to start taking oral contraceptives is a momentous one, and perhaps explains in part why 60 per cent to 80 per cent of unwed mothers have never used any form of contraception. The Hospital for Sick Children's Adolescent Service in Toronto saw 21 such girls last year. None had ever used contraceptives.[5] The record of the so-called sexually liberated female is not much better. A University of Toronto survey showed that only 42 per cent of unmarried coeds who have coitus often, used birth control pills, and 25 per cent used nothing.

A good deal of ambivalence arises from the conflict between attitudes and value system learned from the cradle, and the 'new' values of today's youth. As nurses who work in family planning clinics know, people do not always reveal what they *really* want. A request for oral contraceptives may not mean that a young lady wants protection against conception. She may actually be hoping for counsel *against* sex, which she indulges in because she believes she must to keep her boyfriend or because she erroneously believes all her friends are sexually active. (At Toronto's York University, only one-third of the girls admitted to having intercourse, and only 4.7 per cent had had three or more partners.)

If the young lady suffers from these conflicts and gets only the pills she has asked for, she feels let down. No one was interested or sensitive enough to respond to her unspoken need. What happens? She 'forgets' to take her pills or omits them because they 'make me sick.' Or she may continue to take them and complain of some unlikely body response until she is able to resolve her conflict.

She may stop practicing contraception, rationalizing that 'sex should be natural.' If her guilt feelings are powerful, she can justify unprotected intercourse because being carried away by passion is less sinful than in premeditated (protected) sexual intercourse. Irresponsibility is preferable to sinfulness. As irrational as this behaviour seems, it is well to remember that the moral teachings of parents are not easy to repress - not for any of us.

Some women ask for oral contraceptives and emotionally want a child.[6] These women are more likely to suffer severe side effects, especially nausea, breast swelling, decreased libido, and depression. If they say they do not want another child, at least temporarily, but fear side effects or fear they will forget to take a daily pill, these women should be encouraged to wear an IUD. They may also benefit from expressing their feelings on contraception and reproduction, and should be referred to a social worker or, if the situation demands, to a psychiatrist.

For some women, contraceptive practices, or lack of them, may be totally or partially influenced by their husbands. Some men need a repeatedly pregnant wife to prove their virility. The penalty for avoiding pregnancy for these women may be greater than carrying repeated pregnancies. In this case, counselling only the woman is a waste of time.

Often, if the man has control of contraception, he will not feel insecure about his wife's potential for infidelity. Sometimes the woman is dependent and prefers him to take the responsibility. Thus, it is irrelevant whether or not the health worker believes the condom or the withdrawal methods are the most effective. Many couples have succeeded in limiting their families to two and three children, solely by using one or both of these methods.

Women who dislike touching their genitals will not use female barrier methods. Those who do not want semen to touch them prefer that men use a condom or withdraw before ejaculation. Therefore, they will be unable to tolerate the other methods of contraception and will claim some side effect to justify discontinuing them. The nurse should not try to change a long-standing contraceptive practice without ascertaining the reasons for it; if she does, she may be contributing to an unwanted pregnancy.[7]

RELIGION

Religious taboos against contraception and the use of rhythm and related methods are well known. For the young healthy couple in love, abstinence may be agonizing. The success claimed by those committed to this method is probably due to the alternatives to coitus that permit couples an exchange of sexual pleasure while still retaining their religious scruples. Or they have low coital frequency rates.

All health workers interested in helping couples learn and accept other forms of sexual pleasure will find *The Sensuous Woman* an imaginative and amusing source of different sexual activities.

ABORTION

There are many reasons why contraception fails and abortion, as a back-up method may be required.[8] Availability and knowledge of contraceptives are not always adequate to prevent pregnancy. There are, of course, genuine method failures. Whatever the reason for failure, abortions will always be necessary for some, just because people are human. Whether we like it or not, society will be served and it does not much care who provides the service as long as it is provided. Hence, abortions will be done whether we personally approve or not.

Professional servants of the public are not paid to inflict their personal value systems on others while providing service. The reasons for arriving at the hospital door to have an abortion are numerous and complex, but the need is the same. All individuals are distressed, anxious, and, worst of all, filled with the anguish of regret – whether they show it or not. Sadistic treatment by moralizing nurses and doctors only adds to their burden; it does not remove their need for service. Neither does it prevent the need for a subsequent abortion. Sexuality counselling or, for some, psychiatric treatment, will be more effective.

CONCLUSION

Provision of health care must always include a consideration of personality, environment, and biology. Family planning service is no exception. It requires more emphasis on the personality than on the biology of the individual, on the attitudes toward contraception rather than on the contraceptive itself.

As nurses integrate the family planning and sexuality components of health care more and more into their daily activities, they will better meet the total health needs of society. At the same time, the personal gratification they will experience in providing this aspect of health care will more than compensate for their efforts and will enrich their own lives with a deeper understanding and appreciation of human relations.

NOTES

1 Wood, Clive, and Beryl Suitters, *The Fight for Acceptance; a History of Contraception*, Aylesbury, Medical and Technical Pub. Co., 1970, pp. 19-30.
2 Fortin, J.N. *et al.*, 'Side Effects of Oral Contraceptive Medication: A Psychosomatic Problem,' *Canad. Psychiatr. Ass. J.* 17, no. 1 (February 1972), 3-10.
3 Boria-Berna, Maria C., 'Husband's Role in Birth Control Acceptance,' *Med. Aspects of Human Sexuality* 6, no. 5 (May 1972), 70-114.
4 Bardwick, Judith M., 'Her Body, the Battleground,' *Psychol. Today* 5, no. 9 (February 1972), 50-114, 76, 82.
5 Wolfish, Martin G., 'Birth Control Counselling in an Adolescent Clinic,' *Canad. Med. Ass. J.* 105, no. 7 (October 9, 1971), 750, 753.
6 Sandberg, Eugene C., and Ralph I. Jacobs, 'Psychology of the Misuse and Rejection of Contraception,' *Amer. J. Obstet. Gyn.* 110, no. 2 (May 15, 1971), 227-142.
7 Neubardt, Selig, *Contraception* (New York, 1968).
8 Peel, John, and Malcolm Potts, *Textbook of Contraceptive Practice* (New York, 1970), pp. 169-209.

Summary of contraceptive methods*

Method	User	Effective- ness rating	Advantages	Disadvantages
Birth control pills	Female	Excellent	Easy and aesthetic to use	Continual cost; side effects; requires daily attention
IUD	Female	Excellent	Requires little attention; no expense after initial insertion	Side effects, particularly increased bleeding; possible expulsion
Diaphragm with cream or jelly	Female	Very good	No side effects; minor continual cost of jelly and small initial cost of diaphragm	Repeated insertion and removal; possible aesthetic objections
Cervical cap	Female	Very good	Can be worn 2-3 weeks without removal; no cost except for initial fitting and purchase	Does not fit all women; potential difficulties with insertion
Condom	Male	Very good	Easy to use; helps to prevent venereal disease	Continual expense; interruption of sexual activity and possible impairment of gratification
Vaginal foam	Female	Good	Easy to use; no prescription required	Continual expense
Vaginal creams, jellies, tablets, and suppositories	Female	Fair to good	Easy to use; no prescription required	Continual expense; unattractive or irritating for some people
Withdrawal	Male	Fair	No cost or preparation	Frustration
Rhythm	Male and female	Poor to fair	No cost; acceptable to Roman Catholic Church	Requires significant motivation, co-operation and intelligence; useless with irregular cycles and during post-partum period
Douche	Female	Poor	Inexpensive	Inconvenient; possibly irritating

*SOURCE: Katchadourian, Herant A., and Donald T. Lande, *Fundamentals of Human Sexuality* (New York, 1972), p. 45 (by permission).

SERENA

An alternative approach

to family planning in Canada

One of the things that distinguishes modern life from former times is open discussion of sexual questions. This change especially touches the matter of birth control. In Canada until 1969 this subject was under a Criminal Code section that banned distribution of contraceptive information or materials. With the removal of that legal restriction, public programs are beginning in many communities.

One on-going action program is that of Serena teams, started in 1955 in Quebec, and gradually expanding outside that province. The work of Serena's 250 teaching couples was recently given a boost by a $25,000 National Health and Welfare grant for an information program throughout Canada, to continue building on the base already established by Quebec provincial grants, on the status afforded by Quebec and Ontario public charters, and on the more than 15 years of efforts by Serena volunteers themselves.

The Serena approach to problems of human fertility thus stands as a well-defined alternative in the midst of various public programs now developing in the wake of the 1969 change in the Criminal Code.

FAMILY PLANNING NEEDS

The question no longer is whether human procreation should be responsibly planned. Today the problem is to discern the particular needs involved in such planning. Some needs are identified easily enough in terms of helping couples acquire general information about fertility regulation and the technical aids that may be used. Other needs, however, are less obvious, with the result that their importance may be minimized. These include: respect for individual freedom, adequate information as a basis for conscientious choice, sexual development of conjugal partners and their marital harmony, respect for life and a positive out-look on fertility, and an opportunity for conscious creation ('every child a wanted child').

Moreover, there are other questions that are more or less indirectly related: How can professional and paraprofessional training be expanded? What is the role of volunteers in delivering information and service at the local level? What factors should govern the availability of contraceptives for adolescents? What is the impact of contraceptive technology on sexual attitudes and roles, and on male and female definitions of self? Do some of the limitations of technology, highlighted in the pollution and ecology debate, apply also to contraceptive technology? What is the relation of fertility control to such general social ills as maternal and child mortality, child neglect, family breakdown, poverty, inade-quate housing, etc.? What is the relation of family planning to an overall popula-tion plan for the country and for its particular regions?

SERENA APPROACH

In the midst of such questions, the Serena approach offers:

a Specific, personalized knowledge about the process of the regular biologi-cal fertility-infertility cycle.

b A thorough understanding of the particularities, advantages, and disadvan-tages of all fertility control methods, as a basis for conscientious free choice.

c An increase of self-reliance on the part of couples, based on confidence that they can cope with the decisions to be made regarding their fertility.

d The possibility of full, mutual, and equal sharing by both conjugal partners in decisions regarding their fertility.

e A voluntary, community-based service, whereby couples who seek fertility counselling can receive it from couples in their own milieu.

f A training program for teacher-couples, to prepare them to counsel and assist other couples.

g A share in international research programs regarding human fertility.

The Serena approach thus starts from the view that technical aid is not the only and probably not the most important need to fill, even if it may seem the most urgent. Birth regulation is placed within the cluster of biological, psycho-logical, social, and cultural factors that make up the phenomenon of human sex-ual relationships, and is not taken in isolation. Harmonious integration of fer-tility control into the total life of the couple is seen as an essential requirement for any effective control program. Fertility control is treated as a question of orienting a strong and healthy human dynamism, and not as a matter of intervening medically to arrest a pathological condition. Proposed ways of channelling these dynamic forces therefore start with resources available in the lives of couples themselves, including knowledge, self-reliance, restraint, and mutuality.

FERTILITY KNOWLEDGE

Serena teaching couples are trained to recognize the phases of their own fertility cycle, and to aid other couples to do likewise. Each couple is helped to know and recognize the following facts:

1 The cycle (time between the first day of menstruation until the onset of the next one) is regulated by natural hormones.

2 Ovulation divides the cycle into three phases: time before ovulation (including menstruation), ovulation, and time after ovulation.

3 During each of these phases, the level of the different sex hormones in the body varies. The transition from one phase to the next is governed by the relative amount of these circulating hormones.

4 After ovulation has occurred, the hormone called progesterone is present in greater quantity and is believed responsible for a rise in the basal body temperature (temperature of the body at rest). This high level is sustained until the onset of the next menstruation.

5 The progesterone also prevents the release of another ovum or egg from the ovary. This is a key point: it means that a definite period of infertility exists in each cycle and that it can be determined by the temperature shift.

6 A couple's fertile period extends from a few days prior to ovulation until just after it – taking into account the fact that the male sperm can live in a woman's body up to five days while the ovum lives a maximum of 24 hours. (A World Health Organization report cites figures that 'suggest that the fertile period has a maximum duration of 4 days, but the average is probably much less.')

7 Once ovulation has occurred, it will be followed by menstruation in approximately 14 days, no matter what the overall length of the woman's cycle.

8 Thus it is the time preceding ovulation that changes whenever the cycle changes in length.

9 Ovulation itself is not pinpointed. However, because of the thermal change in the body, it is possible to ascertain that ovulation has occurred and to know that it will not occur again until the next cycle.

10 There are several visible signs (symptoms) that indicate the proximity of ovulation. The most common and reliable of these is the presence, and change in consistency, of cervical mucus.

Observation of these signs in combination with temperature changes in basal body temperature gives the name 'sympto-thermal' to this method.

BEYOND CALENDAR RHYTHM

The systematic grounding of the sympto-thermal method in biological realities makes it quite distinct from calendar rhythm – despite confusing and misleading links often made between them by those who are not informed about their differences.

Calendar rhythm involves an attempt to predict the length of the cycle on the basis of statistical probability. For a large female population, the average length of cycle can be calculated with considerable reliability. However, an individual woman cannot depend on her particular cycle regularly equalling the population average. The sympto-thermal method, in contrast, is based on facts that each woman directly observes in her own cycle. Through such specific, personal information, normal variations in length of cycle can be taken into account accurately and with confidence. The basis is fact, not prediction. From daily temperature readings and observation of other symptoms, each couple can know at all times what phase of the cycle they are in.

KNOWLEDGE AND CONTROL

Precise determination of the fertile period can be a factor in minimizing the need for concern about fertility control. No control problem exists during that part of each cycle when it is known that fertilization is biologically impossible. Beyond that, couples counselled by Serena members are helped to make their own choice about what control method to use.

Serena teaching couples give detailed information about the use, advantages, and disadvantages of all control methods, including abstinence from sexual relations during the time in the cycle when pregnancy will, or is likely to, occur. Abstinence is presented not only as a possible fertility control method but as a way of life for the couple.

COUPLE TO COUPLE

In communities where there are trained Serena couples, their availability for counselling is made known by all the usual means – advertising, marriage preparation courses, personal testimonies, etc. An inquiring couple usually makes contact by telephone, and an information session is arranged for them in a teaching couple's home. These sessions typically last several hours, usually in the evening, so that husband and wife of both couples have time to become acquainted and freely exchange information and questions. Thereafter, the teaching couple remains available to answer questions and give further directions to the newly initiated couple, usually by telephone.

Should a new couple wish after a time to qualify as a teacher couple, they are required to take detailed instructions from a doctor, trained couples, and other specialists including moral counsellors, before being certified by Serena.

HISTORICAL NOTE

The name *Serena* is a contraction from the French *Service de Régulation des Naissances* (Service for Regulation of Natality). As a method of fertility knowledge and control, it was introduced to Canada by Gilles and Rita Bréault of Lachine, Quebec, in 1955, after they had learned of it through contact with family groups in Belgium and France.

Word of their work – counselling couples, and training other couples to become counsellors themselves – spread slowly in a social climate that did not encourage open discussion of family planning. From the outset, the Bréaults emphasized not just fertility control but also the development of conjugal love and fidelity, family solidarity, and the ability of the ordinary couple to understand and handle the question of when to have children.

In 1962 the name Serena was chosen and a more public phase of the work began. Notre Dame Hospital in Montreal accepted the Montreal Serena team for public lectures under the auspices of its gynecology department. Magazine articles and radio programs in 1962 and early 1963 brought more than 2000 letters of inquiry. In 1963, Dr Jacques Baillargeon and his wife, Hélène Pelletier-Baillargeon, published a book, *La Régulation des Naissances*, in collaboration with the Bréaults. More than 65,000 copies have been sold.

During 1964 and 1965 some 40 Serena groups were formed throughout the province of Quebec. A liaison centre was organized in 1965 at Montreal. Other groups were started in New Brunswick and Ontario. Serena Inc. is now legally incorporated in the province of Quebec, having received its letters patent in 1969. Serena Ontario was incorporated by Ottawa area groups in the summer of 1971. There are now more than 250 couples at work. Since the beginning of the service in 1955, more than 32,000 couples have received Serena counselling and follow-up assistance.

SCIENTIFIC TESTING

Scientific study of their work began with a World Population Council grant to Dr Claude Lanctôt, now of the University of Sherbrooke, Quebec. His initial research was with the first thousand couples to whom the Serena approach had been taught. It consisted primarily of a verification of the efficacity of the method as taught. Dr Lanctôt's findings were reported at the first Symposium on Rhythm at Washington in October 1964, at an April 1965 meeting of the Population Association of America, and at a September 1965 meeting of the Scientific Group of the World Health Organization.

Last year Dr Lanctôt and Dr Frank Rice, a statistician at Fairfield University in Connecticut, received a grant from the US Human Life Foundation for a five-country study of the sympto-thermal method involving 1000 couples. Data from 200 Canadian couples following the method are being pooled and compared with information from similar groups in France, Columbia, Mauritius and the United States.

The primary objective of Fairfield study is to repeat, on a larger scale and within the context of the couple-to-couple approach, the work of Dr John Marshall of England,[1] who has done a study of the biological effectiveness of the sympto-thermal method. Secondary goals include study of menstrual cycle activity and variations, analysis of couples' attitudes to sex and to this method of fertility control, and study of the effect on marital happiness of varying periods of abstinence from sexual relations. The study, which will continue until the latter part of 1972, is also expected to contribute to the development of an international collaborative research consortium among the couple-to-couple groups participating in the current research.

RELIABILITY

One objective of this on-going research will be to test further both the theoretical effectiveness and the actual use effectiveness of the sympto-thermal method. Already an impressive body of literature is available on the subject. For example, Dr Christopher Tietze,[2] associate director of the bio-medical division of the Population Council, New York, wrote in a 1970 article ranking contraceptive methods by levels of effectiveness that 'determination of ovulation by means of basal body temperature and restriction of coitus to the post-ovulatory phase of the cycle, also falls within the most highly effective group of contraceptive methods.'

FOR FURTHER INFORMATION

For further information about the training and work of Serena teaching couples, inquiries may be addressed to: Serena Inc., 55 Parkdale, Ottawa, Ontario, K1Y 1E5; 9405 Berri, Montreal 354, Quebec.

NOTES

1 *The Lancet* (July 1968).
2 American Association Planned Parenthood Physicians (April 1970).

CARL F. GRINDSTAFF AND G. EDWARD EBANKS

Vasectomy: Canada's newest

family planning method*

For the past few years, we have taught courses in population study (demography) at the University of Western Ontario. As an integral part of these classes, we compare the various types of birth control methods available to Canadian couples who desire to plan their families. Recently, we received a call from one of our former male students, who exclaimed excitedly: 'Why didn't you tell me it was so great?' Not knowing what 'it' was, we asked. 'Why, a vasectomy of course. Why didn't you tell me it was so great and would be so easy? The day I had the operation, I took my wife shopping and the very next day I was playing ball with my kids. No pain, no trouble, no worry. It was just great.'

While perhaps more enthusiastic than most, this type of reaction is not atypical of men who have chosen vasectomy as their form of birth control. We have just recently completed a study of over 500 men who underwent the vasectomy in London, Ontario, between 1966 and 1970, and overwhelmingly, they exhibit complete satisfaction with the procedure. More than 95 per cent indicated that they would undergo the operation again if they had that choice to make. In fact, over 95 per cent said that they would recommend the operation to any friend who wanted a safe, sure, and inexpensive way of controlling their family size.

Although no comparable statistics are available for the London area, it would appear that the men are rather typical of the general population, but perhaps a bit above average in terms of occupational, educational, and income attainments. About one-third listed their occupation as professional or managerial. The men had completed 10.5 years of schooling on the average and approximately 13 per

*Reprinted from *Canada's Mental Health* 21 (September 1973).

cent had attended university. The median age is 36.4 years. The median family income is $8600 – which at the time of the questionnaire, 1970, is probably higher than the median family income found in the city as a whole. The men are 75 per cent Protestant, 10 per cent Catholic, 10 per cent no religion, and 5 per cent other. The city of London's population in 1961 was about 75 per cent Protestant, but it was also about 20 per cent Catholic. Thus, there is an under-representation of the latter religious group among the men who had undergone the vasectomy. This is to be expected given the official Catholic opposition to such a procedure.

The operation necessary to sterilize a man is a minor surgical procedure which can be performed in the doctor's office in approximately one-half hour, requiring only a local anesthetic. Specifically, the vasectomy involves the cutting and tying of the *vas deferens*, the tubes which carry the sperm from the testicles to the penis, hence preventing the transmission of the sperm to the female during sexual intercourse. Physiologically, this operation does not interfere with intercourse; erection and ejaculation still take place during the sex act, but the sperm are blocked and then reabsorbed by the body tissue. After a successful vasectomy, there is no sperm deposited into the uterus during intercourse to fertilize the female ovum, even though semen secreted by the walls of the penis is ejaculated into it.

POPULATION AND BIRTH RATE

While Canada does not have a population problem comparable to that experienced by most of the world (i.e., a growth rate of two per cent per year due to natural increase), the question of birth control is an important one for many Canadian families. In 1851-61, the crude birth rate in Canada (the number of live births per 1000 people in the population) was 45. In 1971, this rate is approximately 17. Not only have the birth rates decreased but the average family size has declined from a normal five or six children per family at the turn of this century to one of two or three children in the 1970s. In addition, women are completing their child-bearing at an earlier age. Fifty years ago, it was not uncommon for a woman in her late thirties or early forties to have a child. Today, this is a relatively rare event. It is estimated that approximately 75 per cent of all families now complete their child-bearing before the woman in the family is 30 years of age. This new demographic pattern creates an important and serious consideration. At age 30, with the family size complete and with 15 more years of potential child-bearing ahead of them, what can a couple do to prevent the occurrence of additional pregnancies? Vasectomy has been the answer for many.

The number of vasectomies being performed in Canada has increased dramatically in the past five years. For example, the total number of operations in London, Ontario, in 1966 did not exceed 200. In 1971, that figure will rise to more than 1000. We estimate that there are, at a minimum, over 100,000 men in Canada who have had the operation, most of whom were sterilized in the past two or three years. In British Columbia alone, in 1969, nearly 5000 operations were performed. The waiting list of one doctor in London shows that requests for vasectomies are so numerous that there is a waiting period of about four months. In Toronto, one urologist has a backlog of 200 cases.

There are a number of reasons for this increasing popularity. First, it is a cheap method of contraception (costing about $25 in Ontario, OHIP pays the rest). Secondly, it is a simple operation with no known side effects. Alternatively, female sterilization (usually tubal ligation) is a major operation requiring several days hospitalization. Third, vasectomy is very reliable, almost 100 per cent full-proof. This is an important factor especially to couples that have had all the children they want (and sometimes more than they had planned). Many couples desiring contraception for child-bearing termination have tried a number of the mechanical and chemical available methods and for one reason or another found them unsatisfactory. The following response from our study is rather typical: 'As a couple we have been very pleased with the outcome of this operation, knowing there is no fear of pregnancy as we get older and also no ill effects – the pill perhaps is all right for some, but the side effects worried us.' One of the wives said: 'I had no real complaint against the pill except about the last year I had too much fluid build-up, clogging before the cycle and much tension. I never had this at first.'

INCREASED USE

Thus, the vasectomy is chosen as a safe and reliable method. But why is male sterilization on the increase, especially in comparison to female methods? *The Globe and Mail*[1] reported that five years ago most sterilization procedures involved women whereas today 75 per cent of the patients are men. Cost and ease of the operation are factors which favour the male procedure, but these factors have always been relevant. Why has there been this change in the past few years?

Perhaps the main reason is the 'snowball' effect. Once a few men had had the operation and found it satisfactory, they told their friends about the vasectomy and perhaps made some positive recommendations. As more and more people discovered the procedure, the success of the operation was publicized by family planning groups. As a result the mass media, especially the newspapers, began to report on the operation as a birth control technique specially suited for those couples who had completed their family size. The mass media provided a source of information for people who had no previous knowledge of this method of birth prevention. Once this information network was underway, the increase in the number of men having the operation increased at an accelerating rate. The 'snowball' gained momentum.

In addition, there may be a political and social explanation: the increasing importance of the women's liberation movement. More and more women may be encouraging their husbands to take a more positive role in family limitation. Over the past 50 years, most improvements in contraceptive techniques have been 'female-oriented' – specifically the IUD and the pill. Women may see vasectomy as a much safer and reliable method and they ask, what is wrong with employing such a technique? Yet, as a recent Kitchener, Ontario newspaper noted:[2] 'A member of the Women's Liberation Movement in Toronto said many Canadian doctors still refuse to perform the operation [vasectomy] although it is perhaps the best method of birth control from the women's point of view.' This is a right-about-turn from the suffragettes and Margaret Sanger who clamoured for female methods in order to gain the control in the decision on procreation.

Finally, perhaps the male is also more responsive to the need to take an active role in planning one's family because he no longer necessarily equates his masculinity with the ability to have child after child. The cultural definitions of male and female sex roles seems to have undergone dramatic changes in the 1960s and 1970s, and the increasing importance of vasectomy as a birth control measure may simply be one indicator of this overall change. The male-female relationship is developing more as a partnership, with both parties taking equal responsibilities in such areas as economic provision, home care, and family planning. The male may be adopting an image of himself that relates to a birth control responsibility which he must share – and vasectomy is a way of doing that.

We asked the respondents in our study who was the most important person in arriving at the decision to have the operation. Nearly 65 per cent indicated that it was a joint decision between the husband and the wife and over 25 per cent said that the husband was most influential. Only five per cent said that the wife's insistence was the most important factor. The overall response would lend support to both hypotheses of wife encouragement and husband's initiative.

PSYCHOLOGICAL CONSIDERATIONS

The decision to choose vasectomy as the birth control technique can cause fears and worries for the male patient. There is certainly a psychological component present. Any tampering with the sex organs can create the fear of castration. Even though the male knows that the vasectomy operation is not a castration procedure, the fear that something might 'go wrong' may in fact be a very real one, at least at the psychological level. Approximately one-third of all the men in our study expressed some worry, fear or concern prior to the operation about a lessened sex drive, loss of sexual enjoyment, and pain of the operation. However, none of these worries or concerns were subsequently borne out for most men following the operation. Satisfaction was nearly total and universal. Only seven of the men indicated that they would not have the operation if they had the opportunity to do it over again. Three men said that they subsequently suffered nervous breakdowns, but only one felt that the vasectomy operation was related to their problem. Finally, as we indicated previously, 488 of the total 506 males in the sample (over 96 per cent) said that they would recommend the operation to a friend as a safe and satisfactory method of birth control.

All of the patients in our study reported that they had been informed they could no longer father a child. Some, however, expressed concern about this: 'If the operation were reversible, it would remove the concern about not being able to start a new family in case something happened to our children.' At this point in time, there is really very little known about the reversibility of a vasectomy, mainly because there are so few requests for such an operation. Many victims of the Nazis had been sterilized by means of vasectomy, and subsequent efforts to make some of these men fertile again were successful about 50 per cent of the time. A recent study carried out in the United States cited successful reversal of the operation in 18 out of a total of 20 attempts, but such a small number does not allow any definite conclusions as to the reversibility of the procedure. For the present, most doctors tell their patients that the operation will render them permanently unable to procreate.

Most of the men indicated they decided to have the operation because they had achieved their desired family size, and in many cases had exceeded it. The 506 respondents had a total number of 1690 children, an average number of children per family of 3.38. The average number desired by the husband and wife at the time of their marriage was 2.50 and 2.65 respectively. Thus, there was over 30 per cent more children born to these couples than they had originally desired when they were first married.

This inability to achieve the desired number of children is further reflected in the failure of all other birth control methods that had been tried. For example, 140 couples had used the rhythm method at various times for birth control purposes, and 138 pregnancies had resulted. Over 300 couples had employed the pill, and even with this relatively safe method, 27 accidental pregnancies occurred. As one man remarked to his doctor after having the vasectomy: 'Thank you for your assistance in getting the operation done. I am more than pleased. Too bad I hadn't done it two months earlier!' Another couple remarked: 'We were at our wits end as to know what to do, so thanks to this operation we now have peace of mind.'

A bonus accrued to most of the couples after the operation was performed. Nearly 70 per cent of both the husbands and wives said that there had been an increased enjoyment in sexual relations since the operation. Less than two per cent indicated a decrease in sexual enjoyment. One wife expressed her feelings by writing: 'Vasectomy is a sure way. We are happy and satisfied with this. Life has more meaning now. No more "too tired's" or any other means to keep away from him, even though you love him. Thanks for giving us a chance to live in peace. Thanks for giving me back my marriage that I almost lost. From the bottom of our hearts. Thanks.' Another couple said: 'We are pleased with the operation, we have a better understanding of each other's relationships. Since the operation, all of our lives have improved; no nagging mother, more contented husband, happy, healthier wife.' For these people, the vasectomy enabled them to develop an improved physical, emotional, and psychological relationship with each other. Here, sex role changes are brought about by the knowledge that accidental pregnancy is no longer possible. The woman is freer to express her physical and emotional involvement with her husband.

NO-CURE-ALL

However, a vasectomy is not the answer for everyone. One respondent commented: 'Our marriage was not well prior to the vasectomy, it has since sickened and will soon be dissolved by separation.' Another husband reported: 'Since the operation, my nerves have been bad and now I have no sex drive at all.' Thus, a vasectomy is not a cure-all for marital, sexual, personal, and emotional problems. It should be considered only after in-depth discussions between the husband and wife and perhaps also with the doctor. The vasectomy is primarily undergone for birth control reasons, and all other benefits are incidental and cannot be counted upon.

Vasectomy has become a popular method of birth limitation, and this popularity will undoubtedly continue to grow in the near future. For most men who have completed their family size and have undergone the operation, it has been the safe, sure, and satisfactory method of birth control that they had been seeking. In addition, the increasing use of this birth control technique may be an indicator of the changing culture of our society relating to traditional sex roles, and it may in turn result in further sex role modification.

NOTES

1 *The Globe and Mail*, March 28, 1970.
2 *The Record*, November 19, 1970.

MARION G. POWELL

Female sterilization

Couples who have completed their families and are seeking a permanent method of birth control are selecting sterilization, of both the male and the female, as a desirable alternative to the uncertainties of other temporary methods of birth control. It is a means of limiting family size rather than spacing children. Sterilization is an alternative to effective birth control and is not important in national fertility control. The couples using this method of birth control are usually older with completed families. Sterilization is rapidly gaining in popularity in many countries. In the United States, India, and Pakistan, male sterilization particularly is gaining in popularity. It is difficult to obtain figures on the number of sterilizations performed in Canada.

In most countries female sterilization is more popular than male sterilization and has been available for a longer time. In the past, female sterilization was performed for medical indications such as repeated Caesarian sections or serious maternal disease. The number rule of 120, obtained by multiplying the age of the mother and the number of children, has been a method used by hospitals for selecting women for sterilization. The accepted figure of 120 is unrealistic for younger women and for women with few children. The request for sterilization is still too frequently met with a curt refusal or scorn, and elective sterilization is still not a reality in many parts of Canada. Some hospitals require a committee decision in order to carry out a sterilization on a younger woman with no medical indications for the operation. In the past, to circumvent some of the obstacles to sterilization a hysterectomy was performed as an alternative, a procedure which carries a higher risk to the women than tubal ligation carried out using new techniques.

Sterilization is increasing in popularity despite the fears of side-effects and rumours of sequelae in the area of sexuality. There is a need for accurate information to reassure couples seeking sterilization. Many men fear impotence following vasectomy and equate the procedure with castration. These fears have tended to reinforce the practice of the past in which women were sterilized in preference to their husbands. In many parts of the world, including Canada, vasectomy is being performed on many men as a result of the publicity in the press coupled with the simple technique, lower cost, and availability of the operation. Increasing sexual knowledge and increasing concern about world population growth account in large measure for the changing attitude towards sterilization.

Detailed follow-up studies of sterilized women have been done in a number of countries. These studies show that about 90 per cent of women are satisfied with the operation. In the areas of health, marital relationship, and psycho-social adjustment, there was actual improvement or no change. A small percentage experienced some difficulties. The removal of fear of pregnancy resulted in improved sexual relations and in a reduction in tensions within the marriage in most cases. These studies were carried out on women who were sterilized for medical or gynaecological reasons and those who elected the procedure on social or economic grounds. There was no significant difference between the two groups.

Tubal ligation may be performed at the time of Caesarian section or during the puerperium or at the time of abortion. There has been a tendency for physicians terminating pregnancies to coerce the multipara into agreeing to sterilization as a condition for the abortion. While it may be reasonable to discuss sterilization with the woman likely to seek another abortion should she become pregnant in the future, many women are unable to adjust to sterilization under these circumstances and their reaction may be different than if the decision to be sterilized is delayed until some weeks or months after the abortion has been performed.

The shifting emphasis away from the traditional roles for women is allowing them to find alternatives to childbearing and child rearing. As opportunities for women are increasing, the consequences of early termination of child-bearing is making sterilization an attractive alternative to conventional birth control. For the few women who may regret this decision to be sterilized and request that the operation be reversed, many more regret that they had not made the decision earlier and that they did not have fewer children.

There are some women for whom sterilization is not indicated. Gynaecologists who frequently see only the woman and assess her request on a single interview may fail to determine whether her marital relationship is stable. Some women seek sterilization to salvage a failing marriage as couples may use a pregnancy for the same reason. While mistakes have been made in selecting women for sterilization by making the procedure too readily available, many more women have suffered because they have been denied the option and have been forced into bearing unwanted children.

Couples seeking sterilization are usually highly motivated and with counselling and adequate knowledge have very few problems. Those couples who choose vasectomy are often couples who have discussed the question and come to a joint decision. Their confidence in their relationship is more apparent. The choice of vasectomy is often made by the husband out of consideration for the wife. The wife who prefers sterilization may have made the decision on her own, fearing to raise the subject of vasectomy with her husband or fearing the consequences to his health and potency. Attitudes towards sterilization vary in different populations according to culture and social strata. At the present time vasectomy has become acceptable among certain groups of men and the pressure exerted by members of the group on their peers has altered many of the preconceived ideas physicians have had about the type of patient who elected a certain procedure.

Advances in the techniques of female sterilization have reduced the length of hospital stay and the necessity for an abdominal operation. Both these factors were deterrents to many women seeking sterilization. The classical operation of ligating and resecting a portion of the fallopian tubes using the abdominal approach is still widely used by many gynaecologists. A modification of this technique in which the distil end of the fallopian tubes is removed, is becoming increasingly popular. The term fimbriectomy and tubectomy are being used to replace the obsolete term tubal ligation. In removing the fimbriated end of the tubes there is a higher rate of success but the possibility of reversibility is reduced.

A further modification of the above procedures using the vaginal approach is gaining in popularity because of a shorter convalescence and lower morbidity rates. The use of either the laparascope or culdoscope, instruments developed originally as diagnostic aids, has revolutionized female sterilization, and developments in the use of these instruments which permit the surgeon to visualize the tubes through a very small incision have brought sterilization into the out-patient departments, where large numbers of women can be sterilized quickly and safely. Using these instruments the tubes are cauterized or occluded with clips.

Newer techniques using a hysteroscope, an instrument inserted through the cervix permitting visualization of the tubal orifices in the endometrial cavity, are being developed. The tubes may be occluded by cautery or injection of quinacrine. Success rate is fairly high for these procedures and although they are not perfected to the point of being widely acceptable, they show promise for future developments in techniques of female sterilization.

With the increasing popularity of sterilization as a method of birth control there is an urgent need to provide services, both referral and counselling, where couples can be aided in their choice of male or female sterilization. The change in acceptance of this method of birth control by the public has altered the attitudes of professionals and appears to have made the procedure more acceptable to physicians. The method appears to have few drawbacks. It rates very high in effectiveness, very low in side effects. The occasional dissatisfied man or woman should not act as a deterrent to the couples seeking sterilization. The important fact remains that sterilization removes nothing but the ability of the couple to reproduce. Their sexuality and their endocrine structure remain intact. As long as all other methods of birth control have failure rates or side effects serious enough to interfere with their use, sterilization as a terminal method of birth control will continue to be the method chosen by many couples.

FROM *BABIES BY CHOICE*

Babies by choice, not by chance*

The Family Planning Home Visiting Project extended over a period of 17 months from September 1971 to February 1973. Two major questions guided the research and demonstration process: 1 Is there a need for an expansion of family planning services? and 2 If there is, how should such services be delivered? The systems for locating those in need included a large-scale survey approach. This was productive of data which made it possible to draw a profile of contraceptive usage in Vancouver and North Vancouver, quite apart from the evaluation of the outcome of the service delivered. To order the data in manageable form and keep the information on birth control usage distinct from the usefulness of the service given, the findings are presented in two parts.

Volume i describes the study population, methodology, and demonstration procedures. It attempts to give a profile of contraceptive usage and to answer the questions: Did the project reach a target group in need of birth control information and help in using contraception? What are the characteristics of those in need? Who were helped by the project? Whom did the project fail to help?

Volume ii presents the findings to such questions as: Which mode of service delivery proved the most effective in reaching the target group? (Visits to new mothers and therapeutic abortion patients, social worker referrals, and household canvassing will be compared.) Which type of worker, professional or para-

---

Babies by Choice not by Chance published by United Community Services of the Greater Vancouver area.

professional, was best suited to particular social situations? How much service was given with what effects in changes in fertility? How successfully did new users adopt efficient contraception? What is the need for outreach family planning services? How should such services be organized and administered? Volume II was published in June 1973.

HIGHLIGHTS OF THE FIRST REPORT

The neglected child, the abandoned child, the battered child – major concerns in our society – provided the major impetus for this study on outreach family planning services. Not all unplanned children are unwanted, but it seems a safe assumption that children deliberately conceived have a greater chance of being loved and cared for than those not so ordered. How can we help those who wish to limit or space pregnancies but are unsuccessful in doing so? That is the major question which this research project attempts to answer.

A second impetus for the study came from the rapid rate of increase in therapeutic abortions. This expensive and traumatic solution to unwanted pregnancy is resorted to by more and more women. In 1971, the abortion rate for Canada was 8.3 for every 100 live births; in British Columbia, the rate was 19.1, more than double the national average. This represents over 7000 abortions during the year, an increase of 350 per cent over the year before. A large number of these are young single women and the suspicion arises that abortion is being used as a type of contraception.

Why are so many unplanned pregnancies occurring in a society where a great range of contraceptive devices are available? Some clues to the puzzle have already been provided by previous research. Consistently it has been shown that, while low-income families do not desire more children than others, they do in fact give birth to more. Further, there is evidence that this is due to differences in knowledge of and access to methods of contraception. The problem of the unwanted child is, of course, not solely the province of low-income families; but the burden falls more heavily on them than on the affluent.

Other communities have had success in providing outreach services to families who wish to limit and space their children. This project was set up to test a similar approach in the local situation. Two professional and two non-professional workers were carefully chosen and trained intensively for a week in all aspects of modern birth control techniques. These workers then made house calls in selected areas of Vancouver and North Vancouver, talking to mothers of child-bearing age. They discussed specific techniques in simple terms, showed the contraceptives, arranged appointments with a doctor or clinic if requested, and kept in close touch with the family to assist them in adopting a method correctly. *The decision as to how many children they wanted was always that of the family, not the worker.*

In one year of service, 13,000 house calls led to interviews with 2450 women with an average age of 29 years. In the main, these families had their contraceptive plans under control, but several findings suggest the need for an outreach program beyond the present agency-based service. What were these findings?

Many babies still arrive by chance, not by choice. Of the sample families, 18 per cent (451) were inadequately protected against pregnancy. Most of these (284 families) were not using any method of birth control, even though they were sexually active and did not want to have children in the near future.

Unplanned pregnancy is linked to poverty. The 'inefficient users' tended to have had more children and a higher number of unplanned pregnancies, and to be of lower socio-economic status than the general population: 10 per cent of the families had five or more children; 7 per cent had 6 or more unplanned pregnancies.

The pill is no panacea. The most popular method of contraception was the pill, used by 51 per cent of the sample. But, of 1063 women who had at one time in life used the pill, 50 per cent gave it up because of adverse side effects; 9 per cent gave it up because of fear of prolonged use; and 10 per cent gave it up to adopt another method. A total of 720 women (almost 68 per cent) had been dissatisfied with the pill. Of the 595 current users, 22 per cent expressed dissatisfaction.

The IUD is a 'sleeper.' Only 14 per cent of the sample used the IUD as a birth control method. This finding is surprising in view of the fact that some IUDs are safer than some pills and, in addition, cannot be incorrectly used as can the pill. This finding gives rise to speculation about medical practices, particularly in light of the high degree of rejection of the pill. Given the pressures of a busy office, does the comparative ease of writing a prescription influence the frequency with which this method is advocated? Are doctors able to keep on top of recent developments in the field of contraception? Do they have time to discuss with their patients the alternative methods of birth control available to them?

Nine out of ten women prefer doctors! Nearly 10 per cent of the interviewees were referred to a medical resource for the prescription of a contraceptive. This was 4 in 8 of 'inefficient users' and 1 in 7 of 'non-users.' Of those referred, 90 per cent chose a private physician over family planning or drop-in clinics. This, and other information we gathered, suggests that for this group of the population the family doctor is the best line of defence against unwanted pregnancy.

People want to know the facts. A total of 58 per cent of the interviewees requested some information, ranging from questions on particular methods to requests for descriptions of all methods and the way they work. Talks were given to 90 per cent of 'inefficient users' and 75 per cent of 'non-users.'

Sterilization is 'in.' Nearly one-quarter of all families visited had family size controlled by this means. One-third of these were accounted for by surgery not performed for contraceptive purposes (hysterectomy, etc.). One-third were female sterilizations (tubal ligation) and one-third male sterilizations (vasectomy). Worthy of note is the popularity of vasectomy in the sample interviewed, this being on a par with the proportion of tubal ligations. Those choosing sterilization are in general older and have had more children than the rest of the sample. Choice of this method appears to be a last resort when non-use or inefficient use of other measures fail to control family size.

These, then, are the findings of the initial stage of the project. Perhaps the single most important finding to date is the readiness with which the community has accepted a full and frank discussion of family planning. *In the course of 13,000 house calls and nearly 2500 interviews on a most intimate topic, not one telephone call or letter of complaint has been received by the sponsoring agency.* The time seems ripe for a new and forceful effort to harness the forces of fertility.

PART FIVE

ADOLESCENTS AND YOUNG ADULTS

MARION G. POWELL

The pregnant schoolgirl

In the past, the pregnant schoolgirl has been a source of embarrassment and shame to her parents and the community. As a result she has been hidden away and ignored until after the birth of her baby, when she could return to her own community and attempt to reorganize her life as if the previous nine months had not occurred.

Several changes have occurred which have altered the situation for the single pregnant girl. With the provision of welfare services, an increasing number of girls are raising their babies themselves. Fewer girls are leaving the community to take up residence in maternity homes. Abortion is more readily available to these girls. However, despite these changes, pregnancy in a schoolgirl is still a crisis for the school authorities. It has been stated that pregnancy is the leading cause of school dropouts among girls in the early grades of secondary school.

In Canada in 1971 there were 33,057 first births to girls between the ages of 15 and 19. From past experience, based on statistics of previous years, it can be assumed that approximately one-third are illegitimate. An estimate of the number of abortions performed in Canada in this age group in 1971 was approximately 9000.

Pregnancy occurring in the 15 to 19 age group is a frequent and unplanned tragedy. The education of these girls remains an unsolved problem in most areas. Several cities in Canada, including Calgary, Winnipeg, and Kingston, have set up special school programs that permit a girl to continue her education in a school setting. Most school boards will provide a tutor for an hour or two a week at the request of the girl or her parents. Many schools are willing to have the girl remain in school if she wishes to do so. However, many girls are unwilling to take advantage of this opportunity and prefer to drop out.

In 1970 in Scarborough, the eastern borough of Metropolitan Toronto, there were 104 girls aged 15 to 18 years of age who were known to their school administrations to have become pregnant. Following their deliveries only 27 returned to school. That same year 45 per cent of all single mothers took their babies home from the hospital.

In an attempt to find out more about the educational expectations of girls at the time they got pregnant a public health nurse interviewed all teenagers who were delivered of babies at Scarborough Centenary Hospital in the month of October 1970. Of the 12 girls interviewed, the mean age was 16 years and 11 months. One-half were married during their pregnancy, while the other half remained single. Eight of the girls were attending school at the time of conception. The last grade completed was tabulated; four girls had only completed grade 8 and one girl was attending university. On questioning them about their plans for their futures, eight girls had no plans for returning to school and three were hoping to return.

Of the eight girls in school, six of them left without any explanation as to the real reason for their withdrawal. Moreover, the school made no attempt to follow up these girls. Several of the girls stated that they were disappointed in this apparent lack of interest. The two girls who informed the school of their pregnancies were the only two who received home tutoring.

The above sample is very small and no conclusions can be reached. However, it is safe to assume that many school authorities still have this same attitude toward the pregnant schoolgirl. Many girls leave school never knowing that they could have continued or could have been taught at home. Many changes in attitude towards the single parent are apparent in the community but the school seems to be slow in accepting change. It is as difficult today as it has been in the past for the pregnant schoolgirl to continue with her education.

In 1970 abortion was not as readily available as at the present time and some of the girls who carried their babies to term then would be having abortions in 1973. However, many girls who will continue to carry their pregnancies will have need of special educational services. Despite limitations of education budgets, there is urgent need to plan for programs to meet the needs of the pregnant schoolgirl and the single parent in order to allow them to continue their education.

Family planning clinics set up especially to provide birth control for teenagers and easier access to abortions are causing a drop in the number of births to teenage girls. The timing of the first birth is the single most important factor in determining future fertility patterns of women. This first birth has the greatest potential for social change. If all unplanned first births could be prevented, illegitimacy would be eliminated almost entirely and the number of babies born to teenagers would be drastically reduced. Since infants born to mothers below the age of 20 constitute a high risk group, infant mortality would be dramatically reduced also. In addition to the above considerations, unplanned pregnancy in the teenagers frequently leads to a hasty marriage. The impact on the adolescent girl of pregnancy during her school career cannot be ignored but must be recognized as being one with far-reaching effects on the whole course of the girl's life. To prevent such a pregnancy, the barriers which prevent the use of contraception must be broken down. Unavailability of effective birth control to unmarried minors, particularly in small towns and villages, is perhaps the foremost barrier. The lack of knowledge of contraception and the ignorance of the risk of pregnancy are two subject areas for health educators in the schools to look at with a view to changing curricula.

To solve the problem of the pregnant schoolgirl and to provide for her educational needs are challenges facing boards of health and education.

DORIS GUYATT

Family planning and the adolescent girl

For teenage girls 'family planning' usually means planning not to have a family, or birth control. In Scarborough,[1] one of five boroughs in Metropolitan Toronto, a clinic operated by the municipal Department of Health has been serving the family planning needs of teenagers for more than six years. Although the Family Planning Clinic serves all age groups, a very high proportion of its patients is comprised of students, mostly from the borough's high schools but a few from community colleges, schools of nursing, and the universities. Because of the concern over the increasing number of pregnancies among adolescent girls in Scarborough, a survey was begun in October 1971 of all the girls under 20 who came to the clinic for the first time. These girls were asked to complete a questionnaire on their socio-economic background, their attitudes toward premarital sex and abortions, their medical history, their knowledge and use of birth control, and their relationship with their boyfriends.

A research team consisting of Dr Diane Sacks, a pediatrician from the Hospital for Sick Children, and the author, interviewed each girl to obtain additional information. A pilot study was conducted on the first 175 usable questionnaires and selected characteristics were tabulated.

CHARACTERISTICS OF GIRLS ATTENDING CLINIC

The adolescents served by the clinic ranged in age from 14 to 19 years but the most common age was 17. Four-fifths of these girls were students. All but 6 per cent had completed grade 9 or higher. The largest group, about 26 per cent, had just completed grade 12. This is probably a reflection of the sex education program in the schools because the grade 12 course provides extensive information on birth control and members of the clinic staff have served as guest speakers in these health classes. The higher number from the upper grades probably also indicates an increasing sexual involvement among older high school students.

The fathers of the girls in this sample most commonly had received some high school education (35 per cent) but approximately one-fifth were high school graduates and one-seventh had some university or other post-secondary education. Almost two-thirds of the fathers were Protestant in religion and one-quarter were Roman Catholic.[2] About one-tenth were said to have no religion, to be atheist, agnostic or, in a few cases, some uncommon religion such as Buddhist or Bahai.

More than half the girls never attended church and only 17 per cent attended regularly. However, 60 per cent considered themselves somewhat religious. A rather large proportion of girls, more than one-quarter, came from one-parent families. Of these only a slightly higher proportion was pregnant than the proportion from two-parent homes. This difference was not statistically significant.[3]

Ninety per cent of the girls said they had family or local doctors to whom they went for treatment but more than 70 per cent said they would not feel free to go to their doctor for help with birth control. Their major reason for not going to their doctor was that they feared he would tell their parents. Nearly all the girls in the sample had some knowledge of birth control, but in spite of this 42 per cent had never used any method of birth control.[4] The method most frequently used by the girls was the condom, followed by the pill, rhythm, and withdrawal. About two-thirds of the girls were aware of the danger period during the menstrual cycle when pregnancy might occur. Almost 70 per cent of the girls came to the clinic for help with birth control but more than one-quarter came because they thought they were pregnant. Not all of these were pregnant and some who said they came for birth control were tested and found to be pregnant.

Forty-one of the 175 girls were known to be pregnant, 23 per cent of the total sample. An additional 17 girls were checked for pregnancy, 12 of whom were not pregnant and 5 of whom did not return to report. Of the known pregnancies, 4 out of 5 girls decided to abort and were referred to local hospitals. A few girls were referred to clinics in Buffalo, New York, because they wished to forgo the hospital committee procedure or they were only 17 years of age and did not wish to obtain parental consent, which is necessary for those under eighteen to obtain an abortion in Canada. The girls who decided to carry their pregnancy were referred to community services for unmarried mothers. The hardest part of the whole experience of being pregnant for most of these girls was telling their parents of their condition and they would go to any extent to avoid doing so if at all possible.

A disproportionate number of girls aged 15 were pregnant. Although this age group represented only 12 per cent of the total sample, 38 per cent of the 15-year-olds were pregnant. This appears to indicate a need for more stress on birth control in health classes around the grades 9 and 10 level. There is also a need not just to tell girls about methods of birth control but to direct them to a clinic for help. Many of the pregnant girls said they would have come to the clinic for help had they known about it earlier.

Most of the girls in the sample were not promiscuous, although nearly all had a very permissive attitude toward pre-marital sex. A typical answer to the question, 'What do you think about pre-marital sex,' was: 'It's OK if you love the guy.' And another, 'It's alright for some if you know what you're doing and what can happen because of this. For me, I have to know the fellow and care about him. You have to have some kind of strong feeling.' Nine out of ten said they had a steady boyfriend and most had had a lengthy relationship. Some 70 per cent of the girls had had a relationship with their boyfriend of over six months' duration. More than 12 months was the most common response and, of these, many relationships were more than two years' and a few up to four years' duration. Almost 90 per cent described their relationship with their boyfriend as close or very close.

Half of the girls had been at risk of pregnancy for seven months or more and three out of ten had been sexually active for more than twelve months, some as long as four years. They came to the clinic because a friend who had been there recommended it. Former patients often accompanied their friends on their first visit. Other sources of referral were the school nurse and advertisements posted in the high schools. Very few girls came to the clinic because of referrals from social workers, doctors, or teachers. Although 30 girls said they had had some contact with a social worker,[5] only seven said that their social worker had discussed birth control.

Their major sources of information about sex and birth control were school and girlfriends. Mother was mentioned by many girls as a source but in most cases they said mother discussed only menstruation. Doctors were mentioned as a source of information by only 13 per cent of the girls (see Table below).

WHY DO THEY GET PREGNANT?

The question arises that if these girls knew about birth control and facilities were available to help them prevent pregnancy, why did nearly one-quarter become pregnant? There is no simple answer to this question. Experience in working with more than 600 adolescent girls in the clinic leads to the following conclusions:

1 There is a strong biological drive in adolescence which tends to be unrecognized in them by our society, although it is acknowledged in others. Given the

Sources of information about sex

Source	Frequency of response	Percentage of total
School	124	70.9
Girlfriends	124	70.9
Boyfriend	87	49.7
Mother	111	63.4
School nurse	59	33.7
Siblings	42	24.0
Doctor	23	13.2
Social worker	14	8.0
Church groups	8	4.6
Other (books, pamphlets, magazines	52	29.7
No source	3	1.7

opportunity, physically mature young people will mate, and in our society there is a great deal of opportunity. We encourage early dating without chaperones. Our mass media incessantly entreat the young to 'be beautiful' and 'be sexy.' Parents appear to condone this message, but with the additional conflicting advice, 'Don't get pregnant.' Few of the girls understood this force of nature which impels them toward pregnancy. A response which illustrated this lack of insight was as follows: 'Why did I get pregnant? An accident. It wasn't planned or premeditated. It just happened. I'm kind of dumb. I don't really know why it happened.'

2 There appears to be what some writers have referred to as a universal fantasy among adolescent girls that they will not get pregnant. Pregnancy is something that happens to the girl down the street but not to themselves. This fantasy is reinforced if a girl has intercourse several times and nothing happens. She is lulled into a false sense of security and fails to protect herself against unwanted pregnancy. One girl explained, 'I guess it was not thinking enough about it. Actually it was quite stupid because I knew quite a few girls who got pregnant. I guess I just didn't think it would happen to me. Did I want a baby? Fantasizing – yes! Realistically – no!'

3 Some realize they are taking a risk but are afraid to come for help.
a Most girls will not go to their doctor because they are afraid that he will tell their parents. This fear is not always unjustified because cases were reported to the clinic staff in which family doctors had contacted parents. Many doctors are uncertain about their legal position if they prescribe for girls under 18 years without the parents' permission. A girl who used no birth control described her situa-

tion thus: 'I knew pretty well all the methods. What kept me from using something? You'd have to go to the doctor and I thought he'd have to tell your parents – especially for the pill. My boyfriend and I never talked about it. I just never brought myself to think about it. I had intercourse for several months. I figured I'd gone this long, so ...'

b Some girls are afraid the person they go to will refuse help because they are under 18. This also happens. One clinic patient said that before she became pregnant she had been to three doctors, all of whom refused to help her.

c Still other girls are too shy and self-conscious to discuss their problem with anyone. One such girl who became pregnant before seeking help recounted how she had come to the clinic building before but was afraid to ask where the clinic was located.

d Many young girls are afraid of having an internal medical examination. They are sometimes so tense and frightened that they cannot hear the information provided by the clinic staff until the medical examination is over.

4 They use some method of birth control but it fails.

a In a few cases condoms were known to have broken. In others, although condoms were used, they were used irregularly and pregnancy occurred.

b A large number of girls rely upon some kind of rhythm method. This method is not entirely reliable at best and frequently girls are misinformed as to the 'safe' period.

c Many girls rely upon withdrawal as a method of birth control. Probably the oldest method of birth control and the easiest to use, it is also the least efficient.

d Some teenagers begin to use contraceptive pills, experience some initial symptoms and then stop taking them. Others take the pills regularly for a time, then break up their relationship with their boyfriend and stop taking them. This may actually increase their fertility and make them more likely to become pregnant if their relationship is resumed unexpectedly.

5 They are reluctant to use contraceptives.

a Unmarried girls frequently feel guilty about having a sexual relationship before marriage. They can excuse their behaviour if it is unpremeditated, if intercourse just happens, but not if they prepare for it by using some method of birth control. There appears to be a paradox in our culture in that 'nice' girls do not prepare for intercourse but 'nice' girls are not supposed to get pregnant.

b Many girls are afraid of contraception because they have heard unfavourable reports. This is particularly true of the contraceptive pill. The girls often have heard they will gain weight if they take the pill and this discourages them: 'I was afraid to use the pill for a while. I was afraid of the side effects. People were telling me terrible stories and I was afraid my mother would find out.'

c Fear of parental discovery if they use contraception is probably the strongest deterrent of all.

6 A few girls want to get pregnant.

a Some girls express a need to have someone of their own to love and to love them. A girl who had been heavily involved in the drug cult and had decided to abort for this reason was asked if she thought she had become pregnant because she wanted to have a baby to love. Looking directly at the interviewer, she replied without hesitation, 'Someone to love *me*.'

b Other girls want to get pregnant so they can marry and get away from home.

c In a few cases the girl may wish to become pregnant in order to punish her parents. Although this motive does not appear to be as common as the social work literature suggests, for a few girls pregnancy is part of their adolescent rebellion against parental authority.

d Occasionally a girl wishes to get married and uses pregnancy as a means of getting parental consent or, in some cases, as a means of forcing the boy to marry her.

e Some girls romanticize pregnancy. They say: 'Having a baby is the greatest thing in the world.' They do not perceive marriage as a necessary context for having a baby and, in fact, place little importance on who fathers the child. They tend to have a very poor school record and to be enrolled in special vocational schools for slow learners. Perhaps for these girls who cannot compete in other aspects of life, having a baby is one thing they can do as well as anyone else.

f Finally, there are girls who want to become pregnant because it is the thing to do. All their friends have been pregnant. One such girl stated, 'It just seemed like I'd be the next. First Bette got pregnant, then I did and then we expected Jean to but she went on the pill.'

7 Last of all, some girls get pregnant because they are raped. There is no doubt that rape occurs fairly frequently, not as often as parents of pregnant girls may claim, but far more often than is reported to the police. Not all girls who reported to the clinic staff that they had been raped were pregnant but a few were, perhaps 3 or 4 per cent of the pregnant girls seen. Several girls reported incestuous relations with their fathers, but none of these girls was pregnant.

WHY DO THEY NOT GET PREGNANT?

Since about three-quarters of the girls who came to the clinic were not pregnant, it is perhaps more relevant to ask why do these girls *not* get pregnant. Certainly many have had prolonged sexual relationships and have been either completely unprotected or poorly protected. There is no reliable answer to this question at present. All past research has been focused on the group which becomes pregnant.

For the younger age groups, under 15, the explanation may be related to the age at which girls become fertile. It is known that after puberty occurs and the menstrual cycle begins there is a period of possibly a year or more during which a girl is not fertile and cannot become pregnant. However, for the older group the only explanation seems to be that intercourse may have been infrequent or else they were just lucky. Future research may provide other possible explanations.

HOW CAN WE PREVENT UNWANTED ADOLESCENT PREGNANCIES?

The girls in the study group were asked for suggestions regarding ways to get more information and help to teenagers. They suggested more sex education in schools at lower grade levels, grade 8 or 9 at the latest. They wanted not just factual discourses on anatomy in health classes but discussions of the emotional involvement in boy/girl relationships. They said knowledgeable people from the community should be brought into health classes to relate their experiences in the family planning field. They suggested signs be posted in public places and advertisements in the newspapers and on television telling of community clinic services. Finally, they thought their parents should be educated.

Social workers can do their part by counselling their young clients on the methods of family planning, referring them to community clinics and encouraging responsible behaviour in sexual relationships.

NOTES

1 Population 333,750 as of October 1971.
2 The mother's religion was used if the father was absent and his religion was unknown.
3 $X^2 = 0.0412$.
4 Only 7 per cent of the girls were virgins.
5 They defined social worker very broadly, including untrained workers and members of other helping professions.

REFERENCES

1 Bernstein, Rose, *Helping Unmarried Mothers* (New York, 1971).
2 Furstenberg, Frank F., 'Birth Control Experience among Pregnant Adolescents; the Process of Unplanned Parenthood,' *Social Problems* 19, no. 2 (Fall 1971), 192-203.
3 Rains, Prudence Mors, *Becoming an Unwed Mother* (New York, 1971).
4 Roberts, Robert W., ed., *The Unwed Mother* (New York, 1966).
5 Sorensen, Robert C., *Adolescent Sexuality in Contemporary America* (New York, 1973).

MARTIN G. WOLFISH

Birth control counselling

in an adolescent clinic*

Today's physicians were brought up in a social climate far different from that familiar to today's teenager. Adolescent behaviour and attitudes have undergone a remarkable and, at times, a perplexing change. Attitudes to sexuality have altered radically in the past generation. The aseptic, and often antiseptic, virginal image projected by the girl of yester-year connoted premarital continence and marital fidelity. The sexual behaviour of today's adolescent and youth no longer follow the established orthodox patterns.[1] Several options are open to him: intercourse with a single partner, or with many; long-term relationships or successive short-term relationships. While the majority of today's teenagers still adhere to the standards of orthodoxy of their parents, they do not condemn those who have chosen different avenues of sexual expression.

What is the actual extent of the sexual experience of our teenagers? How many of the reports of their sexual proclivities are true? A detailed survey of British adolescents was conducted by Michael Schofield[2] in 1965. In it 934 boys and 933 girls were interviewed regarding their sexual experience and behaviour. Although about one-third of boys had experienced intercourse by secondary school graduation, their sexual relationships tended to be of a sporadic nature. While only one-sixth of girls had had sexual intercourse by that time, they continued to be sexually active. But one must allow for possible further changes in the six years since that report was compiled.

Today, not only does the onset of puberty occur at a younger age in girls[3] (the menarche occurs six months earlier than it did a generation ago) but the age

*Reprinted from the C.M.A. Journal, October 9, 1971.

of financial self-sufficiency has been delayed by society's demands for more education and technological skills. Thus the period of sexual need without orthodox means of satisfaction has become prolonged to a point no longer tolerable to many. Contraception, largely stripped of the religious prohibition of its use, is considered an acceptable means of providing sexual freedom, and pregnancy is looked upon as an unfortunate consequence of lack of knowledge.

These changes in sexual attitudes are obvious at the Teen Clinic, The Hospital for Sick Children, Toronto. In the four years the clinic has been in existence, requests for contraceptive information, diagnosis of, support for, or termination of pregnancy, and the diagnosis and treatment of venereal disease have become no longer an oddity in a children's hospital but an everyday occurrence.

In 1967 we received no requests for contraceptive information and supply. During the past year we have had 31 such requests. This assistance was sought by 10 per cent of the new female patients seen in the Teen Clinic in the past year.

Some patients came directly to the clinic, some were referred by their teachers or school nurse who had become aware of their needs. The local Planned Parenthood Association has referred patients on several occasions. Six girls travelled to Toronto from outside the city, either because of lack of facilities closer to home or because they were unwilling to make their needs known to the family physician. Four girls were accompanied by their mothers. The remainder came without parental knowledge or consent.

The problem of parental consent is worrisome both legally and ethically. Withholding advice and supply unless parental consent is obtained would prevent many girls from seeking such help. The legal status of a minor's rights to medical treatment is vague and uncertain at present. The Society for Adolescent Medicine[4] has adopted a statement that for a minor, parental knowledge and consent are always preferable to self-consent, but if denial of medical treatment due to lack of parental consent would expose the patient or community to risk, then self-consent should be allowed. In our hospital this statement serves as a guideline for diagnosis and treatment in the adolescent, and this includes pregnancy prevention.

Patients seeking contraceptive advice and supply ranged in age from 14 to 19 years with a mean of 16.4 years. Their backgrounds varied from the inner-city core to wealthy areas of Metropolitan Toronto, and from slum schools to expensive 'free curriculum' private schools. The majority of girls were healthy, and were progressing through puberty in a normal fashion. One girl had had a previously diagnosed psychotic illness, and four other girls required care for less serious emotional disturbances. All patients received a thorough physical assessment, including pelvic examination, cervical cytology, and bacteriological study for gonococcal infection. Specimens were obtained for serologic testing for syphilis. One patient was found to have gonorrhoea.

One girl had no previous sexual experience. The remaining 30 patients had had sexual intercourse, usually with no attempt at contraception or only the haphazard use of the rhythm method. All patients were nulliparous, although two were originally examined because of suspected pregnancy.

Although most of our patients have asked directly for contraceptive information or supply, occasionally their need is exposed during the course of a visit for some other reason. Each female patient is asked sympathetically and diplomatically whether she is sexually active and all accept the enquiry with equanimity. How much she knows about conception and its prevention is ascertained.

We are constantly being reminded of the misconceptions many teenagers still have about pregnancy. Dispensing of contraceptives should never be mechanical and impersonal if it is to answer the teenager's need for information and allow her to examine her own attitudes toward sexual activities. The doctor who merely prescribes or dispenses the pill probably gives the young lady licence as well as a feeling of being 'put down' by his lack of interest. In the clinic each patient is exhaustively interviewed regarding her feelings and attitudes toward sex, is encouraged to consider her boyfriend objectively, the impact of her changing sexual behaviour on her own life style, and the possible effect of this on her parents and the parents of her boyfriend. Although we try not to judge, a thorough discussion of a girl's sexual behaviour will, sometimes, allow her to see her sexual feelings differently.

Contraceptive information and supply is always preferable to pregnancy in the unwed teenage schoolgirl. Little is gained if we discourage or scare a girl away, and then have her return pregnant.

One occasionally sees a girl who has what has been described as the 'unwed mother syndrome.' These girls usually come from emotionally deprived backgrounds and, in their quest for a love-object, wish to have a baby. Their sexual licence is directed toward pregnancy, not self-gratification. This syndrome should be recognized early. The girl is searching not for contraception but for someone to love or to love her and these needs must be met before she ceases to be a pregnancy risk.

The various methods of contraception are considered, and discussed with the patient in the Clinic. The 'pill' is usually the only practical method of prevention in this age group. We commonly prescribe a combination of norethisterone and mestranol. That condoms are totally unacceptable to today's youth – male and female – is unfortunate, since the pill offers no protection against venereal disease, whereas the condom does give both partners some safeguard. The diaphragm is too cumbersome for surreptitious sex, foams and jellies are notoriously unsafe, and an intra-uterine device is usually regarded by the gynecologist as unsuitable for the nulliparous teenager.[5] The rhythm method,[6] so trustingly used by many adolescents, generally results in the girl's seeking help only after she is pregnant. The flood of publicity that has been generated about the dangers of the pill, whether true, exaggerated, or false, confuses the young patient.[7,8] She needs the advice of a competent guide.

In spite of the increased availability of methods of contraception, the pregnancy rate has risen among teenagers. The impact of pregnancy on the teenage unwed girl is horrendous. Feelings of worthlessness, hopelessness, and the fear of ridicule by society, and possibly rejection by parents, are profound. Only in the inner-city slum where society accepts an out-of-wedlock child, or in our hippie counter-culture where an unwed mother defies the establishment, is teenage pregnancy acceptable.

We have seen 21 pregnant girls in the past year. Not one had practised contraception prior to her pregnancy. Today's standards of sexual behaviour may be vastly different from those of the older generation, but to understand the young and help them we must have a mind and heart open to their needs.

NOTES

1 Collins, D., 'Options,' Address to The Hospital for Sick Children, Toronto, Canada, May 5, 1971.
2 Schofield, M., *The Sexual Behaviour of Young People* (London, 1965).
3 Zacharias, L., R.J. Wurtman, and M. Schatzoff, 'Sexual Maturation in Contemporary American Girls,' *Am. J. Obstet. Gynecol.* 108 (1970), 833–46.
4 Rigg, C.A., *et al.*, Committee on Legislation, Society for Adolescent Medicine. (Washington, 1970), unpublished data.
5 Kleenman, R.L., *Medical Handbook.* International Planned Parenthood Foundation, third ed. (London, 1971).
6 Tietze, C., and R.G. Potter, 'Statistical Evaluation of the Rhythm Method,' *Am. J. Obstet. Gynecol.* 84 (1962), 692–98.
7 Drill, V.A., *Oral Contraceptives* (New York, 1966).
8 International Planned Parenthood Foundation, Medical Bulletin 2, November 1968, *Thromboembolism and the Pill – New Data.*

KATHLEEN BELANGER AND ELEANOR J. BRADLEY

'Family' planning and the single university student*

Canada, with the exception of the Province of Quebec, has concerned itself very little with the definitive study of social, economic, and cultural factors as they affect or are affected by the use of contraceptive measures. Canadians, however, are just as prone as everyone else to speculate about the supposed relationship between 'family planning' and the 'poverty cycle.' These suppositions, which often seem based on little else than myth and folklore or on research which has become invalid or outdated by rapid social changes and the advent of new methods of contraception, usually resolve themselves into hopeful assumptions that if only the poor had sufficient access to and were actively encouraged to avail themselves of family planning services some kind of magic would take place assuring a positive intervention in the poverty cycle. Unfortunately, facts to support these assumptions are both rare and ephemeral.

The most perceptive of the literature, while touching upon such imponderables as motivation toward or against the use of contraception and the barriers, myths and taboos which may prevent its use, is sadly deficient in presenting the kinds of conclusions which might increase effective planning of either informational or practical services. And the copious facts reiterated by most of the large demographic fertility studies serve only to propound a strange paradox; while historical differences traditionally thought to exist between the fertility and social values of urban and rural, rich and poor, middle, and working class families have become almost homogeneous, the poor continue to have more children than they say they want – in spite of everyone's best efforts.

*Reprinted from the *Social Worker* 38 (February 1970).

A descriptive study[1] in process in the city of Vancouver is attempting to clear away some of the unprofitable conjecture by eliciting the social, medical, economic, and attitudinal differences which may exist between women who use contraceptives and those who do not. The population under study consists of 100 new patients of the Vancouver Planning Clinic as compared to a matching sample of 100 women who have never attended a family planning clinic but who may or may not be using contraceptives.

The preliminary data collection on the total clinic population for one year disclosed the first myth-exploding fact. In that period between April 1, 1968, and March 31, 1969, *67.7 per cent of the new patients requesting service were single women.* Of this group, 43 per cent were university students, 11 per cent unspecified students, and the rest were employed or unemployed single women.

While it would be possible to consider university students as provisionally poor during the process of getting an education, it would be stretching credulity to a ludicrous point to consider them as caught up in a traditionally defined 'poverty cycle.'

Not only were the bulk of clinic services being used by single women, but of the married women in attendance only 14, or 3.5 per cent of the total clinic population, had unemployed husbands. Although it was true that 39 per cent of the employed husbands were either labourers or semi-skilled workmen whose incomes might fall below the poverty line (and there was a small group of husbands with low present income but high future potential: university teaching assistants, post-doctoral fellows), the occupations of the rest ranged upward from salesmen to engineers.

Of the single women who were not students, 30, or 14 per cent of the total clinic population, were unemployed. If we assume a close relationship between poverty and unemployment, even among the poor the single women rather than married women were by far the more dominant users of a 'family' planning service.

THE SINGLE UNIVERSITY STUDENT

As soon as it became evident that the population under study was likely to remain predominantly single, there seemed value in taking a look at the largest and most homogeneous group of clinic service users – the single university students.

There was further interest in separating out this group in light of the findings of a study completed by two medical students who had interviewed 29 physicians about their attitudes toward the prescription of contraceptives. While 11 who prescribed stated they would do so for all single women, the rest were prepared to do so only under certain conditions such as age, parental consent, independence from family and/or previous history of pregnancy or abortion. There was a reason to suppose, also, from statements made by a number of unmarried clinic patients that there was general reluctance to turn to a private physician because of fear of refusal, whether this fear was based on fact or not. That this fear was justified, in some part, was underlined by the experience of several girls, one of whom was able to pin-point the dynamics of her illegitimate pregnancy as a neurotic way of 'getting back at' a hostile, distrustful mother regrettably symbolized for her in the behaviour of a woman physician who not only refused to prescribe a contraceptive but gave her a lengthy talk on the 'sins of youth.'

THE SAMPLE

A sample was chosen of 34 single university students between the ages of 18 and 24, all of whom were new patients to the Family Planning Clinic. A matching sample of single students of the same age group was chosen from within the university community. Each respondent was matched individually and as exactly as possible by date of birth.

An amusing but revealing sidelight which became manifest during early discussion of the total study and increased into incandescence when it came to the contemplation of single women and their use of contraceptives, was the tendency – mainly on the part of male social workers – toward gloomy prediction about the high rate of refusal sure to be encountered by the interviewers. In fact refusals were rare and when one did occur it was usually at the insistence of the man involved. Apparently the respondents found the matter of contraception a far less touchy subject to approach than did some professional people.

SEXUAL ACTIVITY

As would be expected, all the clinic patients were sexually active. In the matching sample, while more than half the girls had what they defined as 'steady' boyfriends only nine were sexually active. Very few of the non-sexually active thought of sexual activity before marriage as 'wrong' in the moral sense; 13 felt their parents' probable 'hurt' or 'disapproval' had been the main deterrent; 9 said they had decided not to have intercourse 'at least for now' because of 'personal beliefs and feelings.' Many made it clear, however, that there was no guarantee against a change of mind, particularly if a 'meaningful enough' relationship developed.

The clinic patients were not, as might have been expected, older than the sexually inactive but somewhat younger. And a significantly higher number of them had definite plans to marry the present boyfriend than had the matching group of girls who were not sexually active but 'going steady.' Not one respondent in the community sample of sexually active girls revealed a firm intention to marry the sexual partner and several said they had 'no intention whatsoever' of doing so – the first graphic indication that these girls were to show substantially different characteristics from the others.

Where there was indecision about marriage within the group of clinic girls this was usually related to 'not feeling quite ready for marriage' or not being sure of the 'viability of marriage as an institution.' There was some wariness of legal ties 'on intellectual grounds,' but this did not seem related to fear of lasting relationships. None of the clinic girls put the pursuit of a career ahead of marriage and the sum of their answers to the questions on family life and the needs of children revealed a strong sense of responsibility and other directedness. While the 'new morality' might be different from the 'old,' it was clearly, for them, a defined morality, one which seemed essentially unrelated to the practice of formalized religion. Although more girls in the community sample (85 per cent compared to 76 per cent) professed a religious affiliation, church attenders in both groups were rare. Only one girl, a Roman Catholic,[3] considered the church to have had a strong influence on her decision not to become sexually active, 11 said its influence was moderate or minimal, and 12 said it had no influence at all.

EDUCATION OF PARENTS

Recognizing that the total population under study was a university one and a generally higher level of parents' education could be expected than would prevail in a broader community sample, the higher the level of education attained by a respondent's parents the more likely, it seemed, she would become sexually active before marriage. In the sexually active group, including both clinic and community samples, 50 per cent of the respondents' mothers had either fully completed or almost completed university education. Only 10 per cent had failed to go beyond elementary school. In contrast, while 44 per cent of the mothers of the sexually inactive had partially or wholly completed university, 24 per cent had not continued beyond grade 8. The percentage of university-educated fathers was about equal for both groups (44 per cent and 40 per cent) but only 10 per cent of the fathers of the sexually active had stopped their schooling at grade 8 in comparison to 23 per cent of the fathers of the sexually inactive.

OCCUPATION OF FATHER

The same kind of picture emerged in relation to the father's occupation. Fifty per cent of the occupations of the fathers of the clinic girls fell into the top 60 of the 320 occupations listed by Blishen.[4] For the fathers of the sexually inactive the incidence fell to 40 per cent. In the clinic group only 10 per cent of the fathers' occupations ranged within the 140 lowest status occupations as compared to 24 per cent of the occupations of the fathers of the sexually inactive.

LEVEL OF SOCIAL FUNCTIONING

In the total group of 68 respondents only two families had been broken by divorce or separation, both in the clinic group. Five respondents within the sexually active community group and four in the sexually inactive had lost one or both parents through death.[5]

The study design did not allow for exploration of how stable in reality the large majority of apparently intact families were. However, the Heimler Scale of Social Functioning[6] administered to each respondent not only revealed a generally high level of healthy social functioning for the total population but a positive view of family relationships as well. The greatest preponderance of high 'positive' scores was found within the clinic group, the lowest in the community sample of sexually active girls. The 'negative' scores showed a less marked but indicative reversal, with the matching sexually active group showing a higher degree of symptomatology than found in either of the other groups – further evidence of their 'difference.'

Answers to a question designed to reveal where a girl's closest relationships lay showed that for the sexually active the boyfriend had most significance. For the inactive, even for those 'going steady,' a female friend was the most prevalent first choice, with mother next. This inclusion of the mother by the sexually inactive could point to either more trust in the mother, or a lingering dependence on her. A speculative view of the general exclusion of the mother by the sexually active girls could lead to any number of suppositions – concern or guilt about sexual activity, a difficulty in communication, or simply a healthy process of emancipation.

PROTECTION AGAINST PREGNANCY

The clinic girls were not only steadier in a long-term relationship with a particular boyfriend than were the girls in either of the other two groups but much more straightforward and assured in their approach to contraception than the girls in the sexually active community group.

While five out of the nine sexually active girls in the community sample were using estrogens, four had requested them from private physicians for purposes other than contraception – acne, painful or irregular menstruation – so that not all would have been given the appropriate medical examination nor would necessarily receive pertinent follow-up care. One girl had obtained a prescription over the telephone. The rest were either not using a method at all, were inconsistent in the use of one, or were relying on one of doubtful safety.

When asked if anyone might disapprove of their sexual activity 65 per cent of the clinic patients were quite sure their parents would, but only 33 per cent of the other sexually active girls were prepared to admit this likelihood. This was greatly at variance with their concern about disapproval as reflected in their reluctance to be straightforward in their requests for contraceptives and the statements made by several of them feeling 'much more at ease' when, on occasion, a physician would volunteer either directly or indirectly that it was 'all right to use the pills for birth control as well as painful period.'

It was clear from their replies to a number of questions that, unlike the clinic patients, they had neither come to effective terms with their sexual activity nor the use of contraceptives and were compounding their difficulties and anxieties by their inability to be direct.

DEPRESSION AND INSECURITY

Further evidence of the high degree of discomfort and insecurity experienced by the matching sexually active group was contained in their answers to the questions on depression and insecurity in the Heimler 'negative index.' While consistently less ready to admit to occasional feelings of depression than were the other girls, the degree of uncertainty and confusion about self they revealed was more than triple that found in either of the other two groups.

AMBITION AND GOAL-DIRECTEDNESS

The clinic patients were found to be more highly ambitious and goal-directed than any of the others. Many of them were contemplating advanced degrees either before or after marriage whereas the sexually inactive, who were on the average older, were more likely to see the achievement of one university degree as a summit. A number of the girls who were not sexually active said that 'just to go to university at all' was their main ambition and expressed gratitude to their parents – often to a mother who had returned to work – for helping to make this achievement possible. It is interesting to speculate how much this feeling of 'owing something' to the parents, as one girl put it, contributed to sexual inactivity.

PREFERRED LIFE STYLE

Differences in preferred life style, both present and future were most marked between the clinic group and the sexually active girls in the community sample. Almost unanimously, the clinic girls and the sexually inactive preferred big city life. In contrast, 44 per cent of the other sexually active girls stated a preference for small towns or rural areas – even as unmarried women.

If married with children, both the clinic and the sexually inactive girls chose 'good schools' as the prime prerequisite of a neighbourhood, in contrast again with the others who thought 'kind and friendly neighbours' and 'proximity to husband's job' were more important. This seemed to lend credence to the supposition that these girls were less self-assured, less sophisticated, less intellectual – perhaps more vulnerable in areas not explored – than any of the others.

SUMMARY

The existence of a family planning clinic in a community does not automatically assure the availability of its facilities to that ill-defined and elusive group of the married 'poor' who are said by most population experts to want fewer children than they produce. Why this facility, at least as it exists in Vancouver, is used much less by the married 'poor' than by single university students has not been explained. The principal reason for the use of the clinic by so many single women is clearly related to their view of it as a benign medical facility which provides contraceptive services they might have difficulty securing elsewhere.

But what reason or combination of reasons keeps the poor away? Do they, in fact, wish to limit their families or is this another myth propounded by the 'experts'? Has the coming of medicare meant that a married woman who was in the past medically indigent may now receive advice and prescription at the same or even less cost than from the family planning clinic? Or is it more likely that 'higher income groups find their own way to this type of facility but the lowest income groups rely more heavily on referral by health and welfare agencies ... and expect health and welfare workers to raise the subject of family planning'?[7]

Is there provable validity to Michael Harrington's thesis that if the poor are given the same 'freedom that the middle class and the rich now have, that a large number of them will voluntarily and freely choose family planning,'[8] or is this, too, more hope than reality? With these concerns and ambiguities in mind, how should the role of a family planning clinic be defined and publicly delineated? What construction, for that matter, can be placed on the use of the term 'family planning' in an age of such rapid social change that it may already become little more than a euphemistic anachronism serving only, through the implications of 'legal marriage' and 'stability' it contains within it, to deny information about contraception to those who may want or need it most? It does seem clear that a very large proportion of the Vancouver Clinic services are now going to a group of young women who, in the main, come from affluent homes and reveal themselves as so highly intelligent, healthy, goal-directed and self-assured, and so capable of making realistic plans for both present and future that they could be expected to deal with their sexuality and its possible consequences in a way that would minimize risks – whether a family planning clinic existed or not.

The same hopeful prediction cannot be made for the corresponding group of sexually active girls who were not clinic patients and who could be seen as highly vulnerable to the risk of pregnancy. Not only did they show an inclination toward, if not, actual promiscuity, at least to the formation of far less stable heterosexual relationships than did the girls in the clinic group, but their qualities of naivety, inconsistency, insecurity and attendency toward a magic 'it can't happen to me' kind of thinking, could produce nothing less than an increase in vulnerability.

If this type and size of population-at-risk can be found in a university community of what scale and nature is the risk-population that may exist in the larger community? And if the poor rarely perceive the family planning clinic as a resource, or do not know of it, how may the barriers to communication be discovered and removed so that the freedom of choice Harrington speaks of can become a reality?

NOTES

The major study, of which this is only a small part, is being conducted under the auspices of the Department of Health Care and Epidemiology, University of British Columbia. Principal Investigators: Eleanor J. Bradley, Dip. SW, CSW, RN, Assistant Professor, and C.J.G. Mackenzie, MD, CM, DPH, FRSH, CRCP (Can.), Associate Professor.
Federal Health Grant 609-7-215, *Social and Medical Factors of Women Attending Vancouver Family Planning Clinics and a Group of Women Not Attending a Family Planning Clinic in Two Areas of the City of Vancouver.*
1 Federal Health Grant 609-7-215.
2 Unpublished report accepted and taken, in part, as the basis for the award of the G.F. Amyot Prize in Epidemiology to Dr Peter Brierley.
3 There were eight Roman Catholics in the total sample, four in each group.
4 Blishen, Bernard R., 'A Socio-Economic Index for Occupations in Canada,' *The Canadian Review of Sociology and Anthropology* 4, no. 1 (February 1967), 4-53.

5 A small side-project designed to study a group of non-university unmarried mothers of the same age-range has revealed a 50 per cent incidence of broken homes.

6 Heimler, Eugene, Heimler Scale of Social Functioning, Rev. II, The University of Calgary School of Social Welfare – Center of Social Functioning, Calgary, Alberta, Copyright Eugene Heimler, 1967.

7 Mackenzie, C.J.G., 'The Vancouver Family Planning clinic: A Case Study,' *Canadian Journal of Public Health* (February 1967), p. 53.

8 Harrington, Michael, 'Poverty, Family Planning and the Great Society,' address delivered at the Annual Meeting of Planned Parenthood – World Population, October 1965, New York City.

MARION G. POWELL

Changing profile of a family planning clinic

Public family planning clinics are a recent addition to public health services in Canada and, with a few exceptions, are only provided in urban centres. In January 1972, in a survey conducted by the Health Research Division of the Department of National Health and Welfare, there were 56 family planning clinics. Of these, 22 were in health units or municipal health departments and the remainder were under the auspices of hospitals and voluntary organizations.

The first clinic was opened in Hamilton in 1932 by the Voluntary Birth Control Association later renamed Hamilton Planned Parenthood. However, apart from a few post-natal and gynaecology clinics in out-patient departments in hospitals, family planning was not considered an essential part of clinic care until the amendment to the Criminal Code in 1969. Those women who were fortunate enough to have a physician who was sensitive to their family planning needs were given a reliable method of birth control such as the pill, IUD or diaphragm. Otherwise, women were dependent on the co-operation of their husbands in providing contraceptive control through the use of abstinence, rhythm, coitus interruptus, or the condom.

With the growing public awareness of the need to prevent unwanted pregnancies, stimulated in many instances by voluntary planned parenthood associations, public health departments began to open family planning clinics in the late 1960s. These clinics were set up to provide birth control for those women who did not have access to private medical care. The service was directed towards the poor on the assumption that the poor have more unwanted pregnancies and more children. By providing clinics it was also felt that the poor would avail themselves of the opportunity to obtain reliable birth control and that this would be a significant factor in lessening poverty. The solution to the poverty problem was not as simple as this and on closer examination it was discovered that many of the poor did not have the large families they were thought to have and that they had been able to obtain birth control. As family planning clinics were opened, relatively few of the target population attended. However, even where there were no clinics, birth rates have declined dramatically over the past decade beginning in 1958. Acceleration of the decline accompanied the widespread introduction of the pill in 1960. More physicians were providing birth control advice and prescriptions, and more of the population had access to private physicians through the provision of medical insurance.

In order to examine the changes that have occurred in the past seven years as family planning services have become more available, and to determine the characteristics of the women attending clinics, the Scarborough Family Planning Clinic was studied, comparing the statistics of the first year of operation in 1966 with the statistics of 1972.

Scarborough is the eastern borough of Metropolitan Toronto with a population of approximately 350,000. It is a suburban community with a large number of government housing complexes. Before the opening of the clinic in March 1966 a survey was carried out of the attitudes of the physicians in the community towards such a clinic. Although two-thirds indicated their approval, in fact they referred very few of the women to the clinic.

In 1966 one-half of the women who attended the clinic were between the ages of 20 to 29, with only 10 per cent below the age of 20, and the same percentage over the age of 40. There were no single women in attendance at the clinic; only 5 per cent had no children and 15 per cent had more than 6 children. The two methods of contraception prescribed with equal frequency were the IUD and oral contraceptives.

By 1970 it was apparent that the clinic was attracting young single women who were either working or attending university. Fewer married women were coming as new patients. However, many of the former clinic attenders continued to return for an annual medical examination and renewal of birth control. The preferred birth control method became the pill and the clinic became a centre for pregnancy testing and problem pregnancy counselling.

In 1972 the number of new attenders was 2023. Four clinics were held each week. Seventy per cent of the women were under the age of 20, with the largest age group being 17 years. Most were high school students referred to the clinic by a friend or the public health nurse in the school. Of all the clients 83 per cent were single. The preferred birth control method continued to be the pill, with only 4 per cent selecting the IUD.

The change in the clientele of the Scarborough Family Planning Clinic dramatically reflects the change in attitudes towards birth control by physicians. More physicians are prescribing all methods of birth control, including sterilization, than a decade ago. Women who choose to attend family planning clinics do so because of lack of access to a private physician owing to age, marital status, or financial situation.

The sexual involvement of teenage girls attending the family planning clinic frequently alienates them from family and family physician and their relationship is usually not discussed openly with their parents. Most young people become independent on the completion of high school, at least in regard to sexual matters. At this point many girls go to a physician and thus leave the clinic. At the present time most college health services provide birth control for students and college-age women use these facilities.

There have been proposals to provide outreach programs and mobile family planning services to bring birth control within easy reach of the rural poor. It is not only the rural groups who need this type of program; the urban ghetto dweller, who is isolated from many community resources, also requires an innovative approach to the provision of family planning services.

The distribution of family planning clinics is uneven across Canada. Most clinics are within areas of large concentrations of population. Most are open only a few hours a week and many still place age, residence, and marital status requirements on the girls coming to the clinics. It is not surprising that the most frequent source of referral to public health clinics is the public health nurse. Large numbers of girls hear of clinic facilities from their friends. A fact that is disturbing is the few referrals to clinics by social and welfare agencies. The inclusion of a social worker from a community agency on the staff of a family planning clinic would no doubt be followed by an awareness on the part of social agencies of the services provided by the clinics.

Availability of family planning clinics and the knowledge of contraceptive methods have had little impact on the number of unwanted pregnancies. In a number of studies carried out on women referred for termination of pregnancy, approximately two-thirds were using no contraceptive at the time of the pregnancy. Looking at the number of young women attending clinics in centres across Canada, one can only speculate about the number of pregnancies prevented and conclude that the clinics are meeting the needs of a large group of the population who would otherwise be deprived of reliable, medically-prescribed birth control.

PART SIX

ABORTION

BENJAMIN SCHLESINGER

Abortion: an introduction

Despite the continuing controversy surrounding its morality, abortion is by no means a new phenomenon, but has been practised in almost every human society. The debate about the morality of abortion has been recorded as far back as Plato and Aristotle, and throughout history various theories concerning the point at which human life begins have been put forward and both rejected and accepted by different peoples. Laws dealing with abortion have ranged from very permissive to very restrictive, reflecting the various stances regarding abortion in different societies and at different times. The Christian Church, especially the Roman Catholic branch, has traditionally regarded abortion as sinful and this attitude was reflected in the laws of most countries in the western world, which until recently have declared abortion illegal.

In Canada, Section 237 of the Canadian Criminal Code was altered in 1969 to provide for legal therapeutic abortion if in the opinion of the therapeutic abortion committee of an accredited hospital the continuation of the pregnancy would or would be likely to endanger the life or health of the mother. The medical profession in Canada has found itself very much in the middle of the abortion controversy. The law has placed on doctors the burden of deciding upon and performing the abortion. As a result the medical profession has had to come to terms with the situation and despite considerable debate and disagreement among its numbers, has formulated a set of resolutions which were adopted at the June 1971 annual meeting:[1]

1 That in the event of an unwanted pregnancy the patient should be provided with the opportunity to have full, immediate counselling services.

2 That Section 237 of the Criminal Code be further amended so that all reference to therapeutic abortion committees be omitted.

3 That the appropriate sections of the Criminal Code apply to the performance of abortions: *a* by persons other than qualified licensed physicians; or, *b* in facilities other than approved hospitals.

4 That faced with a request for an abortion, a physician whose moral or religious beliefs prevent him from recommending and/or performing the procedure should so inform the patient so that she may consult with another physician.

5 If society should decide that the indications for the performance of abortions should include other than those involving a medical opinion, society should be responsible for providing special facilities and staff for carrying out the procedure when it follows from these further indications.

6 That in view of the significant hazards both of morbidity and mortality from induced abortion, the council wishes to recommend in the strongest possible terms that induced abortion should not be considered as an alternative to contraception as a method of responsible family planning.

7 That physicians or other health personnel should not be required to participate in the termination of a pregnancy; and that a patient should not be forced to have a pregnancy terminated.

8 That the professions make every effort to document and study the effects of abortion upon the health and social welfare of the people of the community.

9 That abortion should be defined as the termination of a pregnancy before 20 weeks of gestation.

The Canadian and American Psychiatric Associations have adopted similar positions on the question of abortion. The American statement was approved by the membership, December 12/13, 1969. Their position reads:

A decision to perform an abortion should be regarded as strictly a medical responsibility. It should be removed entirely from the jurisdiction of criminal law. Criminal penalties should be reserved for persons without medical license or qualification to do so. A medical decision to perform an abortion is based on the careful and informed judgments of the physician and the patient. Among other factors to be considered in arriving at the decision is the motivation of the patients. Often psychiatric consultation can help clarify motivational problems and thereby contribute to the patients' welfare.[2]

The Canadian Psychiatric Association is on record as saying that abortion should be removed altogether from the Criminal Code of Canada. They further recommend that it be made a strictly medical procedure to be decided by the woman and her husband if she has one, together with her physician.[3]

The Canadian Association of Social Workers in 1968 drafted a position statement with regard to the proposed change in the abortion law and forwarded this statement in the form of a letter to Prime Minister Trudeau. The letter had three recommendations on the subject which can be summarized as follows:

1 That the law be changed in such a way as to permit a woman who desires an abortion for medical, psychological, or social reasons to be able to obtain the professional help necessitated by her condition.

2 That the law stipulate that the decision concerning abortion be the responsibility of an inter-disciplinary committee composed of doctors, psychiatrists, psychologists, social workers, theologians, and lawyers as required in order that all the elements of the situation be considered in the decision to proceed or not proceed with the abortion.

3 That there be periodic revision of the law concerning abortion and that research programs be put into effect immediately in order to improve the adequacy of the law.

Pelrine[4] records that a number of organizations and groups have called for repeal of abortion laws. Among these are included the Liberal and New Democratic parties, the Canadian Labour Congress, the Ontario Women Teachers Federation, the Confederation of University Women, the Federation of Business and Professional Women, the Ad Hoc Action Committee on the Status of Women, the National Council of Jewish Women, the Board of Directors of the Canadian Nursing Association, and the Royal Commission on the Status of Women in Canada. Space does not allow an individual review of these various statements of position.

It should also be noted that within the context of any social movement directly involving a large percentage of the population various groups representing the opposing positions tend to develop. Similarly, the question of abortion has generated such opposition groups, the most active of which in Canada seem to be Birthright and the Right of Life groups, which have produced a considerable amount of literature outlining their stands.

ABORTION AND PUBLIC OPINION

Various organizations have conducted surveys aimed at determining how the public feels about abortion now that it is legally available. The results of these surveys differ widely mainly as a result of different modes of obtaining data; however, some general trends are apparent.

In October 1970 *Chatelaine* magazine[5] published an article on how Canada's new abortion law was working out and at the same time asked their readers to complete and mail in a questionnaire designed to determine their attitudes to and personal experience with abortion. The results in March 1971 indicated overwhelming support for abortion on demand among the 6030 respondents. The

	Total number/percentage	English	French
The abortion law should be:			
Left as it is	251/4.2	193/3.6	58/8.8
A matter of the decision of the woman and her doctor	4454/73.9	4166/77.6	288/43.5
Changed to include additional reasons	1306/21.7	995/18.5	311/47
Abortion should be granted for:			
Rape, incest	3050/50.6	2748/51.2	302/45.6
Possible damage to fetus	2982/49.5	2699/50.3	283/42.7
Economic reasons	2519/41.8	2304/42.9	214/32.5
Mother's health inadequate to raise child	2794/46.1	2528/47	266/40
Too young	2584/42.9	2370/44	214/32
Unmarried, widowed, divorced	2263/37.5	2061/38.4	202/30.5
Partners planning to separate	2046/33.9	1867/34.8	179/27

two main questions were concerned with how the abortion law should be changed, and for what reasons abortion should be granted. Answers to these questions are tabulated above.

The typical respondent was in the child-bearing years, 21 to 40 (70 per cent), married (80 per cent), lived in a city of 10,000 or more (72.1 per cent), and worked in the home (55.8 per cent). As well, 58.6 per cent of the respondents were Protestant and 20.8 per cent were Roman Catholic. All income groups were represented.

The position that the decision about abortion should be the woman's, with the doctor giving medical advice only, was favoured by 77.5 per cent of the English Protestant respondents, 62.8 per cent of the English Roman Catholic respondents, and 41 per cent of the French Roman Catholic respondents. Support for abortion on demand increased with the age of the respondents from 65 per cent of the under 20 group to 83 per cent of the over 30 group.

It is important to note that 1739 of the 6030 respondents reported having had an abortion and of these 1278 were illegally performed. Personal experience no doubt has a considerable effect on one's attitude to abortion.

The obvious disadvantage to this study is that the data were collected by means of voluntary mail-in questionnaires. As a result the sample is not random and cannot be considered to be representative of the general Canadian population. However, the fact that support for abortion on demand was so overwhelming does suggest a trend towards a change of attitude.

A study with a different focus was done by Boydell and Grindstaff (1970) in London, Ontario.[6] A mail questionnaire was sent to a random sample of 2 per cent of the household heads. A return rate of approximately 50 per cent resulted in 451 questionnaires in usable form. Respondents were asked to assign a penalty to such crimes as illegal abortion. The penalties ranged along a ten-point continuum from no penalty to execution. The general response pattern rarely indicated a jail term for the pregnant female, and the majority of respondents assigned no penalty. A medical doctor who performs such an abortion was sentenced more severely but only slightly so. Less than 25 per cent assigned a prison term and over 40 per cent gave a no-penalty judgment. A non-doctor who performs an illegal abortion was treated very harshly, with over 80 per cent prescribing prison terms.

The responses were further examined along such demographic variables as age, educational level, and religion. It was found that the youngest age groups assigned the most lenient sanctions to the female, while assigning the harshest penalties to the non-doctor performing such an abortion. In general the oldest group gave relatively severe sentences to the female and medical doctor but was most lenient of all age groups in sentencing the non-doctor.

In examining the responses along educational levels it was found that the least educated group tended to be the most severe in assigning sanctions to both the female and the medical doctor performing the illegal abortion. The non-doctor was treated most harshly by the 'some university' category. The researchers had no clear idea as to the nature of this somewhat inconsistent finding.

The researchers found that there was a difference in the severity of the penalties handed out by Roman Catholics and Protestants but the differences were not as significant as might have been expected considering the Catholic opposition to abortion in general. In fact, the proportion assigning no penalty to the doctor performing an illegal abortion is exactly the same for Catholic and Protestant (38 per cent).

This study was subject to certain limitations and these were noted by the researchers. The study sampled household heads and not population in general. This would mean that the sample is weighted heavily with those old enough to be household heads and also with males who are more likely to be household heads than females. Furthermore, women who were household heads would probably not be typical of women in general. However, the study does seem to indicate trends and directions in public attitudes and for that reason has been included here.

The generally liberal attitudes found in the *Chatelaine* and London studies parallel those obtained by a 1971 Canadian Gallup Poll[7] (44 per cent of the respondents were in favour of repealing the abortion section of the Criminal Code) and by a December 1970 survey conducted by the CBC television program *Weekend*[8] (63 per cent of the English-speaking respondents considered the law too strict, as did 32 per cent of the French-speaking respondents).

One Canadian book has been published which deals with the overall abortion situation in this country; it is *Abortion in Canada* by Eleanor Wright Pelrine.[9] This book was written in 1970 when the effects of the 1969 change in law were beginning to be felt. It attempts to answer some basic questions about legal abortion; how it is performed, how much it costs; when it is legal and how it can be obtained. There is also a section dealing with the morality of abortion. The paperback edition of the book includes a new chapter on the 1972 situation. The author is frankly pro-abortion; however, she does provide the reader with a reasonable outline of the abortion situation in Canada from which one can proceed to further study of the subject.

NOTES

1 Canadian Medical Association. 'Resolutions on Abortion,' *Canadian Medical Association Journal* 104, no. 1 (June 1971), 1134.
2 American Psychiatric Association. 'Resolution on Abortion,' *American Journal of Psychiatry* 127 (October 1970), 536-38.
3 Pelrine, E.W., *Abortion in Canada* (Toronto, 1971), p. 3.
4 *Ibid.*
5 Gillen, Mollie, 'Your Replies to the Abortion Quiz,' *Chatelaine,* March 1971, pp. 23-26.
6 Boydell, C.L., and C.F. Grindstaff, 'Public Attitudes Toward Legal Sanctions for Drug and Abortion Offences,' *Canadian Journal of Criminology and Corrections* 13 (1971), 209-32.
7 Pelrine, p. 121.
8 *Ibid.*
9 *Ibid.*

ESTHER GREENGLASS

Attitudes toward abortion

Evidence is accumulating that society's attitudes toward abortion are changing. More and more thoughtful people feel that laws governing abortion must keep pace with our changing social conscience. In 1969, laws governing abortion were 'liberalized' by amendment to the Canadian Criminal Code to allow abortion provided a committee of doctors in an approved hospital believe that the continuation of the pregnancy will or will be likely to endanger the life or health of the woman. The law further states that the therapeutic abortion committee must consist of not less than three members each of whom must be a qualified medical practitioner, and the medical practitioner performing the abortion cannot sit on the committee. A great deal of controversy has arisen over the amendments to the law, with some claiming that the law is too liberal and others arguing that the law as it stands impedes many Canadian women in obtaining abortions. At the present time, there are insufficient facilities to meet the public demand for abortion because not all hospitals are required to establish a therapeutic abortion hospital committee. Pelrine [4] reports that not even one-half of all Canadian hospitals with 100 beds or more have set up a committee to review abortion applications. She further points out that those hospitals with committees are already working to capacity and in some cases are found to turn qualified applicants away because of lack of facilities. Many women who seek abortions in areas where hospitals have not established committees are forced to look for a sympathetic physician elsewhere, finance a trip to a large centre abroad, or failing these measures, are found to resort to the illegal abortionist.

Is there a case, then, to broaden the grounds for abortion in Canada? In a national opinion survey released on March 7, 1970, a Gallup Poll of Canada showed that 43 per cent of the adult population favoured legislation that would permit a woman to terminate pregnancy at any time during the first three months. Moreover, many organizations and individuals urged the Royal Commission on the Status of Women in Canada [5] to liberalize or repeal all abortion laws. On the basis of numerous public hearings and briefs, the commission recommended that the Criminal Code be amended to permit abortion by a qualified medical practitioner on the sole request of any woman who has been pregnant 12 weeks or less. It seems, then, that public opinion has moved in the direction of pressing for more liberal abortion laws. A survey was undertaken and its purpose was, a to ascertain the attitude of representative members of the population toward the decision to have an abortion; b to inquire into the reasons persons give in support of their attitude; c to determine the variables associated with persons favouring a more and a less liberal attitude toward abortion.

Let us look for a moment at the content of some of the views held toward abortion. Many hold the view that the decision to have an abortion should be left entirely to the woman. Since she alone knows her circumstances and her emotional limitations, she alone should be allowed to make the decision. They further argue that in a pluralistic and democratic society, people should be permitted to exercise a maximum degree of individual freedom. According to this view, the law should be amended to permit abortion at the woman's request after she has received the best medical advice available. She of course is free to consult with her sexual partner if she so wishes. At the other extreme, there are those who argue that abortion under any circumstances should not be permitted since it involves the taking of a human life. There can be no doubt that strong religious ideals contribute to sustaining a system of legal sanctions that labels abortion a crime. This view is based on the concept of the 'inviolability of every human life' and the Roman Catholic tenet that the embryo should, from the moment of conception, be considered a human life. Further, there are those who argue that in certain circumstances, abortion may be justifiable. Typically, those holding this view regard the individual as incapable of making the decision to have an abortion. For this reason, these individuals would favour that the decision to have an abortion be left to a committee (present law) which they see as objective, emotionally uninvolved, and informed.

What are the characteristics associated with those who are most likely to disapprove of highly liberalized abortion laws? Similarly, what are the characteristics of persons who are most favourable to abortion? As expected, Catholics are reported to be least favourable to abortion [1], Protestants more liberal toward abortion, and Jews the most favourable [3,7]. Previous research further suggests that those opposing abortion are more likely to participate actively in religious activities (in all religions) and to be less educated than those who hold more favourable attitudes toward abortion [7]. Attitudes toward abortion are probably also related to attitudes toward other aspects of fertility control as well as sexual behaviour. It is possible, for example, that many people oppose abortion because they fear anything which will promote sexual liberation, whether it is the sale of pornographic materials, sex education in the schools, or the distribution of birth control devices. The assumption is that if a woman is threatened with pregnancy she will avoid sexual intercourse.

One might expect that relatively older people are generally more conservative and younger people more tolerant toward abortion. Recent data indicate, however, that younger women are less, not more, favourable toward abortion than older women [7]. It is possible that those who have reached a more advanced stage in the process of family formation experience greater pressure on the control of fertility and are thus more likely to be permissive toward abortion than are younger women who are still at earlier stages of having children.

In this survey, respondents were asked to state whether they thought that the final decision to end a pregnancy by means of an abortion should be a private matter between a woman (or a couple) and a doctor, or that the decision should be left to a therapeutic abortion committee of a hospital. Respondents were also asked if they disapproved of abortion under any circumstances. The nature of the final decision to end a pregnancy by means of an abortion was also examined in relation to the following variables: religion, degree of religiosity (importance of religious activities), attitudes toward use of contraceptives, frequency of use of birth control, age, sex, income level, education, marital status, residential category in which the respondent grew up, racial group, and country of origin.

CHARACTERISTICS OF RESPONDENTS

The sample consisted of a total of 219 respondents, of whom 93 were males and 126 females. The mean age for respondents was 39.9 years with a range of 15 to 86 years; 43 per cent of the sample was Protestant, 22 per cent Catholic, 21 per cent Jewish, 9 per cent either agnostic or atheist, and the remaining 5 per cent was 'other.' When asked how important religious activities had been in their lives over the past year, 45 per cent responded either 'very important' or 'important,' and 48 per cent responded 'not very important' or 'not important at all.'

Representatives of most income levels were included for study. One-half of the respondents had completed either grade school, high school, or some high school. Thirty per cent had attended college, and the remaining respondents had attended graduate school, a community or technical school. Eighty-seven per cent of the males and 48 per cent of the females were employed outside the home (including full- and part-time work). Approximately 35 per cent of the females were housewives with no independent income. The rest of the male and female samples were either studying, retired, or on welfare. Approximately 73 per cent of the total sample were married and 17 per cent of the males and 10 per cent of the females were single. The remaining respondents were either divorced or separated, engaged, widowed, or not married to but living with a member of the opposite sex. While approximately 62 per cent of the sample were born in Canada, 13 per cent were born in the British Isles. One-quarter of the sample were born in one of the following places of origin: United States, Italy, Slavic countries, Greece, Spain, or Germany. While approximately one-half of the sample had spent their childhood in a city or a central area of a metropolitan city, 30 per cent grew up in a rural area, a village, or a large town. At the time of the interview, respondents lived either in the city of Toronto or in one of the boroughs of North York, East York, or York.

RESULTS OF THE STUDY

The results of this survey indicate that attitudes toward abortion are influenced by a number of ethical, social, religious, and practical factors. A large percentage of the sample, 76.7, preferred that the decision to have an abortion be a private matter between a woman, or a couple, and a doctor. Some of the reasons given for this choice were that, since this is a highly personal decision and since the parents have to raise the child, it is the parents who should take responsibility for the decision to end the pregnancy. While some respondents mentioned additional reasons such as 'unhappiness of the unwanted child,' and the problem of over-population, most of the reasons for this choice centred on the rights of individuals to make their own decisions regarding the abortion.

Individuals favouring 'private matter' not only were willing to take responsibility for the decision regarding abortion, they were also most likely to take responsibility for their own birth control and expressed little objection to use of contraceptives. These same individuals tended to state that religious activities were not important to them. Nevertheless, a substantial percentage of the sample for whom religious activities were important endorsed the abortion decision as a private matter. This result is somewhat surprising in the light of the conviction held by most theologians that abortion destroys human life and is therefore prohibited by the Church [2]. The individual who saw the abortion decision as a private matter was most likely to be Jewish, then atheist or agnostic, then Protestant, and to lesser extent, Catholic. The percentage of Catholics endorsing 'private matter' is higher than anticipated when one considers that the Catholic Church has persistently condemned the practise of abortion. While publicly a Catholic person may condemn the practice of abortion because of social pressure, privately it appears that many Catholics believe that the abortion decision should be made by the individual in consultation with a doctor.

A somewhat smaller percentage of respondents, 16 per cent, stated that they thought that the decision to end the pregnancy should be left to a therapeutic abortion hospital committee. In general, the reasons given by those favouring 'committee decision' expressed the need for some kind of control on the number of abortions performed as a means of controlling sexuality. Some of the reasons stated, for example, that 'If granted, too many abortions and promiscuity would increase,' and 'Couples who engage in sexual intercourse should accept responsibility for possible pregnancy.' Indeed, reasons given by those favouring a committee decision also expressed the need for some kind of control of doctors performing the abortion. For example, one reason which was frequently used stated, 'Committee ensures that abortions are not indiscriminately performed.'

Respondents who favoured shifting responsibility for the abortion decision from the individual to a committee were also most likely to have objections to an individual's taking responsibility for birth control. Further, the less frequently the respondent (or sexual partner) practised birth control, the more likely he (she) was to leave the decision to a committee. In direct contrast to the reasoning employed by those favouring 'private matter,' respondents favouring a committee decision saw the individual as not having responsibility for his own fertility and, moreover, saw the need for regulatory control of sexuality. A highly religious individual was more likely than a less religious one to endorse a committee decision. This choice represents, for the highly religious individual, a compromise solution of a social problem fraught with conflicting elements. For one, the highly religious individual recognizes that abortion is prohibited by an authority (the Church), while nevertheless realizing that abortions are being sought and obtained. The solution then is to give the responsibility for the decision to another authority, in this case, the hospital committee, which has the power of either approving or prohibiting the abortion in the light of relevant information. According to this type of reasoning, a decision by an authority body is always regarded as superior to that of the individual.

Some respondents, 7.3 per cent of the sample, stated that a woman should not be permitted to have an abortion under any circumstances. According to most of these individuals, abortion was unacceptable since it involved the taking of a human life. In addition, the possible dangers of the abortion itself for the woman were mentioned as reasons supporting opposition. Abortion was regarded as a poor substitute for birth control and parents were not regarded as objective enough to make the right decision. It is not surprising that 50 per cent of those opposing abortion under any circumstances were members of the Roman Catholic Church. The remaining respondents opposing abortion were primarily Protestant. As expected, 75 per cent of those opposing abortion stated that they were highly religious. While approximately one-half of respondents opposing abortion had no objections to the use of contraceptives, only about 37 per cent of those opposed to abortion reported using birth control to some extent. Approximately 71 per cent of those endorsing 'private matter' and 46 per cent of those endorsing 'committee decision' reported using birth control. It appears that respondents opposing abortion tend to see the individual as *not* having control of his (her) own fertility and they tend not to control their own fertility to the same extent as some other respondents, particularly those endorsing 'private matter.'

It is interesting to note that age significantly affected the nature of the final decision endorsed by males but not by females. 'Private matter' was chosen mostly by males 30 years of age and younger, and by males who were 40 years of age and older. Males between the ages of 31 and 40 were far more likely to leave the decision to end the pregnancy to a committee. Males between the ages of 31 and 40 probably witness pregnancy and child-birth within their own families to a greater extent than males in other age groups. Because of their relatively greater immediate involvement with pregnancy, it is possible that many males feel that they are not objective or unemotional enough to contribute to a sound decision and therefore prefer to leave the decision to a committee. The fact that neither age nor marital status significantly affected the nature of the woman's choice suggests that direct experience with pregnancy and child-bearing do not significantly influence a woman's attitudes toward the decision to end a pregnancy by means of an abortion.

One of the major implications of this survey is that most people (in the Toronto area) are dissatisfied with present legislation regarding abortion because it leaves the decision to have an abortion to a hospital committee. For the most part, respondents in this survey, both female and male, saw the decision to have an abortion as a private matter between a woman, or a couple, and a doctor. Most of the reasons given for this choice centred on the rights of individuals to make their own decisions in a matter which directly affected them.

REFERENCES

1 Blake, J., 'Abortion and Public Opinion: The 1960-1970 Decade,' *Science* 171 (1971), 540-49.
2 Montgomery, B., 'How to Decide the Birth Control Question,' *Christianity Today* (March 1966).
3 Niswander, K.R., M. Klein, and C.L. Randall, 'Changing Attitudes Toward Therapeutic Abortion,' *Journal of the American Medical Association* 196 (1966), 124-27.

4 Pelrine, E.W., *Abortion in Canada* (Toronto, 1971).
5 *Report of the Royal Commission on the Status of Women in Canada*, Information Canada (Ottawa, 1970).
6 Scott, W.A., and M. Wertheimer, *Introduction to Psychological Research* (New York, 1962).
7 Westoff, C.F., E.C. Moore, and N.B. Ryder, 'The Structure of Attitudes Toward Abortion,' *Milbank Memorial Fund Quarterly* 67 (1969), 11-37.

SUSAN WATT

Abortion: A challenge for social work

The singularly inescapable reality of social work today is that no longer can the professional social worker hide behind the mask of a non-judgmental attitude as justification for a failure to make decisive commitment on social and moral issues of the day. Recent literature from American sources indicates that one in five pregnancies in the United States is deliberately terminated by illegal or approved abortions; it is probable that Canadian statistics reflect a somewhat similar situation. By numbers alone, the question of abortion and legislation governing it has become a major social issue which few practising social workers can avoid. This paper will discuss some of the current psychiatric, medical, moral, and social arguments which influence the societal and personal convictions debated about the question of abortion and the Canadian woman.

August 1969 marked a revolutionary change in legislation concerning abortion in Canada when the grounds for legalized (therapeutic) abortions were changed to encompass the life and health of the mother. The changes in the *Criminal Code of Canada* (SC 1969) were such that the performing of an abortion would not be a criminal offense under certain conditions. It was required that ...

1 the pregnancy constitute a threat or be likely to threaten the life or health of the mother;

2 the presentation of such evidence was approved by a majority vote of a committee of three doctors in an approved hospital;

3 the procedure be performed by a qualified medical practitioner in an approved hospital;

4 pertinent records be kept and reported to the Minister of Health as required.[1]

Although the law sounds realistic and clear, the decision to grant a therapeutic abortion can never be one undertaken by simple procedural steps. For each woman in our society today, the question of termination is an emotionally laden one which can only be dispassionately discussed by those not immediately and intimately involved in the decision-making process. This is to say that if our society had traditionally held values supporting abortion, the internal conflicts and social pressures facing the woman considering abortion might not exist or at least would be significantly reduced. It might also indicate that a changing social climate concerning abortion would reduce the psychological and social problems of both the woman requesting and those providing therapeutic abortion services.

Over the past five years, during which mental health has come to be included in many interpretations of the law, psychiatrists have become something of the social and moral gatekeepers of abortion. The Group for the Advancement of Psychiatry in its position paper clarified the intolerable dilemma of psychiatry in the following statement:

Psychiatrists do have a relevant contribution to make to a resolution of the abortion dilemma, but their contribution is limited. When the psychiatrist serves as the deus ex machina of the conflicted social system, he may ease the immediate stress without clarifying or resolving the underlying divisiveness of the community. The unfortunate consequences of this are that society places undue responsibility upon the individual psychiatrist and at the same time shuns its own responsibility to face squarely the serious and sometimes critical issues that have led to such divisiveness.[2]

Longstanding arguments condemning abortion because of the psychiatric sequelae are dying in the face of well documented research which indicates, according to Sloane,[3] that, '... the earlier findings of serious psychiatric sequelae are (a) often based on a statistically biased self-selection of subjects or are simply case studies without efforts to standardize the sample or balance it against a control group; (b) inadequately differentiated as to pre-existing conditions and abortion sequelae; (c) highly variable.'[4]

Generally it would appear that psychiatric contraindications to therapeutic abortion are rare. Similarly, true psychiatric reasons for abortion are few and far between. The only criteria which may have consistent application are the following: 1 profound suicidal or homicidal preoccupation in the patient; 2 chronic schizophrenia or a current acute schizophrenic episode; 3 a lobotomy; 4 repeated post-partum psychosis; 5 severe and/or recurrent affective disorders. The only reasonable psychiatric question is, 'Will the abortion and its effects be more traumatic than pregnancy, childbirth, and forced motherhood?'[5] Implications are clear; the only realistic contribution of psychiatry to the question of abortion lies in the area of contraindications.

What then are the medical considerations surrounding this problem? Abortion, at any stage of pregnancy, involves a surgical procedure with its own surgical risk factor. Up to 12 weeks' gestation a dilation and curettage (D and C) is the method of choice; a suction method after dilation may replace the scraping of a curettage. While a hysterotomy was once the common abortive method for the period from 12 to 20 weeks, saline injections appear to be an increasingly popular method. Failure of an injected abortive solution to generate an abortion may necessitate a hysterotomy. If sterilization is to be undertaken at the time of the abortion, a hysterotomy and tubal ligation becomes the method frequently used. With any indication of disease in the reproductive system, a hysterectomy may be used for the purposes of abortion. Twenty weeks is the commonly held maximum period of gestation up to which time an abortion may be performed.

While a D and C of a non-impregnated uterus is a common and relatively simple procedure, it is risky after conception, for once pregnant the uterus rapidly becomes a blood-engorged organ, soft, swollen, and easily damaged. In addition to the standard complications of anaesthesia, infection, perforation of the uterus, cervical lacerations, bowel damage, and excessive blood loss may result. With the use of a hypertonic saline solution in the method of inter-uterine injection, there is always the risk of introducing the abortive solution into the circulatory system thus creating a potentially fatal situation. A hysterotomy is unquestionably a major surgical procedure running all the risks of abdominal surgery. A complicated D and C can result in the need for a hysterectomy because of the high rate of blood loss if perforation cannot be very rapidly repaired. Minimally, a laparotomy is often required in such cases.

A recent study in an Ontario teaching hospital which performs approximately 55 abortions per week indicated a general complication rate of 13 per cent distributed over the following problems:[6]

	%
Perforation of the uterus	1
Cervical lacerations requiring suturing	1
Perforation of uterus with bowel involvement	1
Anaesthesia complications	1
Post-operative (misc.) complication requiring re-admission	1
Incomplete abortion	2
Excessive blood loss	1
Infection	2
Injection complications	3

While we can assume that these figures reflect a lower rate of complications than with most illegal abortions, they do dispel however the fantasy that an abortion done in hospital is a 'perfectly safe' procedure for the woman. We should also consider the fact that child-birth is not risk-free from a medical standpoint. Pregnancy and delivery complications run at approximately the same rate, although they generally tend to be of a less serious nature.

A medical consideration infrequently discussed is that should a hysterotomy be used, child-bearing will require a caesarean section for future pregnancies. On the basis of current medical opinion a woman will be limited, therefore, to the number of children she may safely deliver. Thus, the implications of a hysterotomy are more involved than the ever-present reminder of an abdominal scar.

The only conclusion which can be stated with reasonable conviction is that a therapeutic abortion is at no time a simple procedure and is not without significant medical risk.

The moral arguments about abortion are more complex and less well documented. Much of the controversy seems to rage over whether or not abortion of a fetus is the murdering of a human life. Each century has seen changing religious and philosophic views on this question. Frequently, the definition of when human life begins is the focal point of a moral debate, with opinions ranging from the position that the moment of conception marks this beginning to the belief that it is not until birth that life commences. Where one stands on this point must, of course, remain a personal judgment but can such an individual decision be thrust upon others?

Many anti-abortion lobbyists champion the cause of the rights of the unborn child but few consider the right of every child to be a wanted child. Also, the right of a woman to choose to assume the great responsibility of motherhood needs to be considered.

It is interesting when considering the moral vantage point to review the distribution of religious affiliations found in the hospital study of therapeutic abortion applicants:

	%
Protestant	49.9
Roman Catholic	33.2
Jewish	2.5
Greek Orthodox	4.8
Other	3.6
None	6.0

A recent study by *Chatelaine* magazine[7] appears also to reflect a changing moral position in the general populace. But though many Protestant churches have altered their policy on abortion, the Roman Catholic and Anglican churches still hold an anti-abortion position. To understate the problem, the moral issues surrounding abortion are heavily emotion-laden, defensible from many vantage points, and as varied as any ethical question could be.

One perspective which is rarely examined is that of the attending medical and paramedical staff. Nurses and doctors function from a basic belief in the integrity of life and its preservation. The deliberate destruction of life by means of abortion is extremely difficult for many of the hospital staff to reconcile with the practice of their professions. It is questionable whether the public has the right to force these professionals into a position which potentially negates a basic tenet of their work. There would be indeed a hue and cry if it were physicians who were advocating the right to abort women considered 'unfit' to have children. The right of the medical and paramedical professionals, who necessarily become involved when abortions are performed in hospitals, must also be protected in considering changes in abortion legislation or policy. Should one have the right to demand the surgical procedure of abortion any more than demanding any other surgical procedure?

The only valid statement that can be made is, perhaps, that no statement at all can be made which is universally satisfactory in clarifying the moral issues around abortion. A question for social workers that is appropriate, however, is 'How can we protect the rights of the people involved in any abortion?' Should abortion become freely available, at what point is abortion infanticide? How can we protect a woman's right to have her child in the face of pressures from others (e.g., the family of the unwed mother, the irate husband, the welfare worker)? How can the personnel affected be protected against professional compromise in the area of abortion?

The last moral issue to be looked at needs some recognition if only to eliminate the argument. Some people have said that liberalization of abortion laws would lead to the 'decay of moral values'; that is, if abortion is available pregnancy will no longer be a deterrent to sexual intercourse. The advent of highly effective methods of birth control has unknit the tenacious fibres of such punitive logic. Failure to liberalize abortion laws on the basis of this argument would, in effect, publicly declare that pregnancy other than that conceived in marriage is immoral.

Finally, we turn to the area of the social implications of abortion. I think it is not an unreasonable statement that most abortions are generated from social rather than medical or psychiatric reasons. *Chatelaine*'s results from the 1780 respondents who admitted having had an abortion would support such a position:

REASONS FOR ABORTION	%	REASONS FOR ABORTION	%
Unmarried status	48	Psychological	11
Physical	5	Social	36

If one includes marital status as a social reason, 84 per cent of the respondents cited social grounds for their abortion. Probably, of the psychological reasons a large percentage could be called social rather than psychiatric criteria.

As a method of birth control, abortion may have its major social impact in the adolescent age group and the lower socio-economic brackets. Consider the age distribution of the abortion applicants investigated in the hospital study described in note 7.

AGE IN YEARS	%	CHATELAINE AGE DISTRIBUTION (%)	
13 to 15	2.8	AT THE TIME OF THE FIRST ABORTION	
16 to 18	13.7	Less than 16	3
19 to 21	22.7	17 to 19	20
22 to 24	18.1	20 to 25	44
25 to 27	15.4	25 plus	32
28 to 30	9.1		
31 plus	18.2		

These statistics appear to indicate that women in their late teens and early twenties are most affected at the present time by abortion.

Illegitimate pregnancy rates are significantly affected. In the hospital study, 57 per cent of the sample were single at the time of this abortion application. Other birth control methods were used by only 58 per cent of *Chatelaine*'s respondents while the hospital study showed the following rates:

DISTRIBUTION (%) OF USE OF BIRTH CONTROL METHODS	
None	61.6
Diaphragm	1.6
Foam or jelly	4.2
Condom	4.7
Rhythm	2.0
Birth control pill	2.4
IUD	1.7
Occasional use of one of the above	14.4
More than one of the above	1.8
Birth control pill 'sometimes'	3.6
Miscellaneous other methods	1.9

As an alternate form of birth control, abortion will reduce the number of children available for adoption. For couples unable to bear children this may become a difficult problem. Despite the apparent satisfaction with abortion as a method of birth control, the cost factor is significantly higher than other reliable methods. A minimum three-day hospitalization for an uncomplicated D and C may cost up to $285.00 in hospital costs alone. Abortion, economically, leaves much to be desired as a method of birth control.

It has been suggested that liberalization of abortion laws would reduce the rate of illegal abortions. An accurate response to this suggestion is difficult to document, but it does seem to have a reasonable foundation and support in clinical impressions.

Two very positive aspects of abortion have emerged when it is used in combination with new diagnostic techniques. We can expect a decline in the number of deformed and defective children born where causality or results can be diagnosed before birth (e.g., defects resulting from german measles in the first trimester, use of genetically disruptive drugs by the mother, etc.). With the development of eugenics and techniques for discovering genetic structures *in utero*, there may also be a decline in hereditary diseases.

Dispersion of valuable resources in terms of personnel and physical supplies also becomes an area of consideration. Because of the scarcity of such resources, we are faced with a decision about their allocation in the light of the demands placed upon them. Appropriate questions may be asked about the increased direction of funds toward abortion rather than toward birth control programs. Unquestionably, abortion is a financial, medical, and social disaster area as a method of birth control. It is only if we view abortion as a 'last ditch' crisis intervention technique that we are able to justify the programs required. 'Futile' hardly describes trying to sell a family planning clinic rather than an abortion clinic to a distraught woman ten weeks' pregnant with an unwanted child.

If as social workers we truly believe in the principle of individual responsibility and social responsibility as compatible forces, then perhaps both positions are viable. Prevention of pregnancy would appear to be more desirable than aborting a fetus; but all the prevention efforts will not see the end of all unwanted or potentially dangerous pregnancies. Similarly, it would be naïve to expect the absence of repeaters for abortion. *Chatelaine's* study[8] clearly indicates that even with restrictive abortion laws, multiple abortions are occurring in over 50 per cent of the population obtaining abortions. Of the women applying for abortions during the hospital study, 4.5 per cent had had at least one previous abortion and several returned within the one-year period of the study. This return rate occurred despite the presence of a conscientious birth control program attached to the termination service which was made available to every woman aborted in that hospital.

This paper does not propose to find a resolution to the many-faceted question of abortion. Rather it is hoped that some of the questions and issues may have been opened to the reader in such a way as to encourage further exploration. We are all entitled to our personal opinions on this subject, rooted in whatever basis we wish. As a professional, however, my conviction is that social workers must have a factual overview and understanding of the medical, moral, legal, and social composites influencing the individual woman, medical practitioner, paramedical person, and society at large. When this is accomplished, social workers will have a relevant contribution to make in guiding legislators in a revision of the abortion legislation, and in providing counselling services to women who feel that they cannot cope with a pregnancy.

Answers, if simple, are intolerably naïve; to many people, the present complexity is just as intolerable. The complexity and seriousness of this issue demands active collaboration among concerned professionals for whom the question of abortion is a current and pressing challenge.

NOTES

1 Allemang, W.H., 'Therapeutic Abortion – Some Considerations of the Current Problem,' unpublished paper given at St Michael's College, 1972, p. 1.
2 Group for the Advancement of Psychiatry (GAP), 'The Right to Abortion: A Psychiatric View,' *G.A.P. Report* 7, no. 75 (October 1969), 203.
3 Sloane, R.B., 'The Unwanted Pregnancy,' *New England Journal of Medicine* 280 (1969), 1206.
4 GAP, p. 211.
5 *Ibid.*, p. 215.
6 The hospital study referred to throughout this paper was undertaken at a large teaching hospital in Ontario during the period from July 1970 to June 1971. N = 928 with the sample including all applicants for therapeutic abortions seen during that period at the out-patient clinic of the Department of Obstetrics and Gynaecology of the hospital. Particular thanks is extended to Mrs Gail Sullivan for her assistance in obtaining data for this study and her willingness to share her extensive experience with abortion applicants.
7 Gillen, Mollie, 'Your Replies to the Abortion Quiz,' *Chatelaine*, March 1971, p. 23. See also Table above, p. 204.
8 The study referred to is described in note 7 above.

ACCRA

Background and structure of ACCRA*

ACCRA is an independent agency formed to serve the interests of the Toronto community. Since May 1971, it has provided counselling services related to the problem of the unwanted pregnancy and all aspects of birth control. We believe that abortion is morally, medically and emotionally an undesirable form of birth control, and that contraception is always vastly preferable. We aim to offer each client the means to gain an understanding of the circumstances which lead to an unwanted pregnancy and to educate her to take effective action which will prevent the need for a repeat abortion.

The rapid increase in the number of persons coming to the counselling service proved the need for this type of agency in the community and by April 1972, in order to establish itself as a more effective service, ACCRA developed a formalized structure and set up an advisory board. This board is composed of representatives from interested groups and professions. It meets once every month and is responsible for the formulation of policies which will enable the agency to expand and achieve its objectives. Application for letters patent incorporating ACCRA as a non-profit organization under the laws of Ontario is at present being negotiated by our legal counsel.

ACCRA has developed, and aims to expand its links with other agencies and professions working in relevant fields. It is recognized as an acceptable agency by the University of Toronto Faculty of Social Work, students for the past two academic years having been placed with ACCRA for their field work projects. Also this year a student from Seneca Community College is attached to ACCRA for her field work placement.

*Association for Contraceptive Counselling and Related Areas

A member of the advisory board, Mrs Ruth Evans, was chairman of the United Church Joint Committee which studied the issue of abortion. The results of this committee's work are outlined in the publication *Abortion Study by the United Church of Canada.* Page 37 of this report indicates the committee's belief in the importance of pre- and post-abortion counselling. The report was presented to and accepted by the 24th General Council of the United Church and the recommendations were re-emphasized by the 25th General Council held in 1972.

The agency presented a brief to the Minister's Commission of Enquiry into Hospital Privileges in Ontario held in 1971. As a result, the report of the commission stated that hospitals in Ontario should make known to the public their policies on abortion. The agency is strongly supported by the YWCA. In June 1972, the YWCA offered office accommodation at their headquarters, and study guides on problem pregnancy counselling have been produced as a result of consultations between Mrs Ruth Evans and counsellors and program directors from the YWCA. There is also free and constant exchange of information between Planned Parenthood and ACCRA.

During 1972, ACCRA representatives were involved in a series of meetings under the auspices of the Social Planning Council of Metropolitan Toronto in which gynaecologists, members of the nursing profession, and social workers from three Toronto hospitals discussed the concern of the hospital service over abortion facilities and counselling. The value of good counselling, particularly in the field of contraceptive education, was recognized and all three hospitals were open to the idea of using trained volunteers to expand hospital services. These discussions are planned to continue in 1973. Our links with other agencies and hospital services would seem to be vital, and the medical profession has already shown its widening recognition of our service by a dramatic increase in referrals to us.

ACCRA COUNSELLING SERVICES

Counselling takes place in a suite of offices at the YWCA, 21 McGill Street, Toronto. Counselling hours are 10 am to 3 pm and 7:30 pm to 9:30 pm each weekday and 10:00 to 12:30 on Saturday morning. An answering service takes care of telephone calls during the time that counsellors are not at the office. The agency employs two full-time people, one a secretary/bookkeeper whose responsibilities include day-to-day office administration, clerical duties and bookkeeping. The counselling staff is headed by a co-ordinator of counselling, Miss Phyllis Curry, PHN who is responsible for organization of training, supervision and support of counsellors, administration of the service and acts as a link between the counselling staff and the advisory board.

All counsellors are volunteers and are drawn from a variety of professions. All are concerned with the problems of the unwanted pregnancy and include public health nurses, social workers, and young women working in the business world. Three of the counsellors are men.

All volunteers are interviewed at the onset by the co-ordinator of counselling before being invited to participate in the training program. The introductory training takes the form of small group meetings. Trainees receive an accurate and comprehensive description of the medical procedures involved in abortion, detailed information on contraceptive devices, their effectiveness and how they work, and a description of human reproductive anatomy and physiology. Films are used to emphasize and illustrate these points as a counsellor must be well-informed if she is to give clear and accurate information, allay fears, and clear up misunderstandings. Participants are encouraged to ask questions, to verbalize their own feelings about unwanted pregnancies and their own attitudes to abortion and contraception, and to take part in sensitivity exercises which introduce them to the non-directive part of the counselling role. The major part of training, however, takes place during actual counselling sessions. The trainee spends a number of sessions as an observer in the office gradually assimilating the counselling, referral, and recording processes until she has enough information, experience, and confidence to try counselling. The inexperienced counsellor always works alongside a trained counsellor to whom she can turn for advice, and no counsellor sees a client on her own until both she and the co-ordinator are confident that she is ready. We have found in practice that, where the co-ordinator has doubts about a trainee's potential skill as a counsellor, the trainee often drops out of her own accord early in the training program.

Counsellors keep comprehensive records. Information about clients is divided into different categories so that valid statistics can be compiled. Every effort is made, however, to avoid a formal question and answer format during the counselling interview and the counsellor is encouraged to use the record sheet only as a guide to make sure that all considerations have been covered. Several counsellors have the necessary skill and training to collate data from these records and this is seen as an important part of the agency's task. Constant evaluation of our service from available data has a vital part to play in developing an increasingly effective community service.

At present there are 28 trained active counsellors and the agency is in the process of expanding this force. A number of new counsellors are involved in the training program and it is planned to have a force of at least 40 trained active counsellors by the end of May 1973.

INTERVIEWING TECHNIQUES

Most interviews last a minimum of an hour but the length and content of the discussion, to some extent, depends on the desire of the client to talk. The counsellor tries to elicit the client's feelings about her situation and to help her explore these feelings of ambivalence, anger, guilt, or whatever emotions she expresses. If it is felt that the client has clearly made up her mind that she wants an abortion, the medical procedure is described, the woman is encouraged to ask questions about it, and the counsellor will try to allay any fears expressed. Wherever possible an appointment is made with a hospital or gynaecologist in Toronto, but clients who can afford it and have landed-immigrant status often prefer to travel to the United States in order to avoid the added anxiety of the two-to-three-week delay that a Canadian abortion involves. All clinics in the United States used by this agency have been inspected by the co-ordinator of counselling.

Occasionally, the counsellor senses that her client has not been able to make a decision and in this case will encourage her to return for further counselling. It is interesting to note that, as well as letters of thanks from clients who have obtained an abortion, we have a number of letters from clients thanking us for help in making their decision to continue the pregnancy. Where it is clear that a client does not want an abortion, every effort is made to refer her to an agency where she can obtain help and support to continue the pregnancy. We would emphasize that at no time would any counsellor put pressure on a client to terminate the pregnancy.

We insist on discussing contraception with each client. The counsellor shows the client various types of contraceptives and discusses their relative effectiveness. Literature on all methods is provided and clients are given information on the location and time of family planning clinics in their area.

The counsellor finally reassures the client of our continued concern for her well-being and all clients are encouraged to call back, either in person or by telephone, after the abortion to discuss their experience and any problems.

ACCRA'S CLIENTS

Since May 1971, the agency has counselled over 1600 women. Some of our clients find us by reading our newspaper advertisements, through friends and other agencies such as Planned Parenthood, but at the present moment over 50 per cent of all referrals come directly from doctors, hospitals, or clinics. In addition, numerous telephone calls are received and callers are given information and referred to the appropriate clinics or doctors for contraceptive help.

At the present moment we see about 40 clients a week. The girls and women, who are encouraged to come with a partner - husband, parent or friend - are those who have not been able to obtain an abortion through existing medical services. Some have no general practitioner, others dare not consult the family doctor for fear their parents will learn of their pregnancy and others have not dared to raise the subject of abortion with a strange doctor when their pregnancy was confirmed. Some have tried and failed to make appointments with hospitals or doctors, and others have seen doctors who have refused to help them to get an abortion.

From analyses of available data, we find that 65 per cent of our clients are under 25; 72 per cent are single, divorced, or widowed; 50 per cent of clients were not born in Canada and 80 per cent of these are new to Canada and often have a cultural background very different from the society in which they now find themselves; 50 per cent of clients are newcomers to Toronto.

Many of our clients would seem to be 'handicapped' or 'underprivileged' in their ability to use existing medical services. They typically have a history of erratic medical supervision and are inadequately informed on matters of effective contraception. Only 30 per cent of our clients claimed to have been using any form of birth control at the time of conception, and of these 80 per cent were using the least effective techniques of withdrawal and rhythm. In only four cases did we find what appeared to be genuine failure of an effective method - the IUD. Thirty per cent of clients had used oral contraceptives at some time; some had discontinued because they believed popular myths linking them with cancer, sterility, or thrombosis. Others had discontinued because of common side effects and had not realized that these could usually be eradicated by the prescription of a different kind of pill. The important fact remains, however, that none of these women sought further medical advice - some because they were new to Toronto and did not know where to go, and others because they had no personal link with a doctor or gynaecologist with whom they could comfortably discuss all aspects of contraception.

For many of our clients then, it would appear that we need to provide more than a supportive and informative link in the pre-abortion period. The continuing increase in the number of clients using our service proves that ACCRA is fulfilling a real community need. The unwanted pregnancy can be regarded as a form of social disease and our primary aim is the reduction of the incidence of this disease. We need, therefore, to be able to introduce our clients to a reliable family planning program to prevent further unwanted pregnancies and, for this reason, we believe that not only must our service be maintained, but also improved and expanded.

I. GENTLES, E.J. KREMER, C.G. LANDOLT AND H.S. MORRIS

Brief for the protection of the unborn child*

INTRODUCTION

More than three hundred and fifty thousand Canadian men and women have put their names to a petition asking Parliament to accord full and equal legal protection to all human life, before as well as after birth. Our demand is based on two principles: first, that every living human being deserves the protection of the law against those who would take his or her life; and second, that all human beings are equal in the sense that taking the life of one can only be justified by conditions that would equally justify taking the life of any other. The life sciences have discovered that each human life can be traced back continuously to conception, and that the unborn child is an active, striving, and specifically human being from the beginning.[1]

At the root of our social and legal system is the shared conviction that each human life has a unique value that cannot be measured. This conviction is embodied in our welfare legislation, which strives to ensure that all people, including the poor, the old, the sick, the disabled, and the unemployed, can live their lives in comfort and dignity. So high a value have we customarily placed upon a human life that we do not hesitate to pour forth extraordinary efforts to rescue those who are in great danger. When a man is lost in the bush or trapped in a mine we call upon the full resources of society to rescue him. No one begrudges the cost of rescue efforts because it is commonly accepted that a human life does

*This is a shortened version of a brief presented to the Parliament of Canada by the Alliance for Life Association on May 9, 1973.

not have a price tag upon it. Because the unborn child does not normally require expensive assistance, all that we ask for him is the protection of the law. Until recently the civil law has moved in the direction of granting him such protection by increasingly recognizing his status as a legal person.[2]

Recently some have attempted to popularize the view that a human being is not worthy of legal protection unless he has achieved some arbitrary degree of maturation or development of the ability to think and communicate. Any such view would also exclude from legal protection the newborn, the retarded, and the senile. Such a view will be rejected by a society that strives to maximize the opportunity for every individual person to develop and employ his or her human capacities, and to protect every individual person against the destructive interference of others.

Abortionists sometimes attempt to evade their dilemma by asserting that there is doubt as to whether the unborn child is *really* a human being, and as to the time at which human life *really* begins. But any legislator or citizen who has such doubts is obliged to consult the available evidence. When he does so, he finds that all available scientific evidence points to the conclusion that from conception onwards the unborn child as an actually living, specifically human being. Under these circumstances, the burden of proof is on those who urge that the protection of the law be withdrawn from the unborn, so that they may be killed whenever an individual mother can find a doctor to perform the act. But advocates of abortion have produced no cogent arguments against the actual humanity of the unborn. Instead they have brought forward trifling considerations of size, location inside or outside the womb, and social recognition, e.g., whether the child has a name or receives a death certificate upon its death.

We believe that you, our legislators, must act quickly to reverse the trend toward the cheapening of human life. If it is right to protect the lives of convicted murderers then it cannot be wrong to protect the lives of those who have committed no crime. Not to protect the innocent unborn against abortion is to descend to a lower form of civilization, in which the weak and defenceless no longer call for the protection of society. More humane societies in the future will wonder at the barbarism of those twentieth-century societies which ignored the unborn and allowed millions of them to be killed.

OPERATION OF THE PRESENT LAW
ON INDUCED ABORTION

A rising abortion rate
Since the 1969 revision of the Criminal Code permitting induced abortions when a hospital therapeutic abortion committee certifies that continuing the pregnancy

	No. of therapeutic abortions	Therapeutic abortions as a percentage of live births
1970	11,152	3.0
1971	30,949	8.3
1972 (January–June)	18,801	10.1

would be likely to endanger the mother's life or health, the number of legally induced abortions performed in Canada has grown at an alarming rate.

The intention of the government in changing the law four years ago was to permit abortion where there was a clear medical indication for doing so. However, an unwanted pregnancy was soon interpreted by some hospitals as 'a threat to health.' Once one abortion had been performed under this broader interpretation, any subsequent refusal to terminate a pregnancy was deemed discriminatory. Abortion in these hospitals then became a 'necessary medical service' available on demand. In some hospitals the number of abortions now equals or exceeds the number of live births.[4] Canada is at present faced with a growing abortion mentality (see table above). Apart from the disrespect for human life which this mentality may generate, there is no sign that the rapidly growing demand for abortion will level off in the foreseeable future. Countries like Bulgaria, Hungary, and Japan, which have had freely available abortion for many years, now experience abortion rates ranging from 40 to 130 for every 100 live births.[5]

Abandonment of contraception
Freely available abortion creates its own expanding market. The easier it is to obtain an abortion, the more lax people become about taking steps to prevent an unwanted pregnancy. It has been found that 60 per cent of women in the Toronto area and 62 per cent of women in the Ottawa-Hull area seeking abortion counselling took no steps to prevent the pregnancy, even though they knew about contraception. Similarly, in Great Britain, which has virtually had abortion on demand since 1967, 91 per cent of the women having abortions at the teaching hospital in Oxford were found to have taken no contraceptive care.[6]

Medical hazards of legally induced abortions
When an 'abortion climate' is created by easy availability of legal abortion, the total effect of large numbers of these procedures on very many women may result in an overall deterioration in health and a greater loss of life than when abor-

tion is not readily available. Organized medicine is not unaware of the risks involved, as the following statement by a medical professional indicates: 'Despite competent care in qualified hospitals, there will be more abortion deaths in the future. Even if abortions were allowed only in the first 12 weeks of pregnancy, there would still be more danger than there is in bearing a child or in birth control pills.'[7]

i Mortality. Obviously, the worst complication resulting from a legal abortion is death, not only of the fetus but also of the mother. In England and Wales, where abortion became freely available in 1967, the mortality rate from legal and illegal abortions has remained steady up to 1969, the last year for which data has been published.[8] In 1969, some 52,000 legal abortions were performed in England and Wales. The estimated number for 1972 is 150,000 – the possible toll on human lives is obvious.

In New York State abortion on request became available in 1970 and since that time the number of deaths from abortion has been on the increase.[9] More women are now dying of legal abortions in New York City than of illegal abortions.[10]

ii Morbidity, immediate complications. Immediate physical complications from abortions legally induced before the end of three months of pregnancy in many of the university teaching hospitals across Canada occur in 5 to 10 per cent of patients.[11]

iii Teenage abortions. Of particular gravity to a government concerned with the welfare of the citizens must be the reports on the effect of legally induced abortion on teenagers in Toronto. In a group of 83 girls between the ages of 14 and 18, the complication rate from suction abortions was 26 per cent, with 47 per cent having problems following saline-induced abortion. In addition, all the girls had some grief reaction and a sense of loss was greater than for older girls.[12]

iv Long-term effects on subsequent pregnancies and children. Canada and the United States cannot provide information on this subject, but well-documented evidence is available from Europe and Japan. Sterility is reported to be present in 4 per cent to 5 per cent of women following legally induced abortion; the occurrence of extra-uterine pregnancies increases by 100 per cent to 150 per cent and the total number of spontaneous miscarriages may rise to 30 per cent.[13]

Prenatal mortality rates (still-births and deaths in the first week of life) appear to double following the liberalization of abortion law,[14] and premature births increase by 40 per cent.[15] A similar trend in prematurity has been noted in Hungary where a direct correlation between the number of induced abortions and rate of prematurity is recorded, rising from 10 per cent if no previous abortion to more than 20 per cent after three induced abortions.[16]

Illegal abortions

It is often said that a more 'liberal' abortion law will reduce the number of illegal abortions, and that conversely a restrictive law will simply compel women to resort in increasing numbers to illegal abortion. There is no evidence to support either of these assertions; nor has any satisfactory evidence ever been adduced to support the oft-repeated statement of abortionists that Canada's illegal abortion rate was (and is) 100,000 per year.[17]

According to the British report, *Unplanned Pregnancy*, the Abortion Act of 1967 has not resulted in a decline in illegal abortions in England.[18] An American study of 11 other countries that have widened their abortion laws points in the same direction. None of the countries studied experienced a decline in the criminal abortion rate after widening their laws.[19] The explanation for the failure of the criminal abortion rate to decrease appears to lie in the abortion mentality which results when abortion becomes freely available. The number of legal abortions rises every year, but there are always some people for whom the legal procedures are not speedy or secret enough. These people turn to illegal procedures – all the more readily as abortion becomes socially acceptable – and consequently the illegal rate does not go down.

However, the one thing that might lower the illegal abortion rate would be a strict limitation on the number of legal abortions in combination with the enactment of constructive alternatives to abortion.

CHANGES IN THE LAW TO PROTECT
THE UNBORN HUMAN CHILD

The World Health Organization of the United Nations in 1948 stated that member nations were to accord the utmost respect for human life 'from the moment of conception on.' In 1959 the United Nations adopted the *Declaration of the Rights of the Child* which supplemented the Universal Declaration of Human Rights. The preamble to this declaration states in part as follows: 'Whereas the child, by reason of his physical and mental immaturity needs special safeguards and care, including appropriate legal protection, *before as well as after birth*' ... (italics the authors'). As a member of the United Nations, Canada has already committed herself to uphold the rights of the unborn child.

The legislature of the province of Quebec has recognized the humanity of the unborn in its amendments to the Civil Code (January 1, 1972), which provide in part as follows:

Article 18

Every human being possesses juridical personality. Whether citizen or alien, he has the full enjoyment of civil rights, except as otherwise expressly provided by law.

Article 19
The human person is inviolable.
Article 338
The persons to whom curators are given are: 1 emancipated minors; 2 interdicted persons; 3 children conceived but not yet born.

Federal legislation should also be enacted which would grant full and equal legal recognition and protection to all human persons before as well as after birth.

We suggest the following recommendations for changes in the legislation:
Recommendation one The homicide provisions of the Criminal Code should be amended to guarantee the protection of the law to the unborn and to those whose status as human beings might at some future time be questioned. Amendments should be added to make the killing of the unborn child non-culpable when continuation of the pregnancy would result in the mother's death.
Recommendation two Assuming that abortion would legally be justified under any circumstances at all, the question would arise of how the decision to abort should be made. Given that the unborn child is a person, he should never be deprived of life except by due process of law. The minimum starting-point for any attempt at due process would be the appointment of guardians to represent the fetus. Such guardians should be appointed by the government, but other individuals, such as the father or other relatives, or indeed any citizen, should also have the right to argue in defence of the fetus. Legal representation would at least guarantee that the unborn child received the maximum protection available under whatever legislation was in force.

It may be objected that due process requires the luxury of time, and that if abortions are to be done they must be done quickly. The law, however, has shown itself capable in other areas of accommodating itself to emergency circumstances, with techniques like the temporary injunction or restraining order. Measures could also be taken so as to ensure that abortion cases were decided with appropriate speed.

The argument for creating a machinery of due process is based on the conviction that the matter of abortion is one of public responsibility, that it is too important to be left solely to the medical profession. Medical knowledge may often bear on aspects of a human problem without determining its solution. For example, in the case of the defence of insanity in a criminal prosecution, medical testimony is highly relevant to the issue of responsibility, but we do not submit the decision to a jury of psychiatrists. Even where the problem appears to be predominantly a medical one, the judgment of society is sought. In principle, the medical profession is rightly reluctant to exchange its historic role of champion in the struggle for life, for the role of even a well-intentioned judge executioner. Physicians as much as anyone stand in need of the due process of law and should realize that the rights of any of us are secure only while those of all of us are secure.

Recommendation three No hospital should be permitted to deny employment to any doctors, nurses, or other personnel who refuse to participate in abortion procedures. Willingness to assist at abortions is becoming a condition of employment and promotion at an increasing number of Canadian hospitals. The law should protect the right of those who are opposed to abortion to adhere to their convictions in their place of employment.

Recommendation four When abortion results in the birth of a live fetus, the law should require that the fetus be treated as a patient and that all appropriate medical steps be taken to preserve its life. The abortion procedure known as hysterotomy results in the delivery of a live fetus which is then killed or left to die. However, advances in medical science have now made it possible to save the lives of significant numbers of babies born as early as 20 weeks after conception. Thus the recommended law would certainly save a number of lives.

ALTERNATIVES TO ABORTION

There is a consensus among medical authorities that a mother's feelings toward pregnancy in the early months are not an indication of her feelings with regard to the baby once it is born.[20] In addition, in a classic study by Aren and Amark,[21] it was determined that only 6 per cent of women who did not go through with abortion after receiving legal permission for the operation regretted giving birth. In the great majority of cases, the women had not encountered the difficulties they had imagined would arise with the advent of the child. Nor had their health been impaired or their marriages rendered unhappy.

It would appear, therefore, that if women carry their so-called unwanted pregnancies to term, there is little detrimental effect on them. Thus, women should be given every encouragement and assistance to continue the pregnancy. It has further been shown that by supporting women throughout the pregnancy the pressures for abortion significantly decrease.[22] We must, then, be willing to adopt social policies that will reach out to these women and aid them in a practical, positive way.

Some of the positive alternatives to abortion are listed below:

1 The implementation of abortion-free birth control programs. Birth control programs can and ought to be powerful allies in the fight against widespread abortion. The association of abortion and contraception as supplementary parts of a birth control program tends to transfer to abortion the respectability enjoyed by contraception. As abortion increases in respectability, efforts to promote birth control inevitably diminish in effectiveness. For this reason the government

should create publicly operated birth control centres from which abortion counselling or referral and all other abortion-related services are excluded. In this way
the virtual monopoly currently exercised in English-speaking Canada by the Family Planning Federation – a monopoly which gives undue prominence to the federation's view that abortion is an acceptable method of birth control – would be
broken.

2 More extensive education in prenatal human life. The discoveries being
made about the life and world of the unborn child ought to be incorporated into
primary and secondary school programs and continuing education programs, as
a basis of respect for human life before birth. Such education can also help to
lay the foundation for a humane and intelligent approach to sex.

3 Counselling services for pregnant women to direct them to the constructive help available to them. A woman who requests an abortion is acting to meet
a crisis in her life – and may be acting in a state of emotional upheaval. Counselling about where she can get various kinds of constructive help should be readily
available to her.

4 Full implementation of a rubella prophylactic program.

5 Increased assistance for parents of handicapped children and public education programs to remove irrational fears of the deformed.

6 Improved homemaker service and daycare centres.

7 More low-income housing suited to family life.

NOTES

1 A review of the literature on intrauterine life shows conclusively that a separate human life is present from conception. This human life matures and
   grows according to an orderly and predictable pattern which begins within
   the uterus and, unless interrupted, continues through birth, maturation, old
   age and death. The human being receives his genetic code at conception, when
   a unique person – different from any other that ever has been or will be –
   comes into existence. The tiny embryo quickly develops the placenta and
   amniotic sac from which it draws nourishment. It has a dependent relationship to its mother, but its existence is nonetheless separate and distinct. It has
   its own blood type and nervous system. Sex has been determined four days
   after conception. Heart beat has been determined at 18 days, and 43 days
   after conception brain waves have been detected. Seven and a half weeks
   after conception the child is completely formed. From this point the only
   change that occurs is in the size and sophistication of use of the parts of his
   body.

See the following: Wolstenholme, F.E.W., and Maeve O'Connor, eds., *Foetal Autonomy: A CIBA Foundation Symposium* (London, 1969); Liley, H.M.I., *Modern Motherhood* (New York, 1969); Ingelman-Sundberg, Axel, and Claes Wirsen, *A Child is Born: The Drama of Life before Birth* (New York, 1967); Arey, Leslie B., *Developmental Anatomy*, 6th ed. (Philadelphia, 1954); Patten, Bradley M., *Human Embryology*, 3rd ed. (New York, 1968); Rugh, Roberts, and Landrum B. Shettles, with Richard N. Einhorn, *From Conception to Birth: The Drama of Life's Beginnings* (New York, 1971); Straus, Reuben, *et al.*, 'Direct Electrocardiographic Recording of a Twenty-three Millimeter Human Embryo,' *The American Journal of Cardiology* 8 (September 1961), 443–47; Marcel, M.P., and J.P. Exchaquet, 'L'Electrocardiogramme du Foetus Human avec un Cas de Double Rythme Auriculaire Vérifié,' *Archives des Maladies du Coeur* 31 (1938), 504–12; Flanagan, G.L., *The First Nine Months of Life* (New York, 1962).

2 See e.g., the recent amendments to the Civil Code of Quebec, quoted later in this brief.

3 Statistics Canada, *Therapeutic Abortions in Canada,* 1971 and January–June 1972.

4 Allemang, W.H., 'Therapeutic Abortion – Some Considerations of the Current Problem,' paper presented to the National Canadian Conference on Abortion, St Michael's College, Toronto, May 25, 1972.

5 Statistics Canada, *Therapeutic Abortions in Canada,* January–June 1972, p. 5.

6 Stallworthy, J.A., *et al.*, 'Legal Abortion: A Critical Assessment of Its Risks,' *Lancet* (1971), 1245; Evans, Ruth, 'Approaches to the Abortion Issue,' paper presented to the Fifteenth Annual Public Health Refresher Course, University of Toronto, February 14-18, 1972.

7 Prof. Walter Hannah, Chief of Obstetrics and Gynaecology at Women's College Hospital, Toronto, quoted in the *Globe and Mail,* April 16, 1972. Professor Hannah is supported by the following official statements of medical associations: *College Statement and Minority Report on Therapeutic Abortion,* issued by the American College of Obstetricians and Gynaecologists, Chicago, Illinois, May 1, 1969; 'Legalized Abortion, a Report by the Council of the Royal College of Obstetricians and Gynaecologists,' *British Medical Journal,* April 12, 1966, p. 850.

8 'Report on Confidential Enquiries into Maternal Deaths in England and Wales 1962-69,' *Reports on Health and Social Subjects No. 1,* HMSO, London, 1972.

9 Hilgers, T.W., *Induced Abortion: A Documented Report,* Mayo Clinic, Rochester, Minnesota, 1973, p. 36.

10 *Bulletin on Abortion Programme*, Health Services Administration, City of New York, September 1972; Ingram, H.S., *Report on Selected Characteristics of Induced Abortions*, recorded in New York State, January to December 1971, New York State Department of Health, August 1972.

11 Personal Communication to Dr Heather Morris, unpublished annual reports from Department of Obstetrics and Gynaecology, Vancouver General Hospital, Calgary Foothills Hospital, Saskatoon University Hospital, Toronto General Hospital.

12 Cowell, Carol, MD, Report to the Meeting of the Royal College of Physicians and Surgeons in Toronto, January 1972.

13 Wynn, Margaret and Arthur, *Some Consequences of Induced Abortion to Children Born Subsequently*, Foundation for Education and Research in Childbearing, London, 1972, p. 11.

14 Klinger, A., 'Abortion Programmes,' in *Family Planning and Population Programmes*. Proceedings of the International Conference on Family Planning Programmes (Chicago, 1966), p. 486.

15 Stallworthy, pp. 1245-49.

16 Horsky, J., 'Induced Abortions: Their Relation to Demographical Indexes and to Health,' World Congress on Fertility and Sterility, *Excerpta Medica*, International Congress Series, 7 (1971), 146.

17 See, e.g., the remarks of Peter Newman and Grace McInnis in *Maclean's*, March and May, 1973.

18 Royal College of Obstetricians and Gynaecologists, London, February 1972, p. 36.

19 Hilgers, T.W., *Induced Abortion: A Documented Report*, Mayo Clinic, Rochester, Minnesota, 1973, p. 52.

20 Eastman, N., and L. Hellman, *William's Obstetrics*, 13th edition (New York, 1966), p. 345.

21 Aren, P., and C. Amark, 'The Prognosis in Cases in Which Legal Abortion Has Been Granted But Not Carried Out,' *Acta Psychiatrica et Neurologica Scandinavica* 36 (1961), 203-78.

22 Murdock, K.M., 'Experiences in a Psychiatric Hospital,' in Rosen, H., ed., *Abortion in America* (Boston, 1967).

LOUISE SUMMERHILL

Birthright

To uphold, at all times, that every mother has the right to all the help needed to carry her child to term, and to foster respect for human life at all stages of development this is the creed and philosophy of Birthright.

WHAT IS BIRTHRIGHT?

We are, in fact, an emergency pregnancy service, operating a distress centre, for girls and women with unwanted pregnancies. There is a well-advertised telephone number and the first contact is usually made in this way - or at times by letter. The telephones are manned by women volunteers, trained to listen with sympathy and complete unshockability.

The girls we help may be high school students, or college students, or office workers. Some are nurses, or teachers, or the product of a broken home; she may be divorced, or may be a married woman with several children, or more often just one or two and afraid she cannot cope with any more; or it could be an extramarital pregnancy. She may live in Toronto, or come from other parts of Canada, or from the United States. The fact is that she is most often single and comes from a good average family background. So she could be the girl next door - or your own daughter.

HOW DO WE HELP?

We have become, in fact, a complete pregnancy service. We have a staff of about 80 volunteers and 30 doctors ready to help. We also work through hospital clinics with girls who have no medical coverage. We arrange pregnancy tests without charge, and when needed we find accommodation, emergency or long-term, and employment, or advice on obtaining these.

We enlist the aid of the community resources, such as the children's aid societies, the family life services, welfare, and maternity homes. When requested, clergy of all denominations are ready to help with counselling and spiritual help.

We have a long list of private homes where a girl can stay as a mother's help until her baby comes, thus providing employment, accommodation, and the moral support of a family all in one. We help in making out medical and hospital insurance forms, and straighten out immigration problems. We can help obtain marriage counselling for married couples, and budgetting advice, and material assistance from the St Vincent de Paul Society. We give maternity clothes and baby layettes. We operate a weekly drop-in centre for single mothers. If necessary we go to the hospitals with the girls when in labour, and visit them there. Most of all, we give sympathetic and compassionate listening and a boundless love. In fact, Birthright, after assessing the needs of the girl, gives whatever help is needed to carry the baby to term.

Birthright offers the positive approach to the abortion dilemma. When we punish the unmarried mother with social ostracism or forced marriage, when help is offered grudgingly and suspiciously, when a girl is left alone to bear the burden of self-recrimination and guilt, abortion is often the only solution she is able to accept. Because we are easily accessible by telephone, girls and women, whose first impulse is to seek abortion, are able to find instead people who can help to take stock of the situation and consider alternative solutions.

A Birthright program cannot be established without effort. It is a question of whether our values are firm enough, or our compassion is strong enough. We who work in the Birthright office are ever acutely aware of the Spirit of God in our midst. The Creator of human life has far more concern than we, and we know, by the miracle of grace and rebirth that we encounter daily in the lives of those who come to us, that He is guiding and inspiring us.

BIRTHRIGHT'S FUTURE

In Toronto, in spite of the many abortions being performed, we are almost frantically busy and our work is spreading, with about 300 centres already operating in the United States, 40 in Canada, and others planning to open.

What does the future hold for Birthright? Only God can know this, but like Abraham we will venture forth and go where God leads us. Let us hope it will be into every city in North America.

Mrs Louise Summerhill, the founder of Birthright, accepts the following statement issued by the Roman Catholic Bishops of New York State as our philosophy on abortion:

The moral law can be outlined this way:
1 Human life comes from God; only He has the authority to take it away.
2 The abortive taking of a child from its mother's womb is gravely wrong because the child has a God-given right to life as well as human rights.
3 When a pathological condition exists, however, such as an ectopic pregnancy, where the child is growing in the fallopian tube, the affected tubal tissue can be removed, even though the fetus will be removed with it. Such cases are medically rare but occasionally do happen. The medical procedure is not an abortion (an immoral act) but a surgical procedure on the fallopian tube (indifferent act) and the intention (to save the life of the mother) is good.
4 The Code of Canon Law (which is the setting down of church rules and regulations) states that all those who knowingly and wilfully become directly involved in an abortion, including the mother, are excommunicated (cut off from the life of the Church and the life of Christ by their act). The effect is similar to a person renouncing his rights as a United States citizen knowingly and wilfully. It is a formal result of a deliberate act by an individual.
5 The taking of a human life under any circumstances always follows the same principles. It is immoral to attack, directly, innocent human life. In some situations, however, the employment of certain therapeutic techniques may entail as a by-product the death of an unborn fetus. In such circumstances, the death of the fetus is the unintended but perhaps inevitable consequence of the therapeutic procedure. This is morally permissible only when there is a proportionate reason. This is nothing more than an application of the traditional principle of the double effect.
6 The unborn child must be regarded as a person in the eyes of the moral law. Taking the life of this person is wrong; hence abortion is wrong. New discoveries in genetics lend support to this traditional position of considering the unborn child as a person. Genetics show that all the substance which produces a new, unique individual is present from the moment of conception. The moral law says the unborn infant is an independent being with a right to independent life and a right to have that life protected by society.

COPE W. SCHWENGER

Abortion as a public health problem

and community health measure

Illegal abortions have in the past posed a major public health problem in Canada, leading to a considerable amount of maternal and infant mortality and morbidity. But because of their very nature they are unreported and remain secret, and hence accurate statistics are impossible to obtain. Various calculations have been made including a commonly reported Canadian figure of 100,000 (20,000–120,000) annually, based apparently on an estimate of one million (200,000–1,200,000) performed each year in the United States.[1] Another Canadian figure of 35,000–40,000 can be obtained from a British gynaecologist's estimate that 10 per cent of all pregnancies (Table 3) are interfered with in some way.[2]

Since the Canadian Criminal Code was amended in August 1969, we have had compulsory reporting in Canada of a very rapidly increasing number of legal or so-called 'therapeutic' abortions (Table 1).

The case will be made in this paper that at least some of these are replacing what were formerly illegal abortions. Concern has been expressed that therapeutic abortion may become a leading and accepted primary method of birth control as has been the case in Eastern Europe and Japan.[4]

There is no doubt in practically everybody's minds that no matter how safe and simple the modern procedures of legal abortion, contraception is still a much more acceptable and certainly a much cheaper method of family planning. Most of these legal (as well as illegal) abortions can be looked on as a failure of contraception. Legal abortions therefore in themselves still pose a considerable public health problem which can be controlled only by the provision of more acceptable, effective, and readily available contraceptives. It is going to take concerted organized community action (i.e., public health action) to bring this problem

TABLE 1

Therapeutic abortions, Canadian residents
(number and rate per 100 live births), Canada 1969-72[3]

Year	Total number	Percentage of live births
1969 (Sept.-Dec.)	542	
1970	11,152	3.0
1971	30,923	8.3
1972	39,500	11.0
	(preliminary)	(preliminary)

under control. Ideally, abortion should be necessary only very occasionally and mostly as a backstop for contraceptive failure under unusual circumstances.

ANTHROPOLOGICAL, EMBRYOLOGICAL,
AND THEOLOGICAL ASPECTS

Devereaux has described the almost universal phenomenon of abortion historically and in primitive societies for such things as rape, incest, unknown father, single mother, poverty, and starvation. Methods resorted to have included lifting weights, putting hot stones on the abdomen, and jumping out of trees.[5]

Out of a total of some 20,000 human ova, less than 400 actually leave the ovaries and of these only 20 or so give rise to offspring – the rest (999/1000) are 'wasted.' It has been also estimated that one-third to one-half of all human embryos cease to live either as a result of lack of development or later so-called natural or 'spontaneous' abortion.[6] This has been called 'nature's way of getting rid of abnormal pregnancies.'

Abortion is a very profound and complicated moral, ethical, and theological question. Attitudes of the church (and of society) towards abortion have in the past centred on the time of 'ensoulment' which for centuries was held to occur after the fetus was 40 days in the uterus. However for about 100 years now, ensoulment has been declared by the Roman Catholic Church to occur at the time of conception.[7]

ILLEGAL AND LEGAL ABORTION

Abortion to most people does not mean the natural or spontaneous kind ('miscarriage') but rather the artificial or 'induced' variety. The distinction as to whether the induced abortion is 'therapeutic' (legal) or 'criminal' (illegal) is purely arbitrary and depends upon the particular law of the land. There is no doubt that there has been a recent world-wide tendency towards broadening the indications for abortions so that they are now generally much easier to obtain. Factors influencing this change include the rising independence of women, the population explosion, and the failure of more acceptable methods of birth control.

Illegal abortions have been said to be the primary method of birth control throughout the world[8] - a frequently quoted calculation is that a total of perhaps 20-25 million abortions are performed annually.[9] Methods which have been documented in Canada include: *a* oral - swallowing quinine, castor oil, etc.; *b* uterine - inserting solids, liquids, and gases; *c* physical - exercising, falling intentionally, etc. They have been performed by boyfriends, husbands, compassionate and/or questionable health professionals, or have been self-administered. Locations have included private homes, hotels and motels, and back-room offices.[10]

As for legal abortion, there are various indications in different parts of the world including *a* medical - to save the life or preserve the health of the mother; *b* eugenic - to prevent hereditary disease and uterine disorder leading to fetal damage; *c* ethical - when pregnancy results from rape, incest, or sexual intercourse with a minor or a person suffering from mental disease or deficiency; *d* socio-medical - too many children coming too quickly, domestic difficulty, financial strain, death or disability of the husband, illegitimacy; *e* abortion on request - decision between the woman and her doctor. It is estimated that more than half the world's population now lives in countries where abortion is available for socio-medical reasons. There are, however, still countries in the world where abortion cannot be done for any reason whatsoever, including saving the life of the mother.[11]

It is usual to divide women seeking abortion into two groups: *a* low risk - includes healthy women up to 12 weeks of pregnancy; the method of choice here is increasingly by uterine aspiration (vacuum curettage) rather than the traditional dilatation and curettage (D & C); *b* high risk - includes all later abortions and early ones performed on women with an abnormal medical or obstetrical history or significant gynaecological disease. The termination of late pregnancies is increasingly by injection of intra-amniotic saline (salting out) rather than the traditional hysterotomy (miniature caesarian).[12]

LEGAL ABORTION IN CANADA

On August 26, 1969, the Canadian Criminal Code was amended to allow a therapeutic abortion to be performed in an 'accredited' or 'approved' hospital in

TABLE 2

Therapeutic abortions by province, Canada, 1971[3]

Province	Number of abortions	Rate per 100 live births
Newfoundland	78	0.6
Prince Edward Island	39	2.0
Nova Scotia	643	4.5
New Brunswick	146	1.3
Quebec	1,881	2.0
Ontario	16,173	12.0
Manitoba	827	4.5
Saskatchewan	756	4.6
Alberta	3,116	9.7
British Columbia	7,045	19.1
Yukon	8	1.8
CANADA TOTAL	30,923	8.3

which the case has been reviewed by a therapeutic abortion committee consisting of at least three qualified medical practitioners who have decided that the continuation of the pregnancy would endanger maternal life or health. Since this time, a considerable increase in therapeutic abortions performed in Canada has occurred (Table 1). These figures do not include abortions performed on Canadian citizens in other countries; for example, from July 1, 1970, to June 30, 1971, a total of 4437 Canadian women were aborted in New York State alone.[13]

Because of these very large and increasing numbers performed there has been a tremendous backlash against legal abortion in Canada (and in the United States). Some of the major issues which are debated are the rights of the fetus versus the rights of the mother (the 'right to life' versus the 'right not to give birth to an unwanted child'), the consent of the spouse or parent as against the consent of the 'liberated' wife or 'emancipated' minor.

Inequalities in the present system have been pointed out repeatedly by various individuals and organizations, e.g., *a* geographic – why should it be over 30 times as easy to obtain an abortion in British Columbia as in Newfoundland? (Table 2); *b* urbanization – why should it be so much easier for a woman in a city than in a rural area where there may be no accredited or approved hospital and insufficient physicians to form a committee? *c* religion – why should it be so much easier for a Protestant than a Roman Catholic woman? *d* socio-economic status – it is still easier for the rich to get a legal abortion than the poor, especially if travel is necessary outside the country; *e* medical control – why should physicians be placed in the position of making moral and ethical decisions?* f definition of health – it depends on the individual committee members as to whether they accept a very broad definition of health (physical, mental, and social) or a relatively narrow one.

One of the major criticisms of the present system involves the growing number of abortions performed on single teenagers. Because of inherent ambivalence and conflicting advice given by their family and others, these young people simply cannot make up their minds until by the time they reach the committee they very often arrive late in pregnancy when the complication rate is high, particularly if it is a first pregnancy.[14]

This points up the scarcity of appropriate counselling on abortion in Canada. In the United States this is built into the process by legislation. In Canada, however, because of the lack of counselling provided in hospitals and by health agencies in the community, certain women's organizations have attempted to fill the gap with their own particular biases. Advice tends therefore to be polarized either very much in favour of abortion or very much against it, causing great distress and additional delay to the women and girls involved.

MEDICAL EFFECTS OF REPLACEMENT OF ILLEGAL BY LEGAL ABORTION

Opponents of abortion have been unwilling to recognize the possibility that the rising numbers of legal abortions may have been replacing previous illegal abortions. What is the evidence for this in Canada (Table 3)?

From 1969 to 1970 the total number of births actually rose by 2341 in spite of an additional 10,610 legal abortions. From 1970 to 1971, although the total births dropped by 9801, the legal abortions rose by a further 19,771. It would seem that at least a high proportion of these legal abortions (particularly in 1970) were replacing what would have been otherwise abortions performed illegally, rather than replacing births which would have otherwise occurred.

Evidence has been available for several years from Europe and more recently from the United States showing the improvement of the health of women and children as a result of more accessible abortion. Deaths and complications as a result of illegal abortion dropped precipitately in New York City after the legislation was changed.[16,17] What has been the effect so far in Canada (Table 4)?

The temporary rise to four deaths due to legal abortions from 1969 to 1970 is not surprising in view of the over twentyfold increase in numbers of legal abor-

*The Canadian Medical Association, the Society of Obstetricians and Gynaecologists of Canada, and the Canadian Psychiatric Association have all voted in favour of abandoning the therapeutic abortion committee and allowing 'abortion on request.'

TABLE 3

Live births, legal abortions, and yearly changes, Canada 1968-71[3,15]

	Total live births		Total legal abortions	
	Number	Change from previous year	Number	Change from previous year
1968	364,310			
1969	369,647	+5,337	542	
1970	371,988	+2,341	11,152	+10,610
1971	362,187	-9,801	30,923	+19,771

TABLE 4

Abortion mortality and total maternal mortality, Canada 1969-71[3,15]

	Abortion mortality			Total maternal mortality	
	Legal	Illegal	Spontaneous	Number	Rate (per 100,000 live births)
1969	0	11	2	77	20.8
1970	4	5	5	75	20.2
1971	2	1	3	66	18.2

tions (Table 1). However, the deaths were cut in half from 1970 to 1971 in spite of the fact that the total number of legal abortions almost tripled (Table 1). This is a familiar picture with increasing competence and experience in the use of early and better selected cases for therapeutic abortion.[18] The mortality rate in Canada for legal abortion in 1971 was only 6.5:100,000 (i.e., 2:30,923). This is compared with a mortality rate from the complications of pregnancy and delivery in the same year of 17.3:100,000 pregnancies (i.e., 63:362,187). On the other hand there has been a very striking tenfold drop over three years in the number of deaths ascribed to illegal abortion: only one death in 1971. The total maternal mortality statistics also look very encouraging.

Another important health indicator is the number of admissions to hospitals because of incomplete abortions. Statistics from California and New York, following their more accessible abortion laws, have shown a marked drop in morbidity due to illegal abortion.[16,17] What is the picture in Canada? Table 5 gives statistics for 1969-71 from the province of Ontario for abortion 'separations.'

TABLE 5

Total abortion separations, therapeutic abortions,
and other abortions, Ontario, 1969-71[3,19]

			Other abortions (separations)	
	Abortion separations	Therapeutic abortions	Number	Change from previous year
1969	15,749	274	15,475	
1970	20,343	5,657	14,686	−789
1971	27,750	16,244	11,506	−3,180

(Separations include all patients who were discharged from or died in hospital; separations occurred from active, general rehabilitation and special rehabilitation hospitals.)

What has been done in this table is to subtract the total therapeutic abortions for Ontario (as reported to Statistics Canada) from the abortion separations (as reported by the Ontario Hospital Services Commission). This leaves a total of 'other' abortions which are made up of spontaneous and illegal abortions. The spontaneous abortions have presumably remained the same so the drop of 3180 represents mainly a decrease in illegal abortions admitted to (or separated from) hospital. This would undoubtedly reflect a decrease of a much larger number of illegal abortions which were not admitted to hospital. This decrease in maternal morbidity bears out the comments of obstetricians in Canada that they are seeing fewer results of criminal abortions ('incomplete' abortions) in hospital.[20]

EFFECTS ON NEONATAL MORTALITY,
PERINATAL MORTALITY, AND ILLEGITIMACY

It usually takes more time for legal abortion to influence the health of children. However, once legal abortions have gone beyond the replacement of previous illegal abortions and are available to women with high-risk pregnancies and resultant high-risk children, they can be expected (and have been shown) to affect infant mortality, neonatal mortality, prematurity and illegitimacy rates.[16,17] Has this happened as yet in Canada (Table 6)?

The drop in the rates of neonatal mortality and perinatal mortality over the past five years shows the greatest reduction from 1970-71, probably reflecting the influence of legal abortion. The relatively small drop experienced from 1969-70 might reflect the fact that legal abortions in 1970 were mainly replacing pre-

TABLE 6

Neonatal and perinatal mortality, Canada 1966-71[3,15]

	Neonatal			Perinatal		
	Number	Rate/1000 live births	Rate change (over prev. year)	Number	Rate/1000 total births	Rate change (over prev. year)
1966	6253	16.1		10,004	25.5	
1967	5628	15.2	-0.9	9284	24.7	-0.8
1968	5376	14.8	-0.4	8727	23.7	-1.0
1969	5138	13.9	-0.9	8308	22.3	-1.4
1970	5017	13.5	-0.4	8192	21.8	-0.5
1971	4485	12.4	-1.1	7352	20.1	-1.7

TABLE 7

Illegitimate births, total number and as a percentage
of total live births, Canada 1967-71[15]

	Number	Rate per 100 live births
1967	30,915	8.3
1968	32,629	9.0
1969	34,041	9.2
1970	35,588	9.6
1971	32,693	9.0

vious illegal abortions as discussed above (Table 3). Unfortunately insufficient information on immaturity as a cause of death in Canada in 1970 and 1971 was available from Statistics Canada at the time of writing.

In the case of illegitimacy, Canada in 1971 had a drop in the total number of illegitimate births for the first time since 1949.[15] The rate as a percentage of total live births dropped for the first time since 1954.[15] The Canadian picture for the past five years is shown in Table 7.

There seems very little doubt that this decrease has been due largely to the increase in legal abortions. The decreases in illegitimacy rates in British Columbia, Ontario and Alberta, appear to be directly related to the proportion of abortions performed in these provinces (Table 8).

Unfortunately I do not have any statistics available to show an expected drop in so-called 'shotgun' marriages (i.e., marriages occurring less than eight months before the birth of the first child). This is the other side of the coin of illegitimacy as evidence of unplanned pregnancy.

TABLE 8

Provincial changes in illegitimacy rates per 100 live births, 1969-71, compared with provincial abortion rates per 100 live births 1971[3,15]

	Change in illegitimacy 1969-71		Abortion rate 1971	
	Rate (% live births)	Rank	Rate (% live births)	Rank
Newfoundland	+1.7		0.6	
Prince Edward Island	+1.4		2.0	
Nova Scotia	0.0		4.5	
New Brunswick	+1.4		1.3	
Quebec	+0.3		2.0	
Ontario	-1.0	2	12.0	2
Manitoba	+0.9		4.5	
Saskatchewan	+2.3		4.6	
Alberta	-0.4	3	9.7	3
British Columbia	-1.6	1	19.1	1

TABLE 9

Live births, birth rates, and fertility rates, Canada, 1968-72[15]

	Live births	Birth rate (per 1000 population)	Fertility rate (per 1000 women aged 15-49)
1968	364,310	17.6	75.8
1969	369,647	17.6	72.5
1970	371,988	17.4	71.7
1971	362,187	16.8	70.5
1972	342,050	15.7	67.7

LEGAL ABORTION AND POPULATION
CONTROL IN CANADA

There is no doubt that the very high incidence of illegal abortion has had a major global demographic impact. The population explosion would have been far greater if there had been in addition to the annual 120 million global births[21] an estimated 20-25 million annual births not prevented by abortion. There is also little doubt that legal abortion has had an impact on reducing birth rates in such places as Japan, Eastern Europe and the United States.[22,23] The same thing is likely true for Canada in the last few years (Table 9).

We have now reached in Canada (temporarily at any rate) and with the aid of legal abortion, the so-called 'replacement' level of population (2.1 births per woman). If we could sustain the present fertility rate and were able to establish a policy of zero net migration, Canada's population would still reach 29 million by the turn of the century.[24] Canadians are beginning to ask themselves whether we may not have already reached or even passed an optimum level of population for Canada.[25]

In spite of the fact that legal abortion is helping to reduce our fertility rate, more acceptable alternative methods of birth control such as contraception and sterilization must be made more readily available and this must be done quickly, as methods of legal abortion become simpler, safer, and cheaper.

PUBLIC HEALTH AND ABORTION

In November 1968 the American Public Health Association resolved that 'access to abortion be accepted as an important means of securing the right to space and choose the number of wanted children. To this end, restrictive laws should be repealed so that pregnant women may have abortions performed by qualified practitioners of medicine and osteopathy.'[26] In October 1970 the APHA published a list of Recommended Standards for Abortion Services.[27] These were updated in November 1972.[28] The APHA stresses that abortion services should be an integral part of comprehensive family planning and maternal and child health care. As such, abortion and contraceptive services should be available together. Health agencies must make every effort to provide easy access to safe abortion services to all who are in need of such services. Counselling must be an integral part of such services and should be 'freely entered into, supportive, non-judgmental and educational.' It is emphasized that abortion should not be relied on as a primary method of fertility control and that contraception and sterilization are preferred as methods of preventing unwanted pregnancies.

In Canada, both the official health agencies and voluntary planned parenthood groups have tended to leave abortion counselling to certain women's organizations with their own particular biases as indicated above, with consequent polarization of advice, unnecessary distress, and dangerous delay. If the woman or girl has decided that she will go ahead with a legal abortion then assistance must be given to get this done as quickly and safely as possible. We have had increasing leadership in the last few years from Canadian official health agencies in the provision of traditional family planning services.[29] However, abortion services have been considered more or less taboo by federal, provincial, and local health departments. Other less adequate counselling and referral alternatives have arisen in the community to fill the vacuum. There is no doubt that we have a public health problem and that public health measures are needed to cope with the problem of unnecessary abortions on the one hand, and the provision of quick and safe abortion if necessary on the other hand. It is time that the Canadian Public Health Association began to provide the kind of leadership given by its sister organization south of the border over the past five years.

NOTES

1 Calderone, M.S., ed., 'Abortion in the United States,' Report on the 1955 Arden House Conference on Abortion (New York, 1958).
2 Rhodes, P., 'A Gynaecologist's View,' in *Abortion in Britain, Proceedings* of a Conference at the University of London, April 1966 (London, 1966).
3 Statistics Canada, Publications on Legal Abortion in Canada: November 20, 1970; April 16, 1971; October 4, 1971; May 3, 1972; December 11, 1972.
4 Schwenger, C.W., 'Why We Need Better Family Planning Services in Canada,' *Canadian Welfare*, May–June 1972.
5 Devereaux, G., *A Study of Abortion in Primitive Societies* (New York, 1955).
6 Corner, G.W., 'An Embryologist's View,' in *Abortion in a Changing World*, International Conference, Hot Springs, Virginia, November 1968, 1 (New York, 1970).
7 O'Donnell, T.J., 'A Traditional Catholic's View,' in *Abortion in a Changing World*.
8 Rockefeller, J.D., in *Abortion in a Changing World*.
9 Mehlan, K.H., *Frequency and Mortality Rate Associated with Induced Abortions on a Global Scale (an Assessment), Proceedings* of the Fifth World Congress of Gynaecology and Obstetrics, Sydney, Australia, 1967 (London, 1967).
10 Pelrine, E.W., *Abortion in Canada* (Toronto, 1971).
11 'Abortion – A World Survey,' supplement to *International Planned Parenthood News*, IPPF (London, March 1972).
12 'Induced Abortion.' Conference held in Yugoslavia, June 1971. International Planned Parenthood Federation, London, England, 1972.
13 Figures obtained from the Bio-Statistics Section, New York State, Department of Health, Albany, New York.
14 Coxwell, C., 'Pregnancy in the Adolescent – Therapeutic Abortion – The Alternative of Choice.' Presented to the Royal College of Physicians and Surgeons of Canada, January 1972.
15 *Vital Statistics, Preliminary Annual Reports*, Statistics Canada, Cat. #84-201, Ottawa 1967-71.
16 Harting, D., and H.J. Hunter, 'Abortion Techniques and Services, A Review and Critique,' *American Journal of Public Health* 61, no. 10 (October 1971).

17 New York City Health Services Administration, 'Bulletin on Abortion Program,' December 1971.
18 Tietze, C., and S. Lewit, 'Joint Program for the Study of Abortion (JPSA) Early Medical Complications of Legal Abortion,' *Studies in Family Planning,* Population Council 3, no. 6 (June 1972).
19 Ontario Hospital Services Commission, *Annual Reports - Statistical Supplements.* Ontario Ministry of Health, 1969-71.
20 Clayman, D., 'Impact on Hospital Practice of Liberalizing Abortions on Female Sterilizations,' *Canadian Medical Association Journal* 105 (July 10, 1971).
21 *Demographic Yearbook 1971.* United Nations, New York, 1972.
22 Brackett, J.W., 'The Demographic Consequences of Legal Abortion in *Abortion, Obtained and Denied Research Approaches,* Newman, S.H., *et al.* Population Council, New York, 1971.
23 *Population and the American Future.* The Report of the Commission on Population Growth and the American Future (The Rockefeller Report). Signet Books, New York, 1972.
24 Romaniuc, A., 'Potentials for Population Growth in Canada. A Long Term Projection,' *Statistics Canada,* unpublished paper presented at a Population Seminar, Toronto, 1972.
25 Schwenger, C.W., 'Towards Living in Harmony with our Environment,' *Canadian Welfare* (July–August 1972).
26 Gold, E.M., 'Abortion - 1970,' *American Journal of Public Health* 63, no. 3 (March 1971).
27 'Recommended Standards for Abortion Services,' *American Journal of Public Health* 61, no. 2 (February 1971).
28 'Recommended Program Guide for Abortion Services,' *American Journal of Public Health* 62, no. 12 (December 1972).
29 Schwenger, C.W., 'Population and Family Planning in Public Health,' editorial in *Canadian Journal of Public Health* 59, no. 7 (July 1968).

RESOURCES

A glossary of family planning terminology*

The following glossary of family planning terms was approved by the National Family Planning Forum last May. It was developed by the Forum's Committee on Terminology, chaired by Dr Louise B. Tyrer, project director of the Family Planning Division of the American College of Obstetricians and Gynecologists.

The glossary is divided into five main sections:
General terminology,
Definitions of categories of family planning patients,
Definitions of categories of family planning visits,
Consumer participation in family planning, and
Medical terms.

The first four of these are arranged conceptually while the last section is ordered alphabetically.

GENERAL TERMINOLOGY

Family planning
Voluntary planning and action by individuals to have the number of children they want, when and if they want them.

Fertility regulation
Medical and nonmedical techniques that enable individuals to engage in voluntary planning and action to have the number of children they want, when and if they want them. These techniques include contraception, infertility diagnosis and treatment, abortion and sterilization.

Population planning
Organized efforts to analyze population variables with respect to size, rate of growth (or decline), distribution and

*Glossary prepared by the National Family Planning Forum; reprinted from *Family Planning Digest* 2, no. 6 (1973).

composition, and their impact upon society as a whole, and to recommend and implement measures relating to these variables so as to optimize what is generally termed, the 'quality of life' for all people.

Family planning agency
An administrative mechanism to carry out family planning programs through family planning projects which deliver family planning services.

Family planning programs
Activities that provide the services which enable individuals effectively to practice family planning. These activities are provided by commercial, governmental, or nonprofit institutions and individual practitioners.

Family planning project
A specifically designed set of activities and services intended to advance achievement of the program's family planning objectives. It may be funded through general revenue or specific grants from either public or private sources.

Family planning services
Services which provide the means to enable individuals to meet their family planning objectives. These services are medical, social and educational.

Medical family planning services
Medical history, physical examination, laboratory testing, consultation, counselling, treatment, including continuing medical supervision, issuance of drugs and contraceptive supplies and appropriate medical referral when indicated. Medical services for family planning include:
Complete medical history at initial examination, and interim history at subsequent visits.
A physical examination for initial visits and annual examination visits.
Thyroid palpation
Inspection and palpation of breasts and axillary glands, with instruction to the patient for self-examination
Auscultation of heart and lungs
Blood pressure
Weight
Abdominal examination
Pelvic, including speculum, bimanual and rectovaginal examinations
Extremities
Others as indicated
Examination and laboratory testing for revisits as indicated.
Laboratory testing for initial visits and annual examination visits.
Minimal testing (1) Hematocrit or hemoglobin (2) Urinalysis (microscopic examination when medically indicated) (3) Papanicoulaou smear (4) Venereal disease testing (serology and GC culture) (5) Pregnancy testing when indicated
Optional testing when medically indicated or financially feasible: (1) Sickle cell screening, (2) Other medically indicated tests
Consultation, including diagnosis, counselling and prescription:
Contraception

Infertility
Sterilization
Related medical problems (including
pregnancy)
Referral to other providers for medical
conditions not treated in the program.

Social and education family planning
services   These services comprise:
Outreach and follow-up
Identification
Location
Contact
Discussion
Appointment for family planning
services
Referral to other agencies for social
services
Facilitation services
Transportation
Babysitting
Nonmedical counselling when necessary
Inclinic instruction and discussion
General community information and
educational activities through all media
to all types of community institutions
and individuals. These activities should
include family life, human sexuality,
and health education; social and demo-
graphic rationales for family planning,
in addition to information concerned
with the specifics of contraceptive
methods.

Family planning clinic
A place or facility at which an agency
provides medical family planning services. It may be a hospital, a health
centre, a mobile unit, a freestanding
site, church or storefront. Physicians'

offices should be considered as clinic
locations only when there is a formal
relationship with an agency. An agency
may operate one or more family planning clinics.

Family planning clinic session
A scheduled period of time during
which family planning services are provided at a clinic location. The clinic
session may be *specialized* where only
services related to family planning are
provided, or *combined*, where family
planning services are offered in conjunction with other health services
such as maternity, postpartum, well
baby, pediatric, gynecologic, or comprehensive health care.

Outreach
Activities which inform prospective
patients of the availability of family
planning services, assist them in avail-
ing themselves of the services, and
schedule and maintain them in the con-
tinuity of the program. They consist of
several distinct processes, namely: recruitment, referral, follow-up and education. Outreach activities may be
classified as direct and indirect.

Direct outreach activities   These include the activities of recruitment, referral and follow-up.
Recruitment attempts to locate and
identify prospective patients, to interview them and discuss their needs, to
provide them with information and
education; and, if desired, to offer
clinic appointments. It may be done

by contacting individuals in hospitals and at maternity and other clinics, by home visiting, at meetings of different community groups, and a variety of other ways.

Referral includes the referral of prospective patients to family planning clinics by other agencies, referral of family planning patients to other medical and social agencies to meet their needs and transfer of family planning patients from one family planning clinic to another, either within the same agency or to another agency.

Follow-up may be accomplished by telephone calls, letters, and home visits to persons who have missed appointments, and should result in rescheduling of appointments. Follow-up may also involve repeated contact between the program personnel and patients for purposes of continuing educational activities and reappointment. (Recruitment and follow-up services may include services which facilitate clinic attendance, such as transportation and babysitting.)

Indirect outreach activities **Education**
Indirect outreach consists of varied informational and educational activities undertaken by the program for the purpose of informing prospective patients about family planning. It may be carried out through publicity, i.e., use of radio, the press, and TV, distribution of literature, lectures and presentations to community groups; and, by more formal methods, such as participation in the teaching programs of various school systems.

Medical indigence in family planning
A medically indigent individual is one who is not eligible for welfare, but for whom the cost of average medical care is precluded, or for whom it would create a great hardship, and therefore, be likely to deter the person from utilizing a particular health service.

DEFINITIONS OF CATEGORIES
OF FAMILY PLANNING PATIENTS

Prospective family planning patient
Any individual at risk of unwanted pregnancy, or who desires pregnancy but is unable to conceive, and is not securing family planning services.

Appointed family planning patient
A patient who has a family planning appointment.

Family planning patient
An individual who receives medical family planning services at a clinic location or other service unit of a program.

New family planning patient
One who receives medical family planning services in a particular program for the first time and is then entered into the program record system.

Continuing family planning patient
A patient who is enrolled in an earlier year, and returns for the first visit in the subsequent reporting year.

Active family planning patient
One who is up-to-date in terms of the

last appointment plus a grace period of three months.

Overdue family planning patient
An active family planning patient who has missed a regularly scheduled appointment (synonymous with delinquent).

Inactive family planning patient
An individual who previously registered and received medical family planning service and who is identified as temporarily not in need of family planning services, i.e., pregnant patients and sexually inactive patients.

Closure family planning patient
A patient who is more than three months overdue for the last scheduled appointment and is not classified as 'inactive' (synonymous with *terminated, dropouts*).

Readmission family planning patient
Any patient who has been classified as a closure from a program and who subsequently returns to the program and for whom records are available.

Transfer family planning patient
Any patient who moves from one clinic to another.

Transfer – within system   Any patient who receives medical family planning services from a clinic and is enrolled in the data system, and who moves from one clinic to another clinic within the same data system.

Postpregnant family planning patient
A patient who registers in a family planning program and receives medical family planning services for the first time within 56 days of having delivered products of conception. This may take place in the hospital immediately after delivery, or at the postdelivery checkup examination in a clinic. This category includes postpartum and postabortal patients.

Total family planning patients
The sum of active patients, closure patients, and inactive patients for the reporting period.

Contraceptive patient
A patient who is actively and consistently using a medically acceptable contraceptive method.

Infertility patient
One who is receiving medical infertility diagnosis and treatment. An infertility patient is classified as a Family Planning Patient.

Other patients
Any patients who receive a medical service other than pregnancy or venereal disease testing at a family planning clinic location, or other service unit of a program, who are not at risk of pregnancy or active contraceptors. This covers the following three categories:

Post-family planning patient   An individual who continues to attend the clinic and receive some medical services, but no longer needs contraception, pregnancy termination, sterilization or infertility services. Included in this group are:

Postmenopausal patients
Tubal sterilization patients
Hysterectomy patients
Patients sterilized by other procedures

Medical patients (miscellaneous) Individuals who receive any medical services through the program or clinic and who are not classified in other patient categories. (Individuals receiving pregnancy or VD tests may be enumerated as 'encounters' but the recordkeeping system should reflect their numbers and demographic characteristics.)

Counselling patient An individual who receives professional medical or social service guidance regarding contraception, infertility, pregnancy termination, sterilization, or related health and social problems from a doctor, nurse or other personnel specifically trained to conduct such a discussion in the clinic; and who does not receive a medical service (except pregnancy testing or VD testing).

Male patients
Male patients should not be counted with other active family planning patients, but should be separately enumerated. Service for male patients may consist of:
History and physical examination in conjunction with the services listed below

Vasectomy
Contraceptive services, e.g., condoms
Medical services, e.g., VD or infertility
Counselling

DEFINITION OF CATEGORIES
OF FAMILY PLANNING VISITS

Initial visit
A visit at which the patient is registered, receives medical family planning services from the program for the first time, and is entered into the record system.

Enumeration visit
NOTE: The reason for including the category of *Enumeration Visits* is to simplify the task of obtaining a 'prime patient' count (an unduplicated count of individuals) for a given reporting period. This category would be unnecessary if, for example, a computer program were written in such a fashion as to scan automatically, for prior attendance, all visits in the reporting period for each particular patient identification number. This category is also probably unnecessary in projects which have only one clinic location, a light patient load, and a limited number of sessions. Under these circumstances, a 'hand tally' system would be easy to maintain, particularly if personnel turnover were minimal.

Enumeration – new family planning patients The sum of all initial visits during the reporting period (symbolized by En).

Enumeration – continuing family planning patients   The total of all first revisits by patients registered in the previous reporting period which occurred during the current reporting period (symbolized by Ec).

Total family planning patients
The sum of enumeration visits of new patients plus enumeration visits of continuing patients. (Total patients = En + Ec.)

Annual examination visit
A visit made by continuing patients yearly, within three months of the patient anniversary date, at which time the patient receives at least the minimally recommended medical family planning services (synonymous with *annual visit, annual revisit*).

Revisit
Any visit during a reporting period by a previously registered patient other than the annual examination visit or supply visit, and at which time the patient sees authorized personnel. Revisits consist either of routine scheduled visits or nonroutine visits for the resolution of unanticipated problems.

Supply visit
A visit by a previously registered patient for obtaining prescription supplies only. (If supply refills are mailed, they should be enumerated separately.)

Total visits
The sum of all visits by all patients

during the reporting period (i.e., initial, annual examination, revisits and supply visits, including the enumeration visit for continuing patients).

Encounter
A contact between a client and a provider of family planning services. The client may or may not be a family planning patient. The encounter may take place in the clinic, outside the clinic, or by telephone. Examples of encounters include: group sessions held for general discussion, lectures, films, a visit to a clinic whose sole purpose is to pick up nonprescription supplies, contact by an outreach worker, response to a telephone inquiry, incidental medical testing, such as pregnancy or VD testing. (Persons receiving such medical services may be classified as encounters, but their sociodemographic characteristics should be obtained and they should be enumerated in the category of *Other Medical Patients – Misc.*) If a person receives counselling of an informative nature, but does not receive any medical services, adopt a contraceptive method, or make a future appointment, the contact is classified as an 'encounter.' For reporting purposes, a 'clinic visit record' is not completed for an encounter. Encounters are tabulated separately.

CONSUMER PARTICIPATION
IN FAMILY PLANNING

Community
The population in the geographic area

served by a particular family planning program.

Consumer
A current or past user of the services of a particular family planning program.

Consumer participation
The act of organized participation in the affairs of a family planning program by consumers or consumer representatives.

Consumer representative
Any member of the community who is selected to present and support the interests of those who utilize the services of a family planning program. This representative may or may not be a consumer.

Advocate
Any individual or group which seeks to speak for and advance the interests of a particular person or group. Examples are consumers, community representatives and professionals.

Consumer advocate
Any member of the community who supports and seeks to advance the interest of those who utilize the services of a family planning program.

Family planning consumer advocate organization
An organized group, one of whose purposes is the representation of the family planning consumer, i.e., welfare rights organizations or community action agencies. The group may be formally selected by the family planning consumers as their representative.

Advisory action
Positive and/or negative recommendations on a particular decision or course of action.

Advisory board
A group of individuals, appointed or elected, who interface with each other, and whose functions are to receive and secure information on particular aspects of the program for the purpose of giving advice to the agency or program, e.g., consumer advisory board, patient advisory board, medical advisory board.

Policy
A definite course of action selected from among alternatives to guide and determine present and future decisions, both programmatic and fiscal.

Policy board
A group of individuals, appointed or elected, whose function is to determine policy for the agency or program. All agencies have some type of policy board, e.g., board of directors, board of trustees, governing body, board of health.

MEDICAL TERMS

Abortion
Expulsion or extraction of all (complete) or any part (incomplete) of the placenta or membranes, without an

identifiable fetus or with a liveborn infant or a stillborn infant weighing less than 500 gm. In the absence of known weight, an estimated length of gestation of less than 20 completed weeks (130 days or less), calculated from the first day of the last normal menstrual period, may be used. Abortion is a term referring to the culmination of the birth process before the twentieth* completed week of gestation.

Abortion, complete
Expulsion of all the products of conception before the twentieth* completed week of gestation.

Abortion, incomplete
Expulsion of some, but not all, of the products of conception before the twentieth* completed week of gestation.

Abortion, induced
Deliberate interruption of pregnancy by any means before the twentieth* completed week of gestation. It may be therapeutic or nontherapeutic.

Abortion, infected
Abortion associated with infection of the intraabdominal genital organs. (If infection is disseminated into the systemic circulation, this becomes a septic abortion.)

Abortion, missed
Abortion in which the embryo or fetus dies in utero before the twentieth* completed week of gestation, but the products of conception are retained in utero for eight weeks or more.

Abortion rate
(Total number of abortions during period/Total number of females 15-44 during period) x 1000.

Abortion ratio
(Total number of abortions during period/Total number of live births during period) x 1000.

Abortion, spontaneous
Expulsion of the products of conception before the twentieth* completed week of gestation without deliberate interference. (Also known as 'miscarriage.')

Abortion, therapeutic
Legally induced abortion before the twentieth* completed week of gestation.

Abortion, threatened
State in which bleeding of intrauterine origin occurs before the twentieth* completed week of gestation, with or without uterine cramps, without expulsion of the products of conception, and without dilatation of the cervix.

*The gestational age criterion of abortion is primarily a legally oriented definition, while the weight criterion is primarily a medically oriented definition.

Afterbirth
Placenta and allied membranes cast or removed from the uterus after the birth of a child.

Age-specific fertility rate
(Total number of live births during a year to female of age x / Total number of females of age x as of July 1 of the same year) x 1000.

Amenorrhea
Absence of the menses.

Amniotic sac
Fluid-filled sac that surrounds the embryo.

Androgen
Hormones that produce masculine characteristics.

Bartholin's glands
Two secreting glands found at either side of the vaginal entrance; also known as greater vestibular glands.

Bulbourethral glands (Cowper's)
Tubular glands that secrete into the male urethra.

Castration
Removal of the gonads.

Cervix
Lower segment of the uterus, a portion of which extends into the upper portion of the vagina.

Chancre
Ulcer or sore caused by the syphilis spirochete.

Chancroid
Sexually transmitted disease of the genitalia, in which painful lesions develop and local lymph nodes are generally enlarged.

Circumcision
Surgical procedure in which the foreskin of the penis is removed.

Clitoris
Small erectile body in the female that is situated at the most anterior portion of the vulva between the labia. It is responsive to sexual stimulation.

Coitus
Heterosexual relationship with entry of the penis into the vagina.

Coitus interruptus
Withdrawal of the penis prior to ejaculation. (It is considered a poor method of contraception.)

Conception
Implantation of the blastocyst. Not synonymous with fertilization (from *Obstetric Gynecologic Terminology*, American College of Obstetricians and Gynecologists).

Condom
Sheath worn over the male penis.

Continence (abstinence)
Refraining from sexual activity.

Contraception
Conscious use by individuals of medically prescribed and/or nonprescription methods that permit coitus with reduced likelihood of conception (commonly known as birth control).

Copulation
Sexual intercourse.

Couvade
Psychological reaction in which men experience many of the symptoms of pregnancy.

Crude birth rate
(Total number of live births during year/Total population as of July 1 of the same year) x 1000.

Cryptorchidism
Undescended testes.

Diaphragm
Dome-shaped device worn over the cervix and used as a contraceptive.

Douche
Cleansing the vagina with a liquid. Not considered effective as a contraceptive method.

Dysmenorrhea
Painful menstruation.

Ectopic pregnancy
Extra-uterine pregnancy.

Ejaculation
Expulsion of the semen from the penis.

Endometrium
Lining of the uterus.

Epididymis
Convoluted tubule connecting the testis to the vas deferens and located on the testis.

Estrogen
Female sex hormone produced by the ovaries.

Fallopian tubes
Two hollow muscular passages that transport ova from the ovaries to the uterus.

Fertilization
Union of the male sperm cell and the female ovum.

General fertility rate
(Total number of live births during year/Total number of females 15-44 as of July 1 of the same year) x 1000.

Foreskin
Retractable fold of skin found over the head of the glans penis; also termed the prepuce.

Gonads
Testes or ovaries; sex glands.

Gonococcus
Bacterium that causes gonorrhea.

Gonorrhea
Sexually transmitted disease caused
by gonococcus.

Gravid
Pregnant.

Gynecology
Medical science that deals with the
prevention or treatment of disorders
of the female reproductive system.

Hydrocele
Condition in which fluid collects in
the scrotum.

Hymen
Membrane that partially covers the
entrance to the vagina.

Hysterectomy
The operation of excising the uterus,
performed either through the abdominal wall or the vagina. This does not
include the removal of the tubes and
ovaries. Hysterectomy is a medically
accepted method of sterilization.

Infant death rate
(Number of deaths of children under
1 year of age during year / Total number of live births during year) x 1000.

Infertility
Diminished or absent ability to
conceive.

IUD (intrauterine contraceptive device)
Device inserted into the uterus to prevent pregnancy.

Leukorrhea
Excessive vaginal discharge.

Libido
Sexual drive.

Live birth
Birth of a fetus, irrespective of its gestational age which, after complete expulsion or extraction from the mother,
shows evidence of life – that is, heart
beats or respiration.

Maternal death rate
(Maternal deaths during period / Number terminated pregnancies during
period) x 100,000 (from *Obstetric
and Gynecologic Terminology*).

Medical backup for family planning
Outpatient and inpatient services, at an
adjacent hospital or medical facility,
available to take care of medical referrals from a family planning clinic,
as well as emergencies arising from
contraceptive use, which should be
arranged through a binding agreement.
A necessary part of a family planning
program.

*Medical supervision in family
planning programs*
Continuing physician supervision of
medical aspects of the program, including physician surrogates functioning in a family planning program. Necessary for all family planning programs
and clinics.

*Medically high-risk
family planning patient*
Two categories of patient: (1) Those
for whom pregnancy would be particularly undesirable because of guarded
maternal or fetal prognosis; (2) Those
for whom one or more methods of
contraception are associated with
increased risk.

*Medically uncomplicated
family planning patient*
Patient who has no medical problems
requiring referral to other medical facilities for evaluation and/or care, and
who has no medical contraindications
to any type of contraception.

Menarche
First menstrual flow; usually occurs
between 10 and 14 years of age.

Menopause (natural)
Transitional phase in a woman's life
when menstrual function ceases as a
result of declining ovarian function
due to aging of the ovaries. It usually
occurs between 40 and 50 years of
age.

Menorrhagia
Excessive bleeding at the time of
menstrual flow.

Metrorrhagia
Uterine bleeding occurring at irregular
intervals.

Neonatal mortality rate
(Number of deaths of infants under

28 days of age during year/Total number of live births during year) x 1000.

Nulliparous
Never having given birth to a child.

Obstetrician-gynecologist
Physician specializing in the care, treatment and delivery of pregnant women,
and treatment of disorders of the female reproductive system.

Oligomenorrhea
Infrequent menses.

Orgasm
Height of sexual excitement.

Ovaries
Two ovoid structures on each side of
the pelvis just below the distal end of
the fallopian tubes. They measure about
3.5 cm in length, 2 cm in width, and
about 1.5 cm in thickness. The ovaries
are the primary source of female hormones and produce ova.

Ovulation
Expulsion of the female germ cell from
a ruptured graafian follicle in the ovary.

Ovum
Female reproductive germ cell.

Penis
Male copulatory organ.

Perinatal mortality
(Number of still births plus number of
neonatal deaths/Number of stillbirths
plus number of live births) x 1000

(from *Obstetric Gynecologic Terminology*).

Post-neonatal mortality rate
(Number of deaths of children from 28 days to one year/Total number of live births during year) x 1000.

Pregnancy
State of a female after conception and until termination of gestation.

Pregnancy termination
Expulsion or extraction from the mother of the products of conception.

Prostate
Gland in the male which surrounds the neck of the bladder and urethra, and whose secretions are a component of the semen.

Rhythm method
Method of contraception in which the partners refrain from intercourse during the fertile period.

Semen
Thick yellowish-white fluid which normally contains the male reproductive germ cells, and is released at the time of ejaculation.

Seminal vesicles
Two sacculated, glandular structures which are diverticula of the vas deferens. They are located behind the prostate. Their secretion is one of the components of semen.

Sexual intercourse
An encompassing term indicating all forms of sexual relations.

Sperm
Male reproductive germ cells.

Spermicide
Chemical substance that inactivates sperm.

Sterility
Absence of the ability to conceive.

Sterilization
Any surgical, chemical or radiological procedure by which an individual is made incapable of reproduction.

Stillbirth
Death prior to the complete expulsion or extraction from its mother of a product of conception, of 20 weeks gestation or more, or weighing more than 500 grams. The death is indicated by the fact that after such separation, the fetus does not breathe or show any other evidence of life such as beating of the heart, pulsation of the umbilical cord, or definite movement of voluntary muscles.

Stillbirth rate
(Total number of stillbirths during year/Total number of live births and stillbirths during year) x 1000.

Stillbirth ratio
(Total number of stillbirths during year/Total number of live births during year) x 1000.

Syphilis
Sexually transmitted systemic disease that may cripple or kill.

Testes
Male gonads; egg-shaped glands, normally situated in the scrotum, which produce male hormones and sperm.

Testosterone
Male sex hormone produced by the testes.

Tubal sterilization
Any surgical or chemical procedure by which the patency of the fallopian tubes is interrupted.

Urethra
Tubular structure that provides for the overflow of urine from the bladder. In the female, it is situated close to the anterior vaginal wall; and in the male, in the penis.

Uterus
Hollow, muscular, pear-shaped organ located in the pelvis between the bladder and rectum. The cervix forms the lower portion of the uterus.

Vagina
Hollow muscular structure in the female extending from the cervix to the vulva.

Vas deferens
Hollow, muscular tube by which the semen, including the sperm, are transported from the testis to the penis to be ejaculated.

Vasectomy
Surgical procedure by which the patency of each vas deferens is interrupted.

Vulva
External female anatomy which includes the labia majora, labia minora, and clitoris.

X-chromosome
Female sex chromosome.

Y-chromosome
Male sex chromosome.

Annotated bibliography*

Adams, David W. *Therapeutic Abortion: An Annotated Bibliography.* Hamilton:
  McMaster University Medical Centre, 1973.
  Nearly 175 items are annotated in this comprehensive bibliography.

Anderson, T.W. 'Oral Contraceptives and Female Mortality Trends,' *C.M.A.
  Journal* 102 (May 30, 1970), 1156-60.
  Death rates for Ontario females aged 15-44 were compared for 1959-61 and
  1966-68 to see if any changes were related to the use of oral contraceptives.

Andison, A.W. 'Conception Control,' *Manitoba Medical Review* (February
  1967), 96-99.
  A plea that every child should be a wanted child.

Bacon, Hugh M. 'Psychiatric Aspects of Therapeutic Abortion,' *Canada's Mental
  Health* 17 (January-February 1969), 18-21.
  A report of nine women who had a therapeutic abortion between 1959-66.

Barrett, Michael, and Malcolm Fitz-Earle. 'Student Opinion on Legalized Abortion at the University of Toronto,' *Canadian Journal of Public Health* 64
  (May-June 1973), 294-99.
  The results of a survey questionnaire on legalizing abortion, mailed in 1968
  and 1971 to a representative sample of students at the University of Toronto
  are discussed.

*Canadian Journals to November 1973

Bishop, Mary F. *From Left to Right: A Brief Sketch of the Philosophy and Development of the Birth Control Movement and Its Continuing Role.* Vancouver: Family Planning Association of British Columbia, 1973. A short overview of the development of family planning in Canada.

Boyce, R.M., and R.W. Osborn. 'Therapeutic Abortions in a Canadian City,' *C.M.A. Journal* 103 (September 12, 1970), 461-66. An examination of 119 therapeutic abortions performed during 1962-68 in a Canadian city of 200,000 population.

Brown, George F. *Population Policy and National Development.* Ottawa: International Development Research Centre, 1972. A plea for a broad approach to population problems.

Canadian Association of Schools of Social Work. *Human Sexuality and Fertility Services: Social Policy and Social Work Education.* Ottawa, 1973. The proceedings of a symposium held in Hamilton, Ontario, October 1972. The topics under discussion include sexual counselling, family planning, contraception, fertility services, and education for social workers in this area.

Canadian Broadcasting Corporation. *The Attitudes of Canadians to Certain Aspects of Population Growth.* Ottawa: Research Department, January 1971. The results of 1093 interviews (English and French) related to growth of population, goals of population growth, and government policies of population control.

- *Public Opinion in Canada on Certain Aspects of the Law Relating to Abortion: A Fact Finding Survey.* Ottawa: Research Department, January 1971. 3450 questionnaires (2030 English, 1420 French), were returned to the CBC. The main findings are reported in this report.

Claman, David A., Barry J. Williams, and L. Wogan. 'Reaction of Unmarried Girls to Pregnancy,' *C.M.A. Journal* 101 (September 20, 1969), 328-34. A study of 316 unmarried pregnant girls, most of whom were under the age of 20, in a Vancouver clinic.

Claman, David A., John R. Wakeford, John M.M. Turner, and Brian Hayden. 'Impact on Hospital Practice of Liberalizing Abortion and Female Sterilizations,' *C.M.A. Journal* 105 (July 10, 1971), 35-41. The effect of therapeutic abortions at the Vancouver General Hospital. The first 500 cases (1965 to July 1970) were analyzed by computer.

Daley, Timothy T. 'The Rights of the Unborn: A CAS Looks at Abortion,'
Canadian Welfare 47 (May–June 1972), 19-21.
A Children's Aid Society examines the issues of abortion as they relate to its
services.

Dodds, Donald J. 'Vasectomy: Performing the Operation and Counselling Your
Anxious Patient,' *Canadian Family Physician* 17 (December 1971), 39-41, 89.
Advice on how to counsel men who request vasectomies.

Doyle, Raymond. 'Family Planning is for Somebody Else,' *Canadian Welfare* 47
(January–February 1972), 12-13, 18.
Some thoughts about family planning and motivation of individuals related
to the topic.

Dwyer, J.J. 'Summary of a Brief to a Board on Abortion Policy,' *Ontario
Association of Children's Aid Societies News* (November 1972), 5-8.
A summary of a 34-page brief on abortion submitted to the Ottawa Children's
Aid Society.

Elahi, V.K. *A Family Planning Survey of Halifax.* Halifax: Department of
Preventive Medicine, Dalhousie University, 1973.
A study of 300 married female heads of households from three soci-economic
groups in Halifax. Family planning knowledge, attitudes, and practices were
examined among these groups.

Fortier, Lise. 'Needed: A Change in Attitudes Towards Elective Sterilization,'
The Canadian Nurse 69 (January 1973), 21-23.
A discussion of sterilization for women.

Garrett, Nancy. *Nurse Education for Family Planning.* Ottawa: Canadian
National Conference on Family Planning, 1972. Paper available from Depart-
ment of National Health and Welfare, Family Planning Division.
A discussion of including this material in courses for nurses.

Gillen, Mollie. 'Your Replies to the Abortion Quiz,' *Chatelaine,* March 1971, 23-26.
A report of a questionnaire filled out by 6000 Canadian women (English and
French). The verdict: overwhelmingly for abortion on demand.

Gendron, Lionel. *Contraception.* Montreal: Harvest House, 1971. The facts about
contraception treated in a good-humoured way. Illustrated.

Gravenor, Colin A. 'Birth Control for Teen-Agers: Is It Legal?' *Canadian Doctor* (October 1972), 103-4.
A lawyer discusses some legal problems related to birth control for adolescents in Canada.

Graver, H. 'A Study of Contraception as Related to Unwanted Pregnancy,' *C.M.A. Journal* 107 (October 21, 1972), 739-40.
A study of 150 women requesting therapeutic abortions in Montreal.

Grindstaff, Carl F., and G. Edward Banks. 'Male Sterilization as a Contraceptive Method in Canada: An Empirical Study,' *Population Studies* (Fall 1973, in press).
A study of 500 men in London, Ontario, who had vasectomies.

Hackett, John D., and Diana Barza. 'The Clinical Management of the Unwed Mother,' *Laval Medical* 12 (January 1971), 83-90.
A study of unmarried mothers at St. Mary's hospital in Montreal.

Hardin, Garrett. 'Population: The Solution is in Our Minds,' *Ontario Naturalist* 13 (March 1973), 10-18.
A wide-ranging discussion of population and birth control. Birth control is not population control.

Health and Welfare Canada. *First National Conference on Family Planning. Ottawa: February 28–March 2, 1972.* Ottawa, 1972.
The proceedings of this conference are included in this document.

International Development Research Centre. 'Population and Health Sciences,' *I.D.R.C. Reports* 1, no. 4 (December 1972).
A discussion of the aims and objectives of the population and Health Science Unit of the Centre.

Kerr, M.G. 'Current Birth Control Methods,' *Canadian Family Physician* 17 (September 1971), 37-41.
This article covers details of contraceptive methods and their use.

Knapp, Robert D. 'Abortion, a Threat to the Medical Profession,' *Canadian Family Physician* 17 (September 1971), 51-53.
How abortions are a threat to doctors.

Landsberg, Michelle. 'Our Shocking Failure in Birth Control,' *Chatelaine* (November 1972), 58 and 106-8.
Why some Canadian women do not use proper birth control.

Le Bourdais, Isabel, and Vivian MacDonald. 'Abortion: Two Views,' *Chatelaine* 46 (November 1973), 38, 105-7.
Two writers discuss the positive and negative sides of abortion in Canada.

Livingstone, E.S. 'Vasectomy: A Review of 3200 Operations,' *C.M.A. Journal* 105 (November 20, 1971), 1065.
A report of 3200 vasectomies performed over 11 years.

London Board of Education. *Family Planning: A Curriculum.* London, Ontario: London Free Press, 1972. (PO Box 2280, London, Ontario, $2.00).

MacKenzie, C.J.G. *Teaching Population Dynamics, Conception Control, Human Sexuality and Related Subjects in Canadian Medical Schools.* Ottawa, Canadian National Conference on Family Planning, 1972. Available from Department of National Health and Welfare, Family Planning Division.
A suggestion for inclusion of more content related to family planning in the medical schools in Canada.

MacKenzie, C.J.G., G.P. Evans, and J.G. Peck. 'The Vancouver Family Planning Clinic: A Cost Study,' *Canadian Journal of Public Health* 58 (February 1967), 53-60.
A review of 15 months' experience in a family planning clinic in Vancouver.

MacKenzie, C.J.G. 'The Vancouver Family Planning Clinic: A Comparison of Two Years' Experience,' *Canadian Journal of Public Health* 59 (July 1968), 257-65.
A comparison of the use of a clinic for a two-year period.

MacKenzie, Paul, and Linda Dawes. 'Physicians and Family Planning,' *Medical Aspects of Human Sexuality* (Canadian edition) 3 (July 1973), 16-22.
A survey of 143 private doctors in eastern Ontario regarding the provision of family planning services.

Marko, John. 'The Investigation of Infertility,' *Canadian Family Physician* 16 (April 1970), 54-57.
A description of the necessary tests for investigating fertility.

Milton, Isabel C. 'Contraceptive Practices Past and Present,' *The Canadian Nurse* 63 (October 1967), 1-3.
A historical overview of contraceptive practices.

Milton, D.M., and S.C. Macleod. 'Recent Advances in the Management of Infertility in Women,' *Canadian Family Physician* 16 (September 1970), 51-56. Reviews the procedures on how to deal with women and their husbands in cases of infertility.

Mountain, Eileen. *Teaching Family Planning in Canadian Schools of Nursing.* Ottawa, Canadian National Conference on Family Planning, 1972. Available from Department of National Health and Welfare, Family Planning Division. A discussion of the present status of teaching family planning in Canadian Schools of Nursing.

Mulvaney, J. Neil. 'Voluntary Sterilization: A Lawyer's Perspective,' *Medical Aspects of Human Sexuality* 2 (March 1972), 37-40.
A lawyer examines the legal implications of voluntary sterilizations in Canada.

Page, H.G. 'Changes in the Fertility Pattern in Quebec,' *Canadian Journal of Public Health* 58 (May 1967), 197-203.
A discussion of the decline in fertility in the province of Quebec.

Palko, M.E., R.H. Lennox, and C.R. McQuarrie. 'Current Status of Family Planning in Canada,' *Canadian Journal of Public Health* 62 (November-December 1971), 509-19.
A review of family planning activities in Canada up to 1971.

Patriarche, Elizabeth M. 'The Victoria Family Life Education Program,' *Canadian Family Physician* 18 (September 1972), 72-75.
A description of a family life education program in Victoria, British Columbia.

Ptolemy, Connie Gray. 'Family Planning Interpretation: The Nurse's Role,' *Canadian Journal of Public Health* 60 (October 1969), 402-8.
A discussion of the nurse's role in family planning.

Review of Abortion Legislation and Experience in Selected Countries, 1970. Ottawa: Research and Statistics Directorate, Department of National Health and Welfare, 1971.
19 countries are reviewed. An extensive bibliography is included in this paper.

Rogers, Joan M., and David W. Adams. 'Therapeutic Abortion: A Multidisciplined Approach to Patient Care from a Social Work Perspective,' *Canadian Journal of Public Health* 64 (May–June 1973), 254-59.
A description of the inclusion of a social worker as a fulltime member of the patient-care team related to therapeutic abortion.

Rozovsky, Lorne Elkin. 'Legal Abortions in Canada,' *Canadian Hospital* 48 (February 1971), 39-41.
A discussion of legal abortions.

Schlesinger, Benjamin. 'Social Work Education and Family Planning,' *The Social Worker* 41 (Summer 1973), 93-99.
A review of a course on family planning offered at the Faculty of Social Work, University of Toronto.

Skuy, P. 'It All Began in Egypt with an Rx Dated 1850 BC,' *Drug Merchandising* (January 1970), 1-3.
A concise history of contraception.

Smith, Stuart L. 'Canadian Doctors: Victims of the Abortion Laws,' *Canadian Family Physician* 16 (October 1970), 58-61.
The author examines the moral dilemma facing doctors regarding abortions.

Szasz, George. 'Sex Education of the Family Physician,' *Canadian Family Physician* 18 (March 1972), 48-50.
The importance of sex education for the doctor.

Todd, Iain A.D. 'Vasectomy,' *The Canadian Nurse* 67 (August 1971), 20-23.
An overview of vasectomy and its psychological effects.

Toronto Board of Education. *Human Sexuality: Family Planning, Birth Control, Abortion.* Toronto, 1972.
Resource guide for Health Education courses in high school.

Tyson, J.E.A., and H.H. Washburn. 'Canadian County-sponsored Family Planning: A Second Survey,' *Obstetrics and Gynecology* 35 (March 1970), 377-80.
A study of patients attending a county family planning clinic in Norfolk-Haldimand County in Ontario.

United Community Services of the Greater Vancouver Area. *Babies By Choice*

Not By Chance. Vol. I, *Contraceptive Practices,* Vancouver, 1972. Vol. II, *Outreach Services,* Vancouver, 1973.
An evaluation of outreach family planning services.

Waisglass, Barry R. 'The Sexual Behaviour of "Street People" in Ottawa: A Report of a Survey Conducted in the Summer of 1971,' *University of Ottawa Medical Journal,* 2-9.
Eighty-four males and females were interviewed about their attitudes towards various sexual experiences, including contraception.

Wilson, Edward. 'The Organization and Function of Therapeutic Abortion Committees,' *Canadian Hospital* 48 (December 1971), 38-40.
How abortion committees should function in Canadian hospitals.

Wilson, R., G.W.O. Moss, E.G. Laugharene, and E.M. Read. 'Family Planning in a Co-ordinated Hospital and Community Health Setting,' *Canadian Journal of Public Health* 58 (December 1967), 527-34.
A description of a family planning setting in Toronto, Ontario.

Wolfish, Martin G. 'A Clinic for the Ambulatory Adolescent,' *Clinical Pediatrics* 12 (January 1973), 13-17.
A description of an adolescent clinic, which would include family planning services.

– 'Adolescent Sexuality,' *The Practitioner* 210 (February 1973), 226-31.
A discussion of the work of the adolescent clinic at the Toronto Sick Children's Hospital and sexuality counselling.

World Health Organization Publications.
Spontaneous and Induced Abortion. Technical Series #461, 1970. 51 pp.
Abortion: World Health Statistics Report, 1969, 22, no. 1. 80 pp.
Abortion Laws: A Survey of Current World Legislation, 1970. 78 pp.
Health Aspects of Family Planning. Technical Report Series #442, 1970. 50 pp.

Yuzpe, Albert A., H.H. Allen, and J.A. Collins. 'Total Sterilization: Methodology, Post-Operative Management and Follow-up of 2,934 Cases,' *C.M.A. Journal* 107 (July 22, 1972), 115-17.
A discussion of total sterilization performed during a two-year period in London, Ontario.

BENJAMIN SCHLESINGER

A paperbound book library

on family planning

The following 75 titles, which have been selected up to September 1973, make up a good basic library on the broad area of family planning.

American Friends Service Committee. *Who Shall Live?* New York: Hill and Wang, 1970.

Burt, John J. and Linda A. Brower. *Education for Sexuality: Concepts and Programs for Training.* Toronto: W.B. Saunders, 1970.

Callahan, Daniel, ed. *The Catholic Case for Contraception.* Toronto: Collier-Macmillan, 1969.

Canada. Department of National Health and Welfare. Family Planning Division. *Papers of the National Conference on Family Planning,* 1972.

- *Family Planning Resource Guide,* 1972.

Canada. Department of Health and Welfare. *Rx Bulletin: Oral Contraceptives.* Ottawa, I (December 1970), no. 10.

Canadian Women's Educational Press. *Women Unite.* Toronto, 1972, pp. 109-25.

Carmen, Arlene, and Howard Moody. *Abortion Counseling and Social Change.* Valley Forge, Pa.: Judson Press, 1973.

Chamberlain, Neil W. *Beyond Malthus: Population and Power.* Englewood Cliffs, NJ: Prentice Hall, 1972.

Chasteen, Edgar R. *The Case for Compulsory Birth Control.* Englewood Cliffs, NJ: Prentice Hall, 1971.

Cherniak, Donna, and Allan Feingold. *Birth Control Handbook.* Montreal: McGill University Student Society, 1970.

Commission on Population Growth. *Population and the American Future.*
New York: Signet, 1972.

Consumers Union of the United States. *Consumers Union Report on Family
Planning.* Mt Vernon, New York: Consumers Union, 1962.

Cooke, Robert E., ed. *The Terrible Choice: The Abortion Dilemma.* New York:
Bantam Books, 1968.

Dodds, D.J. *Voluntary Male Sterilization.* Toronto: The Damian Press, 1970.

Draper, Elizabeth. *Birth Control in the Modern World.* London: Penguin Books,
1965.

Ehrlich, Paul. *The Population Bomb.* New York: Ballentine Books, 1968.

Feldman, David M. *Birth Control in Jewish Law.* New York: New York University Press, 1968.

Gendron, Lionel. *Contraception.* Montreal: Harvest House, 1971.

Gillette, Paul J. *Vasectomy: The Male Sterilization Operation.* New York:
Paperback, 1972.

Gorman, Joanna F., ed. *The Social Worker and Family Planning.* Washington,
DC: US Department of Health, Education, and Welfare, Public Health Service,
1970.

Grindstaff, Carl F., C. Boydell, and Paul Whitehead, eds. *Population Issues in
Canada.* Toronto: Holt, Rinehart and Winston, 1971.

Group for the Advancement of Psychiatry. *The Right to Abortion: A Psychiatric
View.* New York: 1969.

Guttmacher, Alan. *Birth Control and Love.* New York: Bantam, 1970.

Haselkorn, Florence, ed. *Family Planning: Readings and Case Materials.* New
York: Council on Social Work Education, 1971.

– *Family Planning: The Role of Social Work.* New York: Adelphi University,
1968.

Hauser, Philip M., ed. *The Population Dilemma.* Englewood Cliffs, NJ: Prentice-
Hall, 1963.

Hawthorn, Geoffrey. *The Sociology of Fertility.* London: Macmillan, 1970.

Heer, David M. *Society and Population.* Englewood Cliffs, NJ: Prentice-Hall, 1968.

Henripin, Jacques. *Trends and Factors of Fertility in Canada.* Ottawa: Statistics
Canada, 1972.

Himes, Norman E. *Medical History of Contraception.* New York: Schocken,
1970.

Hubbard, Charles William. *Family Planning Education: Parenthood and Social
Disease Control.* Saint Louis: C.V. Mosby, 1973.

Journal of Marriage and the Family. 'Special Issue: Sexism in Family Studies'
33 (August 1971), Part I, and Part II (November 1971).

Journal of Marriage and the Family. 'Special Issue: Family Planning and Fertility Control' 30 (May 1968).

Journal of Marriage and Family Living. 'Special Issue: Family Planning in Modernizing Societies' 25 (February 1963).

Journal of Medical Education. 'Special Issue: Family Planning and Medical Education' 44 (November 1969).

Journal of Social Issues. 'Special Issue: Family Planning in Cross-National Perspective' 23 (October 1967).

Joyce, Robert E., and Mary Joyce. *Let Us Be Born: The Inhumanity of Abortion.* Chicago: Franciscan Herald Press, 1970.

Kalback, Warren E., and Wayne W. McVey. *The Demographic Bases of Canadian Society.* Toronto: McGraw-Hill-Ryerson, 1971.

Katchadourian, Herant A., and Donald T. Lunde. *Fundamentals of Human Sexuality.* Toronto: Holt, Rinehart and Winston, 1972.

Kendall, Katherine A., ed. *Population Dynamics and Family Planning.* New York: Council on Social Work Education, 1971.

Kennedy, David M. *Birth Control in America: The Concern of Margaret Sanger.* New Haven: Yale University Press, 1970.

Keyl, Anna. *VD: The People to People Diseases.* Toronto: Anansi, 1973.

Kleinman, R.L., ed. *Medical Handbook.* London: International Planned Parenthood Federation, 1968.

Lader, Lawrence. *Abortion.* Boston: Beacon Press, 1966.

Laing, W.A. *The Costs and Benefits of Family Planning.* London: PEP Broadsheet #534, February 1972.

Lawrence, Marcie, ed. *Prevention of Pregnancy in Adolescents.* New York: Planned Parenthood of New York, 1970.

McCalister, Donald V., Victor Thiessen, and Margaret McDermott, eds. *Readings in Family Planning.* Saint Louis: C.V. Mosby, 1973.

Mace, David R. *Abortion: The Agonizing Decision.* New York: Abingdon Press, 1972.

Manisoff, Miriam T. *Family Planning Training for Social Service.* New York: Planned Parenthood – World Population, 1970.

Meadows, Donella, Dennis Meadows, Jorgan Randers, and William H. Behrens III. *The Limits of Growth.* New York: Signet Books, 1972.

Medawar, Jean, and David Pyke. *Family Planning.* London: Penguin Books, 1971.

Marsden, Lorna. *Population Probe: Canada.* Toronto: Copp Clark, 1972.

Morgan, Robin. *Sisterhood is Powerful.* New York: Vintage Books, 1970.

Neubardt, Selig. *Contraception.* Toronto: Pocket Books, 1968.

Newman, Sidney H., et al., eds. *Abortion, Obtained and Denied: Research Approaches.* New York: The Population Council, 1971.

Noonan, John T. *Contraception (Views of the Catholic Church).* Toronto: Mentor Books, 1967.

Orthopharmaceutical Corporation. *Understanding Conception and Contraception.* Raritan, NJ, 1967.

Paupst, James C. *The Pill: A True Perspective.* Toronto: Clarke Irwin, 1972.

Pelrine, Eleanor Wright. *Abortion in Canada.* Toronto: New Press, 1971.

Peterson, William, ed. *Readings in Population.* New York: Macmillan, 1972.

Pickering, N., and E. Johnston. *Like It Is.* Kingston, Ontario, Box 1511, 1971.

Pierson, Elaine. *Sex is Never an Emergency.* New York: Lippincott, 1971.

Planned Parenthood, Ottawa. *Family Planning.* Ottawa, 1971.

Pollak, Otto, and Alfred S. Friedman, eds. *Family Dynamics and Female Sexual Delinquency.* Palo Alto, Calif.: Science and Behavior Books, 1969.

Rainwater, Lee. *And the Poor Get Children.* Chicago: Quadrangle Books, 1960.

- *Family Design: Marital Sexuality, Family Size and Contraception.* Chicago: Aldine, 1964.

Ransil, Bernard J. *Abortion.* (Catholic Viewpoint.) Toronto: Paulist Press, 1969.

Regier, Henry, and J. Bruce Falls. *Exploding Humanity: The Crisis of Numbers.* Toronto: Anansi Press, 1969.

Schur, Edwin M., ed. *The Family and the Sexual Revolution.* Bloomington, Ind.: University of Indiana Press, 1964.

Varela, Alice M., ed. *Family Planning.* New Brunswick, NJ: Rutgers, The Graduate School of Social Work, 1968.

Westoff, Leslie Aldridge, and Charles F. Westoff. *From Now to Zero: Fertility, Contraception and Abortion in America.* Boston: Little Brown, 1971.

Wrong, Dennis H. *Population.* New York: Random House, 1956.

Yale University Committee on Human Sexuality. *The Student Guide to Sex on Campus.* New York: Signet, 1970.

Young, Louise B., ed. *Population in Perspective.* Toronto: Oxford University Press, 1968.

Other sources

Many films on family planning, birth control, sexuality, and sex education are now available from various sources in Canada.

THE NATIONAL FILM BOARD distributes through its regional offices both French and English versions of *Methods of Family Planning, Purposes of Family Planning,* and *About Conception and Contraception.* There is no charge for the films, but the borrower must pay return postage. A few films on sex education are also available from the National Film Board.

THE CANADIAN FILM INSTITUTE (1762 Carling Avenue, Ottawa) has prints of all the films which until now have been available from the Family Planning Division, as well as other films on sexuality and related subjects. Rental charges vary from $5.50, for a short (1–11 minute) film, to $12.00 for films 60 minutes or over in length.

MOST PROVINCIAL DEPARTMENTS OF HEALTH AND WELFARE have been provided with prints of several films by the Family Planning Division for distribution within the province. In most cases, loan arrangements can be made through provincial directors of health education.

MANY LOCAL FAMILY PLANNING ASSOCIATIONS have also been provided with single prints of *About Conception and Contraception.*

MORELAND-LATCHFORD PRODUCTIONS (299 Queen St. W., Toronto), whose Family Living and Sex Education series is well known, have prepared three series of sound filmstrips from the original films. Two of the series consist of five films and five cassettes and retail for $65.00. The other has six filmstrips and cassettes and sells for $75.00.

Purposes of Family Planning The realities of everyday living in a variety of life-styles are presented in a series of dramatic sequences to demonstrate the essential social, economic, health and emotional factors involved in the consideration of family planning by different kinds of people for their own individual purposes (14 minutes). Colour.

Methods of Family Planning People of various ages, nationalities, and economic levels visit family planning clinics and doctors to learn about the eight effective methods of family planning. Prefaced by straightforward explanation of human reproduction, this film combines comprehensive animation with live action to present vital information with taste and sensitivity (18 minutes). Colour.

CITY FILMS (40 University Avenue, Suite 206, Toronto) are soon to take over distribution of films previously available from the Family Planning Division and the Family Planning Federation of Canada. About 35 different titles are included in this group. Rental charge to family planning associations or their designated agents is $5.50. Service agencies or other groups should ask to be named as an agent of the local family planning association or of the Family Planning Federation of Canada in order to take advantage of this special rate.

ASSOCIATION FILMS (333 Adelaide St. W., Toronto), distributes a new film on student attitudes towards birth control entitled *It Couldn't Happen To Me,* which was produced by Dr E. Herold at the University of Guelph. Rental charge is $25.00 weekly. *Sexuality and Communication,* the well-known Chernick film, is also available from this company at a cost of $15.00 per booking.

MATERIALS FOR FAMILY PLANNING EDUCATION

TEACHING MATERIALS*

Understanding (Abridged). This book contains excellent illustrations and detailed information on the female reproductive system, including the menstrual cycle, conception, pregnancy, and methods of conception control ($2.15 each copy).

ORTHO Pelvic Model. Made of clear pastic, with coloured sections. This model gives both a full view and a cross section of the uterus and adjacent structures – an excellent teaching aid for both professional and lay groups ($7.95 each).

ORTHO Family Planning Teaching Kit. A complete assembly of contraceptive information which includes, in addition to relevant literature, an oral contra-

*Available from Department E, Ortho Pharmaceutical (Canada) Ltd., 19 Green Belt Drive, Don Mills, Ontario.

ceptive dispenser, condom, intrauterine device, diaphragm, and jelly, contraceptive foam, etc. – a must for anyone involved in family planning education ($4.95 each).

GYNNY Pelvic Teaching Model. With the aid of this new medical teaching model and its 16 interchangeable structures, the instructor is able to describe fully the techniques of pelvic examination, clinical problems, family planning methodology, and nursing procedures ($280.00 each).

BIBLIOGRAPHIES

Book List 1972. The Family Planning Association, Margaret Pyke House, 27-35 Mortimer Street, London W1A 4QW, England.

Family Planning Resource Guide. Family Planning Division, Department of National Health and Welfare, General Purpose Building, Tunney's Pasture, Ottawa, Ontario K1A 1B5.

Glassen, Paul H., Helen J. Hunter, and Henry J. Moyer. *Social Work Education for Family and Population Planning: Topical Outlines and Annotated References.* Ann Arbor: Social Work Education and Population Project, University of Michigan, 1973.

Guide to Information Sources in the Fields of Population, Family Planning. Katherine Dexter, McCormack Library, Planned Parenthood World Population, 810 Seventh Avenue, New York, NY 10019.

Human Sexuality: A Book List for Professionals. Sex Information and Education Council of the US Inc., 1855 Broadway, New York, NY 10023.

Planned Parenthood Publications. Planned Parenthood – World Population, 810 Seventh Avenue, New York, NY 10019.

Population and Family Planning: Analytical Abstracts for Social Work Educators and Related Disciplines, by Katherine Brownell Oettinger and Jeffrey D. Stansbury, International Association of Schools of Social Work, 345 East 46th Street, New York, NY 10017.

Selected References for Social Workers on Family Planning: An Annotated List. Compiled by Mary E. Watts, Public Health Service, Maternal and Child Health Service, US Department of Health, Education, and Welfare, Rockville, Maryland 20852.

MAJOR CANADIAN ORGANIZATIONS
RELATED TO ASPECTS OF FAMILY PLANNING

Alliance for Life. 17 Queen Street East, Suite 235, Toronto, Ontario M5C 1P9
Birthright. 600 Coxwell Avenue, Toronto, Ontario M4C 3C1

Canadian Women's Coalition to Repeal the Abortion Laws. PO Box 5673,
    Station A, Toronto, Ontario
Family Planning Federation of Canada. 96 Eglinton Avenue East, Suite 204,
    Toronto, Ontario M4P 1C9
Family Planning, Health, and Welfare, Canada. General Purpose Building,
    Tunney's Pasture, Ottawa, Ontario K1A 1B5
Right to Life. 12 Richmond Street East, Suite 611, Toronto, Ontario M5C 1N1
Serena. 55 Parkdale Avenue, Ottawa, Ontario K1Y 1ES
International Development Research Centre. PO Box 8500, Ottawa, Ontario
    K1G 3H9

CANADIAN PERIODICALS CONTAINING
FAMILY PLANNING ARTICLES

Canadian Doctor. National Business Publications, Gardenvale 800, Quebec
Canadian Family Physician. College of Family Physicians of Canada, 1941
    Leslie Street, Don Mills, Ontario 405
Canadian Hospital. Canadian Hospital Association, 25 Imperial Street, Toronto,
    Ontario
Canadian Journal of Public Health. Canadian Public Health Association, 1255
    Yonge Street, Toronto, Ontario
Canadian Medical Association Journal. CMA House, Box 8650, Ottawa,
    Ontario, K1G 0G8
Canadian Nurse. Canadian Nurse Association, 50 The Driveway, Ottawa,
    Ontario K2P 1E2
Canadian Psychiatric Journal. Canadian Psychiatric Association, Suite 203,
    Lisgar Street, Ottawa, Ontario K2P 0C6
Canadian Welfare. Canadian Council on Social Development, 55 Parkdale
    Avenue, Ottawa, Ontario K1Y 1E5
Medical Aspects of Human Sexuality. Jay Kay Publications, 1 Heath Street
    West, Toronto, Ontario
The Social Worker. Canadian Association of Social Workers, 55 Parkdale
    Avenue, Ottawa, Ontario K1Y 1E5
ZPG Newsletter. Toronto Zero Population Growth, Department of Zoology,
    University of Toronto, 25 Harbord Street, Toronto, Ontario M5S 1A1

PERIODICALS OUTSIDE CANADA
CONTAINING FAMILY PLANNING ARTICLES

American Journal of Public Health. American Public Health Association, 1015
Eighteenth Street NW, Washington, DC 20036

ASA Reports. Association for the Study of Abortion, 120 W. 57th Street, New
York, NY 10019

Association for Voluntary Sterilization. 14 W. 40th Street, New York, NY
10018: Newsletter, reprints, pamphlets

Bulletin. Association for Voluntary Sterilization, Inc., 14 W. 40th Street,
New York, NY 10018

Demography. Population Association of America, 1126 East 59th Street,
University of Chicago, Chicago, Ill. 60637

Eugenics Quarterly. American Eugenics Society, Inc., 230 Park Avenue, New
York, NY 10017

The Family Coordinator. National Council on Family Relations, 1219 University
Avenue SW, Minneapolis, Minnesota, 55414

Family Planning Digest. National Center for Family Services, Department of
Health, Education, and Welfare, 5600 Fishers Lane, Room 12A-33, Rockville,
Maryland 20852

Family Planning Perspectives. Planned Parenthood Federation of America,
515 Madison Avenue, New York, NY 10022

Health Services Report. US Department of Health, Education, and Welfare,
Health Services and Mental Health Administration, Room 4A-5A, Parklawn
Bldg., 5600 Fishers Lane, Rockville, Maryland 20852

The Family Planner. Syntex Laboratories, Inc., 3401 Hillview Avenue, Palo Alto,
California 94304

Family Planning News: Worldwide Notes on Family Planning. Pathfinder Fund,
1575 Tremont Street, Boston, Mass. 02120

International Planned Parenthood News. International Planned Parenthood
Federation, 64 Sloane Street, London SW 1, England

Journal of Marriage and the Family. National Council on Family Relations,
1219 University Avenue SE, Minneapolis, Minnesota, 55414

The Milbank Memorial Fund Quarterly. Milbank Memorial Fund, 40 Wall Street,
New York, NY 10005

Perspectives. Center for Family Planning Program Development, Technical
Assistance Division of Planned Parenthood - World Population, 545 Madison
Avenue, New York, NY 10022

Planned Parenthood News. Planned Parenthood - World Population, 810 Seventh
Avenue, New York, NY 10019

Population Bulletin. Population Reference Bureau, Inc., 1755 Massachusetts
  Avenue NW, Washington, DC 20036
Population Profile. Population Reference Bureau, 1755 Massachusetts Avenue
  NW, Washington, DC 20036
Population Studies: A Journal of Demography. Population Investigation
  Committee, London School of Economics, Houghton Street, Aldwych,
  London, WC 2, England
Publications. American Social Health Association, 1790 Broadway, New York,
  NY
Research in Reproduction. International Planned Parenthood Federation, 18-20
  Lower Regent Street, London, SW 1, England
Siecus Newsletter. Sex Information and Education Council of the US, 1790
  Broadway, New York, NY 10019
Studies in Family Planning and *Current Publications in Population and Family
  Planning.* Population Council, 245 Park Avenue, New York, NY 10017

Contributors

Cenovia Addy, Social Services Consultant, Family Planning Division, Department of National Health and Welfare

Cheryl Argue (Mrs. MacLeod), Social Worker, Metropolitan Toronto Children's Aid Society

Michael J. Ball, Director, University Health Service and Assistant Clinical Professor, Department of Community Medicine, University of Alberta

Kathleen Belanger, Research Associate, Family Service Centres of Greater Vancouver

Mary F. Bishop, President, Family Planning Association of British Columbia

Eleanor I. Bradley, Assistant Professor, Department of Health Care and Epidemiology, Faculty of Medicine, University of British Columbia

Elaine Dawson, Former Director of Educational Services, Ortho/Pharmaceutical (Canada) Ltd.

Edward G. Ebanks, Associate Professor, Department of Sociology, University of Western Ontario

Lise Fortier, Associate Professor, Department of Obstetrics and Gynaecology, Université de Montréal

Nancy Garrett, Research Officer, Canadian Nurses Association

Ian Gentles, Assistant Professor of History, Glendon College, York University

Esther Greenglass, Associate Professor, Department of Psychology, York University

Carl F. Grindstaff, Assistant Professor, Department of Sociology, University of Western Ontario

Doris E. Guyatt, Research Officer, Ministry of Community and Social Services, Province of Ontario

W.J. Hannah, Associate Professor, Department of Obstetrics and Gynaecology, University of Toronto

Elmar J. Kramer, Associate Professor of Philosophy, St Michael's College, University of Toronto

C.J.G. MacKenzie, Department of Health Care and Epidemiology, Faculty of Medicine, University of British Columbia

C. Gwendolin Landolt, Lawyer, Toronto

Lorna R. Marsden, Visiting Assistant Professor, Department of Sociology, University of Toronto

Heather S. Morris, Gynaecologist, Women's College Hospital, Toronto

Marion Powell, Head, Population Unit, School of Hygiene, University of Toronto

Benjamin Schlesinger, Professor, Faculty of Social Work, University of Toronto

Cope W. Schwenger, Professor of Community Health, School of Hygiene, University of Toronto

Louise Summerhill, Founder, Birthright (Canada)

Constance Swinton, Assistant Professor, School of Hygiene, University of Toronto

Virginia Thompson, Social Worker

Susan Watt, Director of Social Work, Etobicoke General Hospital

Margaret Whitridge, Health Studies Officer, Epidemiology Services, Health Protection Branch, Department of National Health and Welfare, Ottawa

Martin G. Wolfish, Chief, Division of Adolescent Medicine, Hospital for Sick Children, Toronto

Acknowledgments

The author wishes to thank the following authors and publishers for permission to reprint their material.

Cenovia Addy, The Federal Family Planning Program: Some Implications for Social Work.

Cheryl Argue, and Benjamin Schlesinger, 'Family Planning and Social Work Practice,' *Australian Social Work* 7 (August 1972), 27-35.

Association for Contraceptive Counselling and Related Areas, 'Background and Structure of ACCRA,' 1973.

Michael J. Ball, 'Obstacles to Progress in Family Planning,' *Canadian Medical Association Journal* 106 (February 5, 1972), 227-31.

Kathleen Belanger, and Eleanor J. Bradley, '"Family" Planning and the Single University Student,' *The Social Worker* 38 (February 1970), 18-23.

Mary F. Bishop, 'Voluntarism in Family Planning in Canada,' a paper delivered at the First National Conference on Family Planning, Ottawa, March 2, 1972.

CBS Educational Division, 'Chart on Summary of Contraceptive Methods,' 1973.

Department of National Health and Welfare, Family Planning Division, 'Recommendations of the First National Conference on Family Planning,' and 'First National Conference on Family Planning: A Summary,' Ottawa, 1973.

Elaine Dawson, 'Conception Control in Family Planning,' *Canadian Nurse* 63 (December 1967), 3-7.

G. Edward Ebanks, and Carl F. Grindstaff, 'Vasectomy: Canada's Newest Method of Family Planning,' *Canada's Mental Health* 21 (September 1973).

Lise Fortier, 'The Role of Doctors in Family Planning in Canada,' a paper presented at the First National Conference on Family Planning, March 1972.

Nancy Garrett, 'Choosing Contraceptives According to Need,' *Canadian Nurse* 68 (September 1972), 37-41.

'A Glossary of Family Planning Terminology,' *Family Planning Digest,* 2, 1973, 8-12.

Esther Greenglass, 'Attitudes Toward Abortion,' unpublished paper, 1972.

Doris E. Guyatt, 'Family Planning and the Adolescent Girl,' unpublished paper, 1973.

W.J. Hannah, 'The Family Doctor's Role in Preventing Unwanted Pregnancies,' *Canadian Family Physician* 18 (August 1972), 70-72.

Information Canada, *Report of the Royal Commission on the Status of Women in Canada,* 'Responsible Parenthood,' 1970, pp. 275-88, and *Brief from the Family Planning Federation of Canada to the Senate Committee on Poverty: Poverty and Family Planning,* 1971.

Medical Aspects of Human Sexuality, 'Is Family Planning in Rural Areas Adequate?' 2 (March 1972), 9-12.

Lorna R. Marsden, 'Family Planning and Women's Rights in Canada,' unpublished paper, 1973.

Marion G. Powell, 'The Pregnant Schoolgirl,' unpublished paper, 1973.

Cope W. Schwenger, 'The Need for Family Planning and Population Control in Canada,' unpublished paper, 1973.

Serena Inc., 'An Alternative Approach to Family Planning,' pamphlet, 1972.

Louise Summerhill, 'What Is Birthright?' unpublished paper, 1973.

Constance Swinton, 'Population and Family Planning: An Overview,' unpublished paper, 1973.

Virginia Thompson, 'Religious Views on Family Planning,' unpublished paper, 1973.

United Community Services of the Greater Vancouver Area, 'Babies By Choice Not By Chance,' 1973, pp. I-IV.

Susan Watt, 'Abortion: A Challenge to Social Work,' unpublished paper, 1973.

Margaret Whitridge, 'Venereal Disease in Canada,' *Living* (Winter 1973), 10-12, published by *Health and Welfare, Canada.*

Martin G. Wolfish, 'Birth Control Counselling in an Adolescent Clinic,' *Canadian Medical Association Journal* 15 (October 9, 1971), 750-51.